LYLE SAXON

To James Smythe –
with deep appreciation
for your support and
encouragement. It is
a pleasure working
with you –

James Thomas
10-28-91

Lyle Chambers Saxon

LYLE SAXON

A Critical Biography

by

James W. Thomas

SUMMA PUBLICATIONS, INC.
Birmingham, Alabama
1991

Southern Literary Series
vol. 3

Editorial office:
3601 Westbury Road
Birmingham, AL 35223 USA

General information and orders:
P.O. Box 20725
Birmingham, AL 35216 USA

Back cover photograph: "Courtesy The Historic New Orleans Collection, Museum/
Research Center, acc. no. 1981-324-2-47"

Cover background photograph: "Courtesy The Historic New Orleans Collection,
Museum/Research Center, acc. no. 1979-325-5221"

Front cover photograph courtesy of Melrose Collection, Cammie G. Henry Research
Center, Eugene P. Watson Library, Northwestern State University of Louisiana

Frontispiece photograph courtesy of Rodolph Fuchs Collection, Cammie G. Henry
Research Center, Eugene P. Watson Library, Northwestern State University of
Louisiana

To the memory of my father

TABLE OF CONTENTS

CHRONOLOGY

1868	Katherine Chambers born in Baton Rouge
1870(?)	Hugh Allan Saxon born in New Orleans
1891	Lyle Chambers Saxon born, September 4, in Bellingham, Washington (?)
1907	Saxon enters Louisiana State University
1910	Chambers bookstore sold
1911 or 1912	Saxon's first newspaper job, with Baton Rouge *State-Times*
1914 or 1915	Saxon moves to New Orleans, writes for *The Trade Index*, *New Orleans Item*, and *The Daily Picayune*
1917	Saxon is cub reporter for *Chicago Daily News*
1918	Back in New Orleans, Saxon writes for *New Orleans Item*
1918 or 1919	Saxon begins work for *The Times-Picayune*
1919(?)	Saxon first moves to French Quarter, lives at 612 Royal Street
1920	Saxon buys home at 536 Royal Street
1921	"At the Gates of Empire" serialized in *The Times-Picayune*
1923-24	Saxon writes fiction for *Times-Picayune* Sunday magazine

1926   March—"Cane River" published in *The Dial*
            October—Saxon moves to New York, takes apartment at
                3 Christopher Street in Greenwich Village
            Saxon is lampooned in *Sherwood Anderson and Other Famous Creoles*

1927   March—"Cane River" selected for *O. Henry Memorial Award Prize
                Stories of 1926*
            March—"Voodoo" published in *The New Republic*
            May—Saxon sent to Louisiana to write flood articles for *Century Magazine;*
                accompanies Coast Guard on rescues
            Yucca House at Melrose plantation becomes available for Saxon to write
            "The Centaur Plays Croquet," published in *The American Caravan*
            October—*Father Mississippi* published
            November—"Cane River" selected for *The Best Short Stories of 1927*

1928   October—*Fabulous New Orleans* published
            Saxon hosts William Faulkner in Greenwich Village

1929   October—Saxon praises *The Sound and the Fury* in his *New York Herald
                Tribune* review
            October—*Old Louisiana* published

1930   October—*Lafitte the Pirate* published

1932   Saxon gives up Greenwich Village apartment, begins spending considerable
            time at Melrose

1934   Saxon publishes several features in *The Times-Picayune*

1934-35   Saxon makes lecture tour of Louisiana and Texas

1935   Saxon becomes director of the W.P.A. Federal Writers' Project in Louisiana
            Saxon organizes the Negro History Unit of the Writers' Project at Dillard
                University

1936-37   Book reviews for *The New York Herald Tribune*

1937   July—*Children of Strangers*, Saxon's only novel, published by
                Houghton Mifflin

July—Saxon's picture appears on the cover of *The Saturday Review of Literature*, which favorably reviews the novel

Saxon buys home at 534 Madison Street in the French Quarter

1938   Cecil B. De Mille's film *The Buccaneer* is based loosely on Saxon's *Lafitte the Pirate*

New Orleans City Guide, first W.P.A. volume, is published

1938-39   Saxon hospitalized for appendectomy, several complications and other illnesses

1941   *Louisiana: A Guide to the State* is published

1942   New Orleans office of W.P.A. Federal Writers' Project closes

1943   Saxon chosen to complete W.P.A. report in Washington, D.C.; end to Writers' Project

Saxon returns to Louisiana and takes position with the State Library Commission; begins editing folklore book

Saxon hosts Gwyn Conger-John Steinbeck wedding at his Madison Street home

1945   *Gumbo Ya-Ya* published, folklore book edited by Saxon, Edward Dreyer, and Robert Tallant

Saxon sells Madison Street home, abandoning plans for restoration and for his retirement there

1946   Saxon's last published work, an article on Mardi Gras for February 4 *Times-Picayune*

Saxon broadcasts Mardi Gras parade over national radio

Saxon dies on April 9 after several weeks in the Baptist Hospital in New Orleans; pneumonia and other complications follow surgery for cancer of the bladder

1948   *The Friends of Joe Gilmore*, Saxon's unfinished memoirs, published posthumously

ABBREVIATIONS

BRMA	Baton Rouge *Morning Advocate*
BRST	Baton Rouge *State-Times*
NOSI	*The New Orleans States-Item*
NOTP	*The Times-Picayune*
NYHT	*The New York Herald Tribune*
NYHTB	*The New York Herald Tribune Books*
NYTBR	*The New York Times Book Review*
LSL	Louisiana State Library
LSU	Louisiana State University
NSU	Northwestern State University of Louisiana
TU	Tulane University
"CPC"	"The Centaur Plays Croquet"
"CR"	"Cane River"
CS	*Children of Strangers*
FJG	*The Friends of Joe Gilmore*
FM	*Father Mississippi*
FNO	*Fabulous New Orleans*
"GE"	"At the Gates of Empire"
GYY	*Gumbo Ya-Ya*
LG	*Louisiana: A Guide to the State*
LP	*Lafitte the Pirate*
NOCG	*New Orleans City Guide*
OL	*Old Louisiana*

INTRODUCTION

OVER THE PAST FIFTEEN YEARS, while working intermittently on the subject of this book, I have been asked countless times: "Who is Lyle Saxon?" A friend of mine quipped a few years ago: "Just think—before your work on Saxon, his name was not a household word." Needless to say, of course, it is still far from a household word. Indeed, his is surely not a familiar name to most serious students of American literature today. From the late 1920s to the early '40s, however, Saxon was one of Louisiana's best-known and most-beloved writers, and his literary reputation far exceeded the boundaries of the region where he lived and about which he wrote. He does not seem now to be well remembered even in Louisiana, where, he was fond of saying, he became "internationally famous locally."

This study is a critical introduction to Lyle Saxon's life and work. I will attempt herein to tell the reader who Lyle Saxon is and to demonstrate why I think the relative obscurity of this Southern writer is unmerited. I will review critical reactions to Saxon's major work, focus on his many literary friendships, summarize much of the primary material, analyze some of his best work, and appraise Saxon's overall achievement. My emphasis will be on the author's fiction.

Lyle Chambers Saxon (1891-1946) was reared in or near Baton Rouge and attended Louisiana State University from 1907 to 1912. He worked for the New Orleans *Times-Picayune* in the 1920s, writing book reviews and stories for the Sunday magazine. At this time he resided in the Vieux Carré and associated with Sherwood Anderson, William Faulkner, Roark Bradford, William Spratling, Oliver La Farge, and the other writers and artists who lived in or visited the Quarter.

After resigning from the New Orleans newspaper, Saxon went to New York. Living in Greenwich Village, he had a few prizewinning short stories published in *The Dial* and *The Century Magazine*, wrote book reviews for the *Herald Tribune*, and became acquainted with such prominent literary figures as Theodore Dreiser, Edmund Wilson, and Elinor Wylie. At his Christopher Street apartment he played cordial host to numerous young Southerners who had come north seeking publishing opportunities; Saxon was among those who befriended Faulkner when he first came to New York. During his years in the Village, Saxon wrote four books dealing with his native state: *Father Mississippi* (1927), *Fabulous New Orleans* (1928), *Old Louisiana* (1929), and *Lafitte the Pirate* (1930). *Children of Strangers*, the author's only novel, was published in 1937. The book was widely and lavishly praised, but was controversial—dealing with miscegenation and exposing the rigid castes of rural Louisiana. *Children of Strangers* is distinctive for its frank and objective treatment of the black-white relationships and for its sensitive portrayal of the blacks of the Cane River country.

While attempting to write additional fiction, Saxon assumed the position of Louisiana director of the W.P.A. Federal Writers' Project. This monumental task resulted in the publication of three volumes in the W.P.A. series. Saxon was one of the most effective state directors of the project, and the three Saxon-edited books were lauded all over the country. His own literary career was curtailed during this time, however, and he published no new fiction the last nine years of his life. He became the literary lion of New Orleans in the 1940s, cultivating friendships with John Dos Passos, John Steinbeck, Thomas Wolfe, Edna Ferber, Sinclair Lewis, and many others who visited him in his suite at the St. Charles Hotel. He suffered from many serious illnesses over the years and died of cancer in 1946.

Although no one of the above facts about the literary or personal life of this writer might warrant such a study as the present one, taken together they seem to me to be ample evidence that the long neglect of this Louisiana writer is unfortunate. I do not foresee herein the discovery of a new major Southern writer, a writer of the stature of many of Saxon's friends. Nevertheless, considering together Saxon's own literary achievements, his friendships with an astonishing number of prominent writers, his astute critical judgments, and his important role in the W.P.A. project, he does seem unduly neglected. During his lifetime, his short stories were included in prestigious anthologies compiled by such editors as Addison Hibbard, Robert Penn Warren, Willard Thorp, Van Wyck Brooks, and Lewis Mumford; his novel was hailed as a literary gem by some of the most highly respected journals of England and America; and his proclamation in the *Herald Tribune* that *The Sound and the Fury* was "a great book" was one of the first wholehearted endorsements Faulkner's novel received.

In the final analysis of this "lesser literary light," I would suggest that Lyle Saxon's own achievement was limited not only because of his work with the W.P.A. and his many extended illnesses, but also because he grew lazy, he suffered many heartbreaks in his personal life, and he was a procrastinator. As a young man he showed great promise and skill as a writer of fiction. In his middle years he knew, entertained, and perhaps inspired not a few great writers. In the end, however, he somehow lost the time and the strength to write the things that may well have made him, like so many of his illustrious friends, a truly first-rate literary artist.

As might be surmised, printed material on Lyle Saxon is limited. He has been the subject of a few graduate theses over the years. Very little has been published in scholarly journals, and many of the articles I examined, appearing in *Life* and other general interest magazines, are often superficial or confusing. For critical comment on Saxon's works, I have relied primarily on contemporary reviews. Several years ago, I was able to obtain a great deal of information regarding the author by interviews with his friends and in letters from those who knew or worked with him. Even so, many details of Saxon's life remain elusive; my sources were often quite contradictory on matters as fundamental as the author's birthplace and his sexual orientation. Saxon never married, and very few close relatives survived him by many years. Many of those with whom I spoke, those who knew Saxon well, are deceased now. I will long remember the vivid pictures of Saxon that they gave me, and I should be pleased if, by this study, the author's personality does not die with the last of his friends.

In preparation for my work, I was able to examine a great deal of primary material. The Tulane University Library has an abundant collection of letters, manuscripts, and clippings which were of use to me. This material was donated, upon Saxon's death, by his two aunts in Baton Rouge. The Louisiana State Library in Baton Rouge has a Saxon Collection; especially useful here is an early manuscript of a long work serialized in *The Times-Picayune*. The Louisiana State University Library materials I examined include manuscripts of *Lafitte the Pirate* and *Children of Strangers*. Finally, I profited greatly from letters, clippings, and manuscripts at Northwestern State University in Natchitoches, Louisiana. This Saxon material was originally a part of the Cammie Henry or Melrose Collection at the University. Henry, Saxon's patroness and owner of Melrose plantation, kept over 250 scrapbooks on Louisianans and Louisiana lore; several contain items exclusively on Saxon, and these were of tremendous value to me.

I am also appreciative of several of my former professors at the University of Tennessee at Knoxville for their help and encouragement when I first worked on Saxon as the subject of my doctoral thesis in 1975. To Professor Allison R. Ensor I am especially grateful, for he was willing to allow me to investigate an obscure name and was very encouraging to me all along the way. This study grows out of my earlier work on Saxon at the University of Tennessee, and part of my discussion of Saxon's long struggle to complete his novel is adapted from my article on that subject published in *Southern Studies*.

Finally, I am deeply indebted to my wife, Katherine Welch Thomas, who has been wonderfully supportive of this and other pursuits of mine over the years, and to Professor Morris P. Landiss, late of David Lipscomb University. Professor Landiss lived near New Orleans during the 1930s, vividly remembered who Lyle Saxon was, and forty years later "introduced" me to Saxon one day over a cup of coffee.

—*J. W. T.*

1

HERITAGE:
TOWARD A JOURNALISTIC CAREER

IN HIS INTRODUCTION TO *Old Louisiana*, Lyle Saxon complains of an interesting problem: trying to discern true history from among too many histories. Many accounts of Louisiana plantation days exist, Saxon points out, but they only compound the problem; they are often pretentious and evade the truth. He laments further: "It has been harder to get at the truth than one might suppose . . . ."[1]

Getting at the truth of Saxon's own early years is likewise harder than one might suppose. Conflicting accounts of his birth and early years abound, and some seem as pretentious and evasive as the histories that frustrated Saxon in writing *Old Louisiana*. Sources agree that the writer was born on September 4, 1891, and that he was reared in or near Baton Rouge, Louisiana. Further details admit controversy.

Surely Saxon was aware of the conflicting stories surrounding his birth and early years, but he seems to have had no interest whatsoever in correcting them. In his unfinished attempt at autobiography, *The Friends of Joe Gilmore*, for example, he refers only once to his precollege days. He writes simply: "My people were simple people and never lived in the grand manner . . . ."[2] He closes this reminiscence with the simple statement that his boyhood was "on the quiet side." Many friends of Lyle Saxon tell of his reluctance to discuss his boyhood. Former L.S.U. professor Harris Downey, who knew Saxon well during the 1930s, remarked: "It's very strange, but Lyle never talked about his youth or family backgrounds."[3]

I will begin, then, with a look at these "family backgrounds" about which the author himself had virtually nothing to say. Quite a few facts emerge to shed light on the relevant circumstances prior to Saxon's birth. Despite the conflicting information and problems in reconstructing the author's youth, tracing his family heritage—his ancestors and their activities—is not quite so difficult. Several sources yield information on the Saxon family history.

The author's paternal grandmother, Elizabeth Lyle Saxon (1832-1915), was the Saxon relative who achieved the greatest degree of fame during her lifetime. Mrs. Saxon was, among many other things, a late nineteenth- and early twentieth-century advocate of women's rights. Her granddaughter (and Lyle Saxon's cousin), Muriel Saxon Lambert of New Orleans, remembered her as "one of the pioneer suffragettes of the whole United States."[4] An article in the Baton Rouge *State-Times* describes Elizabeth Lyle Saxon as one who, with Susan B. Anthony and others, "bombarded Congress in the name of women's rights."[5] Virginius Dabney's study, *Liberalism in the South*, lists her as one of the important suffragist leaders of her day,[6] and the general consensus is that she was primarily responsible for the passage of legislation in Louisiana whereby women could hold property in their own names.

Elizabeth Lyle Saxon was also a writer. She wrote for the old *New Orleans Times*, and surely typical of her subject matter is an item of 1879 entitled, "The Rights of Women." She also wrote poetry and, in 1905, authored an interesting volume called *A Southern Woman's War Time Reminiscences*. This book, in addition to providing several facts about Lyle Saxon's ancestors, is an account of the days immediately before and during the Civil War—including a picture of prewar fever reminiscent of Howells's "Editha" or Clemens's "The War Prayer." This volume also contains descriptions of Mrs. Saxon's "visions"; she reveals the manner in which she sensed clairvoyantly the deaths of her father and brother well before the events occurred. She looks forward to the day when time, "aided by science and unfettered by bigotry," will bring about the development of a sixth sense.[7] Very often in the book, however, Elizabeth Lyle Saxon is busy enough employing her five senses in "many tongue battles in favor of women," for she views slavery as it relates particularly to her sex, rendering womankind especially miserable. Her extraordinary support of Beecher and Wendell Phillips, "Southern in every vein and fiber of being though [she] was," stems from this association of slavery with the degradation of women.[8]

Elizabeth Lyle Saxon's precise position in wartime politics is difficult to assess. She mentions in her book that one of her maternal relatives, Major William Crutchfield, was "the eccentric Unionist of Chattanooga" and that he once wrote to her that he was a Unionist "body, boots and breeches."[9] Mrs. Saxon grew up in Wetumpka, Alabama, however, and most of her relatives were Confederates. Her husband, Lyddell A. Saxon (1824-1901), born in South Carolina and reared in Wetumpka, was a very successful dry goods merchant and an ardent Union man. Possibly he developed these sympathies when he and Mrs. Saxon moved to New York six years before the war. Lyddell Saxon's death notice mentions that the couple returned to the South at the beginning of the war but that Mr. Saxon, whose strong Union sentiments made him very unpopular, soon returned to New York while Mrs. Saxon remained in Memphis.[10] This wartime schism, the article continues, "rendered the lot of the devoted husband and wife quite sad, but after a time [in about 1864] Mr. Saxon joined his wife at Memphis . . . ." Prior to their separation, the couple had a daughter and a son. The death notice indicates that the family moved to New Orleans in 1866, and it was evidently there that Lyle Saxon's father, Hugh, was born.

In addition to Hugh, Elizabeth and Lyddell had three children who reached maturity. The oldest child is listed in the account of Lyddell's death as Mrs. Ina Saxon Murray of Memphis. The second child is about twelve years old during much of the narration in *A Southern Woman's War Time Reminiscences* and thus was born about 1851. This son, Walter L., was also a merchant and is described in his father's death notice as "a leading man in business and public affairs" in New Orleans. The fourth child, named Lyle after his mother, was an attorney; he died in Dallas in 1939. An article appearing in a Dallas newspaper at his death mentions this elder Lyle Saxon's obtaining his law degree at Tulane University and serving his legal apprenticeship under Edward J. White, one-time Supreme Court Justice.[11]

Unfortunately, far less information is available regarding Lyle Saxon's father than regarding his uncle Lyle or the other children of Elizabeth and Lyddell Saxon. Hugh Allan Saxon, the third oldest child, was born sometime after 1865 because, according to Elizabeth's book, only the first two Saxon children had been born by the end of the war. Hugh was very likely born in New Orleans, moreover, because the family had moved there within about a year after the end of the war. His niece, Muriel Saxon Lambert, told me that her Uncle Hugh lived longer than anyone in the family, dying sometime in the early 1950s, at which time he was in his eighties. This indicates, therefore, that Saxon's father was born somewhere around 1870 in New Orleans.

About the same time, Lyle Saxon's mother, Katherine Chambers (1868-1915) was born into a prominent Baton Rouge family. Betty Chambers Campbell, a distant cousin of Lyle Saxon, many years ago compiled a great amount of information on Saxon's maternal ancestors.[12] The earliest Chambers she has information on is Saxon's great-great grandfather Jacob Chambers (fl. 1800), who founded the first Methodist church in the Baton Rouge area. Jacob's son, whom Campbell calls Michael I (c.1800-1844) for the sake of clarity, was born in South Carolina and married a New Yorker, Elizabeth Clein, in 1835; their child, born in 1838, is Michael II, Lyle Saxon's maternal grandfather. By this time the family had settled in the Baton Rouge area, and all subsequent Chamberses were Louisianans.

The Michael Chambers family was a large one. An 1880 census of East Baton Rouge Parish lists seven children; Lyle Saxon's mother, Katherine Chambers, is the second oldest and is listed there as "Kittie" (almost always spelled with a -y ending elsewhere). One of Kitty's brothers, Ralph Chambers, is the youngest child listed in the census. Ralph had two daughters, one of whom married author Robert Cantwell. Two of Kitty's sisters, listed as Lizzie and Maude, would play a major role in Saxon's upbringing. These two aunts of the author never married and would survive him by a few years. Along with his grandfather Michael Chambers II, Saxon was directly influenced by these women among his maternal relatives. For much of his young life he was to be under the direct supervision of his grandfather and his aunts, Maude and Lizzie Chambers.

By about 1890, ten years after this census, Hugh Allan Saxon, from New Orleans, and Katherine Chambers, from Baton Rouge, had grown to maturity. Each was about twenty years old. Each was a member of a large and prominent family, and each had some very distinguished forebears. Somehow and somewhere they met before 1891; and at this point certainties end, and conflicting reports, sometimes proffered vehemently, begin.

Not everyone whom I spoke with was convinced that Katherine Chambers and Hugh Saxon were married when Lyle Chambers Saxon was born on September 4, 1891. Muriel Saxon Lambert indicated in an interview that the marriage did indeed take place. Those who tell this version of what happened in 1891 point out also that shortly after Lyle Saxon's birth in Baton Rouge, a divorce was granted, and Hugh left Louisiana. The Marriage License Index of Orleans Parish does record the issuance of a license to Hugh and Katherine in New Orleans on December 10, 1890; apparently no record of divorce exists, however.[13]

Many others I talked with seem to feel that no marriage ceremony and, of course, no subsequent divorce ever took place between the two. Thomas C. Atkinson, who knew Saxon and the Chambers family quite well during his own days at L.S.U. (1928-1933), told me that he feels certain that Hugh and Katherine never married.[14] A co-worker with Saxon on the W.P.A. Writers' Project corroborated this opinion when he recalled that during his New Orleans associations with the author, the project workers generally felt that Saxon's illegitimacy was the reason for his noticeable reluctance to discuss his early years.[15] Thomas Atkinson also told me that Saxon was actually not born in Baton Rouge and claimed that he had heard Saxon state this fact many times. Edith Atkinson, once librarian of the Louisiana Collection at the State Library, writes that almost any "old timer" around Baton Rouge knew that Saxon only gave Baton Rouge as his birthplace as part of the "story" surrounding his early years.[16] Many years ago Thomas Atkinson was told by the Chamberses' closest friends what he considers to be the truth of the matter. "Kitty Chambers went away from Baton Rouge with this man, Hugh Saxon," Atkinson related, "and not long thereafter, she came home and brought the baby with her." The story the Atkinsons had heard in Baton Rouge seems entirely possible and, at least, does not depend on records for its support. Cathy Harvey presents compelling evidence that Saxon was born in Bellingham, Washington, where Hugh and Katherine had traveled, probably to visit Elizabeth Lyle Saxon, then a resident of nearby Whatcomb, Washington.[17] At any rate, a few weeks or months after the author's birth, Hugh Saxon was gone, and Katherine Chambers Saxon, as she was thereafter known, remained to rear her son with the help of her father and sisters. None of those who remained in Baton Rouge would hear from Hugh again.

Hugh Saxon may have left Katherine for a number of reasons, but one of them was evidently not the proverbial "other woman." He did marry (again or for the first time, depending on the source) several years later, but Muriel Saxon Lambert pointed out that no one ever suspected he had fallen in love with another woman. It is possible he simply fled the responsibilities of fatherhood or perhaps, like Tennessee Williams's Mr. Wingfield, fell in love with long distances. Lyle Saxon's father went first to New York, where he married and worked on a newspaper, and then to California. By 1901 he had become city editor of the *Los Angeles Herald*. Lambert, who often saw her Uncle Hugh when he would visit her family in New Orleans, recalled that in his later years in California, Hugh played "bit parts" in several motion pictures. Hugh survived his son by at least five years, but, Lambert added, he did not attend his son's funeral; and, as far as she can recall, the two never met after the father left in 1891. "Lyle would absolutely never see his father," she stated, "because Lyle adored his mother."

Not only did Saxon's father pursue a career in journalism, but his mother also wrote for a newspaper after the separation. With the Baton Rouge *State-Times* she was society editor and "writer of local interest events."[18] Kitty Chambers Saxon, characterized by the same newspaper as "dainty, quick-witted,"[19] wrote short stories and poems also—at least for her own amusement. In a notebook bearing her name and dated October 12, 1892, are several original verses and unfinished stories. The final entry in this book is a copy of the anonymous child's verse, "Bob White," with this inscription written in her hand: "Lyle's recitation—his own choice— April 5, 1895."[20] Everyone whom I talked with about Kitty Saxon felt that she was a devoted mother and an extremely kind woman.

Exactly where Katherine Chambers Saxon reared her son is another aspect of the author's background which is open to question. Various accounts of the author's Southern childhood are suspiciously similar and pat, and some of them would be embarrassing to contemporary Southerners. Several sources allude to Saxon's being reared on a four-thousand-acre plantation with three-hundred-and-sixty Negroes (the acreage and black population vary occasionally),[21] and one account of his youth contains this description: "His childhood was spent on a plantation near Baton Rouge . . . . It was a happy, care-free life, with dogs, ponies, and little 'niggers . . . .' "[22]

Such stories of Saxon's boyhood have lasted for decades. In Joseph Blotner's biography of William Faulkner, for example, Mr. and Mrs. Carl Carmer allude to Saxon's having been reared "on a large Baton Rouge plantation," and even in a 1989 Faulkner biography Saxon is described as "from a well-to-do family, with a plantation background."[23] On this matter, most of the people with whom I talked have quite different viewpoints regarding Lyle Saxon's alleged family plantation, and, again, nothing Saxon said or wrote is of any real help.

In the opening chapters of his first book, *Father Mississippi*, Saxon describes, in the first person, a somewhat idyllic plantation life, complete with honeysuckles, magnolias, "aunts and uncles," dogs, and, of course, the Mississippi River. This passage surely contributed to the accounts of his "happy, care-free" youth—especially since, in his preface, Saxon tells the reader that he his going to relate life on a Louisiana plantation "as I remembered it."[24] Eventually everyone has to evacuate the plantation which, in the end, is lost in the river's flood. Prior to this, however, the narrator rhapsodizes:

> I remember the plantation . . . . Yea, Lord! Oh, how well do I remember the plantation. I lived there in the summer, but in winter I had to go to school in town. Not that I liked school less, but I loved the plantation. It was like heaven, I thought, a perfect place. (*FM* 6)

After the Mississippi inundates the old home, the narrator says: "The river had taken the land again. The plantation of my childhood no longer existed" (*FM* 58).

That the plantation of Saxon's childhood ever existed is doubtful, to say the least. Surely it is possible that his Baton Rouge schooling and his mother's newspaper work could have been accomplished, as the narrator in the passage above says, without living year-round in the city. In addition, the river did overflow and cause the loss of some homes in 1903, and the boy in *Father Mississippi* could easily be about eleven years old, Saxon's age in 1903. Allowing for some poetic license, then, it is conceivable that Saxon, in this initial section of *Father Mississippi*, "told the truth, mainly." Most of Saxon's friends I talked with had heard the plantation story. No one I talked with, however, had any firsthand knowledge of a Chambers plantation, and some were very suspicious of the description of the old homestead. Thomas Atkinson claimed that the plantation story was "pure fiction" and said that he had heard Saxon laugh about his early chapters of *Father Mississippi*. "Lyle enjoyed the fictional side of his biography," Atkinson added. This comment is interesting when compared to a remark Saxon makes in an interview about the writing of his novel. The author confesses that he enjoyed writing the novel more than his previous non-fiction works because in writing pure fiction, he did not have to be hampered by sticking to the facts.[25] When relating the events of his days on the old family plantation, Saxon very probably told his story unhampered.

The boyhood days that Lyle Saxon spent in Baton Rouge are described in a *State-Times* article of 1938. The reporter recalls Saxon as a "grave-eyed youngster" who would ride through the streets of Baton Rouge on a white, one-eyed pony.[26] This same account characterizes Saxon as an "unusual child" who "liked old people and . . . was always listening to their stories perched on the steps as they rocked in a chair on the front porch . . . ." This picture of the boy's love of stories from the old-timers, perhaps suspiciously facile in light of Saxon's later books in which such yarns are repeated, is nevertheless quite probable—especially since the boy was reared in a household headed by his grandfather. Although this *State-Times* account implies that the boy was somewhat introspective and eccentric, no information regarding Saxon's childhood indicates anything out of the ordinary.

Yielding to the temptation to describe still another person of letters as "having grown up among books," I feel sure this cliché is applicable in the case of Saxon. His grandfather, Michael Chambers, in addition to being Baton Rouge city treasurer, was the proprietor of the city's first bookstore, described as having been "for years an institution" in Baton Rouge.[27] Almost every account that mentions the family bookstore notes the boy's spending a great part of his youth there reading. One writer comments that Saxon encountered many useful things there as well as many things a boy should not have read.[28] Robert Cantwell writes that his wife's aunt, Lizzie Chambers, recalled the excitement in the household when riverboats would bring new boxes of books to the store and all the girls (Lizzie, Kitty, and Maude) would read the latest novel by Henry James.[29] Saxon's friend Harris Downey recalled that James "was a favorite of Lyle's" and that Saxon had introduced him to James's works. Whether or not he read James during his boyhood in Baton Rouge, Saxon evidently read a tremendous amount during these days. Another account quips that he read "everything from the early works of James Branch Cabell to the paper-backed novels of Laura Jean Libbey and Nick Carter."[30] Edward Dreyer, who knew Saxon well during his last years and wrote a biographical sketch at the end of *The Friends of Joe Gilmore*, writes that Saxon and his closest boyhood friend, George Favrot, were "voracious readers."[31] Dreyer claims that the boys read Ibsen and the Russian authors and that their literary tastes were advanced for their ages. Whatever fired his imagination during these years, the books Saxon read surely played a part in what was evidently a very early decision to write. He once told a group of journalism students: "I can't remember when I didn't like to write . . . . I've always wanted to write."[32]

Lyle and his friend George Favrot did not spend all their time in literary pursuits, however. Dreyer, who explains that he is repeating tales that Saxon was fond of telling "varying them, whenever necessary, to suit a special audience," recounts some of the pair's Baton Rouge pranks. The boys once wrote spurious letters to the lovelorn who subscribed to a matrimonial bureau and, in perhaps their finest achievement, dressed two stone angels in a Baton Rouge convent in the garb of a streetwalker.[33] Saxon, it should be noted here, was a great raconteur and probably knew his Mark Twain as well as his Henry James. If the exploits of Lyle and George sound perhaps too much like those of Tom and Huck to be taken as totally factual, they do indicate, at least, a side of Saxon's youth different from the image of the bookstore habitué or grave-eyed youngster.

The three Chamberses, other than Saxon's mother, who were charged with the upbringing of the boy in these days were all to play a larger role in his future than Kitty Chambers Saxon. Francois Mignon, one of Saxon's closest friends with whom he lived intermittently late in his life, told me that the author loved his grandfather very much and was devoted to him.[34] Grandfather "Mike" Chambers lived to be quite old, became quite infirm, almost blind, and was bedridden for years.[35] In a passage in one of Saxon's letters to a friend in New York, the author pokes fun at the old man's plight, yet shows a genuine affection for him too. Saxon writes: "Speaking of birthdays, Grandpa had one on the twelfth. One million, I think, but I'm not sure."[36] Saxon next describes the scene when someone, possibly a neighbor, brought Mr. Chambers a cake "(which he couldn't eat) covered with birthday candles (which he couldn't see) and talked and talked to him until the poor old fellow must have been dizzy." When the well-wisher left, Saxon continues,

> she paused and shot her final arrow of idiocy: "Well, goodbye . . . I hope you live another year!" And I, aghast, wondering how he would feel before such a sluttish remark . . . but he, as soon as the door had closed upon her, said gaily: "God, but that woman is a damned fool!" which cheered me tremendously and we laughed together. Grandpa still has his flashes you see.

Throughout the years Saxon was evidently not always able to maintain a sense of humor or a feeling of warmth for his aunts. Elizabeth (Lizzie) and Maude Chambers were both nurses, Maude serving as public school nurse for several years in Baton Rouge. Betty Chambers Campbell describes her first meeting with Saxon's aunts at a very formal afternoon tea and remembers them as "very proper ladies receiving us in the parlor."[37]

Lizzie (1863-1951) was older than her sister Kitty, and Maude (1876-1960) was younger. Francois Mignon told me that the impression he got from his friend Lyle was that, over the years, they "drove him crazy" with their eccentricities. However they affected him, his life was, for better or worse, continually influenced by them throughout the years.

It seems very likely that neither Lizzie nor Maude, these "very proper ladies," had approved of the relationship, regardless of what it was, between their sister and Hugh Saxon. In an unfinished manuscript at Tulane University, Lyle Saxon tells the story of a girl named Mary Nelson. He describes the girl's relationship with her two aunts. In one scene, he identifies them as "the aunts who had quarrelled with her mother because she had married Nelson [the girl's father]."[38] Regardless of whether or not this relationship in Saxon's story was based on the Chambers aunts' attitude, there seems to be little doubt that an effort was made to save face for Kitty in Baton Rouge. A longtime resident of the city quotes a 1905-06 Baton Rouge city directory in which Kitty Saxon is listed as the "widow of Hugh A," a thoroughly proper explanation for her lack of a husband.[39]

Saxon's paternal relatives were far less a part of his early years than were the Chamberses. As a boy, nevertheless, he evidently made several trips from Baton Rouge to New Orleans, where many of the Saxon relatives lived at this time. The elder Lyle Saxon, the uncle for whom he was named, and his well-known grandmother lived there in the early part of this century. Edward Dreyer writes that "little Lyle," as he was called to avoid confusion in New Orleans, was a great admirer of Elizabeth Lyle Saxon.[40] The only surviving account of a meeting between them is a Saxon tale, which Dreyer recounts as he recalled hearing it, in which the grandson and the great lady discussed religion. According to the story, Mrs. Saxon asked the boy if he believed in a personal God, to which he replied, "No." The grandmother surprisingly said, "Good . . . . Now we can go on from there," and rapport was immediately established between the two.

If Saxon really made this statement to his grandmother as a youth, his feelings about God and religion were established early. As a boy, Richard Bradford, novelist and son of Roark Bradford, knew Lyle Saxon well; Bradford makes the interesting observation: "God knows what Lyle's religious background was. I believe that he had a Methodist or Baptist background of some sort and had rejected it early on."[41] The background was Episcopalian, but nothing Saxon was to write, even very early in his career, was to reflect any orthodox religious beliefs or this belief in a personal God his grandmother asked about. Frequently, in fact, he was to ridicule what he considered the superstitious tenets of various sects. Lyle Saxon seems to have said no to religion early and without thunder, then, and seems to have remained comfortable in his unbelief. Religion, it seems, was simply never an important part of his life.

When Saxon traveled to New Orleans in his boyhood, religious discussions with his grandmother surely were not foremost on his mind. In the early chapters of his *Fabulous New Orleans*, he describes a boy's first Mardi Gras. This narrative, in the first person like the initial chapters of *Father Mississippi*, describes "the grandfather" turning "the boy" over to a black manservant who shows him the seedy aspects of the city at festival time. Saxon later commented that this story was autobiographical "to a certain extent."[42] The statement in the first chapter of *Fabulous New Orleans* is simply: "And this is my first impression of the fabulous city, when I went there with my grandfather for Mardi Gras, twenty-five years ago."[43] Whether "the boy" and his subsequent adventures are purely fictive or represent what literally happened to Lyle Saxon about 1903, the writer of these early chapters of *Fabulous New Orleans* surely viewed the Crescent City as "fabulous" and continued to do so until his death there more than forty years later.

By 1908, before his seventeenth birthday, Lyle Saxon was in print for the first time. The visits to the fabulous city, however, had not produced a Louisiana Chatterton. Saxon's initial published work consisted of three photographs in the *St. Nicholas* magazine for children. Saxon's friend and former *Publisher's Weekly* editor Josiah Titzell writes that the young Saxon was extremely proud of his photography and that "if you had seen Lyle Saxon as a boy . . . , he would probably have shown you his collected works—two issues of *St. Nicholas*."[44] The photographs, winners in a contest, actually appeared in three issues of the magazine, in February, July, and October of 1908.[45] One was merely published without an additional award, but two are prizewinning entries. For the first he received a gold badge, and for the second a cash prize; both of these are pictures of town scenes with children playing. The third depicts an old man alone in a skiff on the river.

At this time the Chamberses and Kitty and Lyle Saxon lived on St. Louis Street in Baton Rouge. This is the address Saxon sent with his photographs to *St. Nicholas* and is also where they lived as far back as 1905.[46] Very probably they lived at this address the entire time Saxon grew to maturity in Baton Rouge. St. Louis Street is four blocks from the Mississippi River and in easy walking distance of where the old Chambers Bookstore was located, on Third Street. Growing up in this setting, then, a few short blocks from his grandfather's bookstore and from the river of which he was always in awe, Lyle Saxon understandably could not remember when he did not want to write.

Although she lived until 1915, Kitty Saxon was evidently not well over a long period of years. By the time her son was a teenager, she was dying of cancer. Saxon's friend Francois Mignon told me that the author took a part-time job in a drugstore during his high school days to help pay for her expensive and unsuccessful medical treatments. Mignon, along with almost everyone I talked with who knew Saxon well, commented on the author's devotion to his mother. He evidently spoke more often about her than about anyone or anything else in his early days. Edward Dreyer writes that he told many "delightful tales" about Kitty and their relationship.[47] The author's cousin, Muriel Saxon Lambert, told me: "It broke his heart when his mother died before he had attained all the success and fame . . . . His goal in life was to do something special for his mother." The same Saxon fragment about Mary Nelson's girlhood, wherein she describes the two aunts in the passage quoted above, contains an interesting passage about the child's very ill mother. Saxon describes Mary anxiously watching as her mother, called "Kitty" in the story, tries to rest:

> Kitty Nelson had grown worse during the summer—she was scarcely able to move from the hammock—and lay for hours with her eyes closed, and tears trickling from under her black lashes. Mary would stand for long minutes, watching the rise and fall of her mother's white robe, and then feeling inclined to cry herself, she would slip away.[48]

"Mary," the young girl in this fragment, emerges as a more vivid and memorable character than "the boy" of happier stories and happier days on "the plantation" and at Mardi Gras. In spite of the autobiographical claims for the boy in *Father Mississippi* and *Fabulous New Orleans*, moreover, Mary and her memories are probably far more real.

Lyle Saxon remained in Baton Rouge through his college years. He entered Louisiana State University on September 20, 1907, just after his sixteenth birthday, and began studying agriculture.[49] His name appears, as "L. C. Saxon," among the "Agricultural Class" in the L.S.U. yearbook,

Gumbo, which was issued in the spring of 1908. This was apparently a precollege group, for Saxon spent five years at L.S.U. and was probably a member of the freshman class of 1908-09.

The 1909 yearbook contains one illustration by the boy who had won prizes for his photography. This drawing, signed "Saxon '12," appears on a page introducing the law school section.[50] It somewhat disproportionately depicts a young man standing by a stack of books (entitled, not very subtly, "Lex" and "Law") with a smug expression on his face and a halo floating over his head. Most drawings in this yearbook are far less crudely done, and Saxon's seems ample evidence that his future in art was not bright. The picture does, however, show a sense of humor on the part of the freshman.

The next year at L.S.U., 1910, was the author's third there, and his name appears in *Gumbo* (again as "L. C. Saxon") as a member of the sophomore class. He continued to be referred to as "L. C. Saxon" during his days at L.S.U., but soon decided to drop his middle name or initial in referring to himself. Saxon's cousin, Muriel Saxon Lambert. told me that her father, the elder Lyle Saxon, would tease young Lyle when he would visit, telling the boy he should use the "L. C." or the middle name since his New Orleans uncle could commit a murder and a Baton Rouge college student would be arrested for it. Lambert did recall that the author thought his name had a good sound to it and that he used to say that simply "Lyle Saxon" was "a marvelous nom de plume although it's my real name."

Just as Saxon traveled occasionally to New Orleans during his early youth, he continued periodic visits while at L.S.U. He spent brief periods with the Saxon relatives in the larger city during these years. Lambert recalled that although her family saw Lyle only rarely at this time, she and her girl friends, whom he would date on his visits south, considered the young college student "gorgeous." This is one of many accounts of Saxon's good looks or of women finding him very attractive.

After the author's sophomore year in college, in the summer of 1910, something occurred that must have saddened him considerably. Michael Chambers sold the bookstore to John Albert Anderson, who reopened it under his name in the fall of 1910. Anderson's son, Dr. Sherburne Anderson of Baton Rouge, explains in a letter that at that time Chambers Bookstore was the only store in the city basically devoted to books.[51] No one with whom I have talked knew exactly why Michael Chambers, then in his seventies, sold the store to someone outside the family. Conceivably, Lyle Saxon may have been offered the managing of the store, but it is very likely that a more dramatic step was necessary. The Chambers family financial problems, not only as a result of Kitty's illness, could have been serious by this time and, surely, would be a very real concern to Saxon for the next several years. During the author's days at L.S.U., at any rate, his boyhood haunt and a Baton Rouge landmark passed out of the family hands.[52]

The next year at L.S.U., Saxon was surely a junior, although, inexplicably, in the 1911 *Gumbo* he is listed as a sophomore for the second consecutive year. In this yearbook his name appears in a club for the first time. The German club has as one of its members "L. C. Saxon," but the young man is not listed in any of the three literary clubs. Although not a member of these latter groups, Saxon certainly was still interested in literature during his college years. Dr. W. A. Read, distinguished professor of English at L.S.U. for many years, was a favorite of Saxon's who was remembered with affection,[53] and there were other associations he enjoyed as well. He and his boyhood friend, George Favrot, also at the university, visited in the home of one of their English instructors quite often. Mercedes Garig, the first woman ever appointed to the L.S.U. faculty, recalled years later how the young men would come to read the books in her library and would often discuss literature with her outside the classroom.[54] This association evidently meant a great deal to Saxon. Twenty years later he would dedicate his fourth book to Garig, and he continued to visit her for many years after his college days. In a letter Saxon wrote less than two months before his death, he describes a recent visit to "Miss Mercedes" in Baton Rouge.[55]

Sometime during his days at the university, Lyle Saxon obtained a part-time job which was a fulfillment of what he had wanted to do since he was a child. He became a writer for the Baton Rouge *State-Times* sometime before 1912. His job was evidently limited to one task: reviewing vaudeville shows at the Columbia Theatre in Baton Rouge.[56] Years later, Saxon confessed to a group of high school students that he was "a little bit afraid" on this first newspaper job.[57] He also advised these journalism students to get some experience as soon as they could—even if it was in the form of some minor job on a newspaper. While still a college student and with a long journalistic career before him, Lyle Saxon had done precisely what he advised these students to do when he went to work, "a little bit afraid," for the *State-Times*.

In the spring of 1912, the young part-time newspaperman was probably less than thrilled with the past four years of college. For one thing, he had not been able to pursue journalism in his course work at L.S.U.; the subject was not introduced into the curriculum until 1913. He was also unhappy with the compulsory military training program at the university. "He always said," his friend Dreyer writes, "that on the day he finished his training he went home, took off his cadet uniform, and threw it away, hoping he would never have 'truck with that kind of nonsense' again."[58] Dreyer also explains that the young Saxon had always hoped to go to an Eastern college, but the family finances would not permit his leaving home. One early sketch of Saxon's life indicates, in fact, that he did not graduate; apparently he lacked a single course to complete requirements for the baccalaureate degree.[59] At any rate, young L. C. Saxon, pictured in the yearbook among the graduates from the Teachers' College in 1912, surely was more ready than ever to leave Baton Rouge and find a more congenial situation elsewhere.

Some very disparate jobs outside of his native state were the first full-time occupations the young man attempted. Saxon's first job was apparently as a salesperson for a paint company in Mobile, Alabama.[60] He next took a high school teaching position in Pensacola, Florida. Francois Mignon recalled that he heard Saxon say little about his teaching experiences and that the author did not enjoy his days in Florida.[61] Leaving in 1913, he took his next position in Texas where, according to Dreyer's account, Saxon "had something to do with making blueprints for engines."[62] According to one who knew Saxon well at Melrose plantation, the author suffered a romantic disappointment in Texas. Joseph Henry recalled that Saxon was spurned by a young woman in Beaumont.[63] Aside from this personal disappointment, these early years out of Louisiana were seemingly somewhat inconsequential—certainly so far as Saxon's literary productions were concerned.

The next year, 1914, Saxon perhaps spent back in Baton Rouge, where his mother had grown critically ill. Late that year, or some time early in 1915, however, he had moved to New Orleans, the "fabulous" city he loved. He worked on *The Trade Index* (the publication of the New Orleans Board of Trade) and apparently contributed articles as a free-lance writer for both the *New Orleans Item* and *The Daily Picayune*.[64] By 1917 he was on the move again, this time heading north.

The apprentice reporter's next stop was Chicago. Saxon himself later described this position, with the *Chicago Daily News*, as that of a "cub."[65] In the same article, his description of a typical day in Chicago during his time with the *Daily News* reveals less than ideal working conditions:

> I can remember how I used to stagger down Michigan boulevard in the middle of winter—the wind from the lake fairly sweeping me (a little hothouse Louisiana flower) off the street. I would walk along one block swearing that I wouldn't make the next one—but I had a tough city editor to think about facing without a story—so I'd push myself on by sheer will power . . . . Well, anyway, it was a job.

Saxon would later complain similarly of New York weather, but this Chicago assignment was surely a welcome step professionally, even if not geographically.

One of the earliest newspaper clippings relating to Saxon in the Louisiana State Library provides a good deal of information about some of the cub reporter's activities in Chicago.[66] This item is an account, written in a lighthearted vein, of the failure of a comedy that Saxon had written for a local theater. The farce, withdrawn after one week's run, was not light enough for the audiences, and "a war playlet [was] substituted." Saxon's play, "The Peacock," the article continues, was the product of "a young newspaper man . . . who is chiefly known by his 'Intimate Interviews' with celebrities and his 'Mr. Werff' stories" in another paper. Saxon would continue to interview famous personalities throughout his career, but the "Mr. Werff" stories, whatever they were, would not be continued or resurrected later for the New Orleans papers.

One activity of these Chicago years that Saxon would attempt later, however, was the writing of a play. "Epitaph," a one-act play discussed in the next chapter, was a product of his *Times-Picayune* days. Much later, in an interview following *Children of Strangers* in 1937, Saxon comments on his desire to write a play next—"something that may be forgotten or may mean an immediate short cut to national and international fame."[67] The author's failure ever to achieve success in this genre may have been a disappointment to him, as the failure of "The Peacock" may have been; but, at least in regard to the latter, he seemed to be less than overwhelmed with grief. The Chicago newspaper article about "The Peacock" ends with

Saxon's reaction to the closing of his play at the theater: " . . . he laughingly remarked that he was 'too prostrated to give out a statement to the press.' "

The young reporter surely could not have remained in Chicago for as long as he once claimed. Although he says in a 1937 Baton Rouge *State-Times* article that he worked "several years" on the *Chicago Daily News*,[68] it is unlikely that he was there much longer than from mid-1917 to mid-1918. Other claims regarding his journalistic career are difficult to explain as well. One source states that he worked on newspapers in Cleveland and in Washington, D.C.[69] In a brief description of his accomplishments prior to 1927, moreover, the editor of *The Best Short Stories of 1927* claims that Saxon had worked on newspapers in "several American cities."[70] Even though these claims would indicate some journalistic experience besides that in Chicago and New Orleans, the reports of Saxon's reporting, it seems, have been greatly exaggerated.

Although many of his friends were serving in the military about this time, Saxon was exempted from service because of poor health.[71] Considering his attitude toward the military training at L.S.U., it seems unlikely that he took any drastic steps on his own to serve, such as exploring possibilities like the Canadian Royal Air Force to get "over there." Saxon's boyhood friend and college classmate George Favrot, however, served in France and decided to remain in Paris after the war. He became an expatriate and wanted to pursue a career in fiction. When Favrot left for Europe, however, Saxon never saw him again. George died in Paris, having published one short story sometime around 1918.

The 1918 examination for the military draft, and perhaps other medical examinations, indicated that Saxon was in danger of becoming a consumptive. Dreyer's account describes the author's successful recovery in the "ozone belt" in rural Louisiana and is filled with several of Saxon's favorite anecdotes about the senile old lady with whom he boarded during this time. Once, for example, she climbed unnoticed into the attic and, upon being missed, was frantically searched for and given up for dead or worse. According to Saxon's tale, she was finally located in the attic "wearing a hat that had been discarded thirty years before, sitting in a dusty arm-chair that had only one leg, and engrossed in an old bound copy of *The Southern Gentlewoman*."[72] After a brief stay in this household, and with the danger of tuberculosis passed, Saxon returned to New Orleans.

One more interlude, consisting of two or three jobs, stood between Saxon and his many accomplishments during the long association with *The Times-Picayune*. His first work upon the return to New Orleans in the summer of 1918 was as a reporter for the *New Orleans Item*, the newspaper he had been associated with as far back as four years earlier. Saxon also worked, before the end of 1918, with Harry Hopkins, then director of the New Orleans Red Cross office. Saxon later wrote that he "ran a Red Cross office . . . working for Harry Hopkins"[73]; actually he handled all the publicity for the local Red Cross. Either in this or another position under Hopkins in 1919, Saxon helped organize the Federal Board for Vocational Education in New Orleans. These early connections with Hopkins would certainly do him no harm in the coming years when he began the Louisiana Federal Writers' Project, a subdivision of the W.P.A., which Harry Hopkins headed for Roosevelt. Almost all accounts of Saxon's newspaper career list 1918 as the beginning date of the work on *The Times-Picayune*, yet he apparently was not a full-time employee until the next year. He probably continued the work with Hopkins in conjunction with his *Item* and *Times-Picayune* assignments for a year or two; thus, by whatever combination of part- and full-time vocations, Saxon's workload was extremely heavy in these years.

With his youth in Baton Rouge behind him, Lyle Saxon's literary career was about to begin in earnest as he started work on the great *Times-Picayune*. As R. W. B. Lewis once said of Whitman, he would now steadily bury his youth—not by steady revision of his works as in the case of the poet, but by ignoring his personal past and embracing instead the mammoth myth and lore surrounding his state and the Mississippi River. During his college years and his early newspaper work, he had experienced the selling of the bookstore, his mother's failing health and death, the family's financial decline, and the separation from his beloved friend Favrot. The land and the river he loved, by contrast, might well have seemed immutable to him, and he would focus his attention on them.

From whatever source or sources—whether from his grandmother, his grandfather's bookstore, his friend Favrot, his parents' journalistic careers, or his own abilities and interests—had come the inspiration to write. He was sure quite early that he wanted to write, and from everything he would ever say about "fabulous" New Orleans, he seems to have been equally sure of where he wanted to write. As he began as a reporter on *The Times-Picayune*, he may have felt toward the city as the boy in *Father Mississippi* had felt toward the plantation: that this was "heaven . . . a perfect place." In 1918 he could not have imagined that after a few very successful years, he would grow weary of newspaper life and leave *The Times-Picayune* for the literary possibilities of New York. That departure was far in the future, though; and, surely, to the twenty-seven-year-old reporter, New Orleans was paradise enough for a while.

ARRIVAL:
NEW ORLEANS NEWSPAPERMAN

DURING LYLE SAXON'S YEARS as a full-time employee of the New Orleans *Times-Picayune*, the young newspaperman worked at a number of different tasks. Various accounts of his positions with the newspaper indicate that he was, roughly in chronological order, general reporter, feature writer, feature editor, literary critic, Sunday editor, and city editor.[1] Understandably these positions were at once satisfying and frustrating to Saxon. He was pleased with many assignments and quite proud of some of his stories in the newspaper; he was discouraged and disillusioned by others. By the time his full-time association with *The Times-Picayune* had ended, at any rate, he was an experienced journalist, a budding writer of fiction, and surely one of the most widely known people ever associated with the newspaper.

Early in his career at *The Times-Picayune,* Saxon was given somewhat important interviews with well-known personalities of the day, such as Lord Dunsany, Billy Sunday, and Theda Bara. He may have achieved his first real notice, however, with a story he wrote on December 4, 1919. During the early morning hours on that day the French Opera House burned beyond repair. The building, often described as the place where opera was introduced to America, stood on the corner of Toulouse and Bourbon streets and had been a chief source of pleasure for Saxon since his boyhood. One of the author's W.P.A. co-workers discloses that the night the old structure burned, Saxon and a friend arose from their beds, rushed to the fire, and sat on the curb, watching brokenheartedly the destruction of the building.[2] In a letter to his Aunt Maude in Baton Rouge, Saxon himself reveals his feelings on this night:

> I want to tell you that I nearly cried over that fire. I was there from the
> beginning, of course, as it is only one block from where I live—And I
> was very much upset over it, as I had always loved the old building, and
> the opera that it contained.
>
> . . . .
>
> This year, especially, I enjoyed it, as I had passes for every perfor-
> mance, and used to go nearly every night . . . . I was there the last
> night.[3]

The morning of the fire Saxon, obviously in an emotional state,
composed the obituary for this building and wrote what would be one of his
most famous pieces for *The Times-Picayune*. The article traces what the
opera house had meant to Orleanians of all ages and ends with the comment
that with the loss of this building, "The heart of the old French Quarter has
stopped beating."

Saxon's story of the fire, quoted in a history of *The Times-Picayune*
twenty-five years later,[4] surely owes much of its fame and longevity to its
inclusion in *Fabulous New Orleans* (280-81). The final line, quoted above,
is, of course, dramatic and memorable. The rest of the article, however, is
closer to melodrama and is described apologetically by Saxon himself as
"florid."[5] In a letter to his Aunt Maude, written only a few days after the
fire, he confides:

> I worked terribly hard on that story, and thought it was complete and
> full of information, but I didn't think much of the sob-stuff at the
> top—it was too sloppy, I thought. However, as a good many people
> wrote me about it, I am glad I wrote it.[6]

The "sob-stuff" is indeed a little sloppy as Saxon begins flamboyantly:
"Gone is all the glory . . . gone in a blaze of burning gauze and tinsel, a
blaze more splendid and more terrible than Walpurgis Night . . . ." What is
noteworthy here, perhaps more so than the article itself, is the fact that
despite Saxon's emotional involvement with the incident, he was able
almost immediately to view his writing objectively and was at the same time
happy to have written something that gained him some recognition at the
newspaper.

Another assignment that fell to Saxon at *The Times-Picayune* in
December of 1919 was evidently one about which he was in no way happy.

In the same letter to Maude Chambers regarding the story of the fire, Saxon complains that his boss has played a "dirty bastard's trick" and given him "this damned Doll and Toy Fund." In a spirit not exactly commensurate with the joyous season, Saxon explains the details of this *Times-Picayune* Christmas project. The entire process was under his supervision, and, as he states in the letter quite frankly, it was "maddening." Saxon was in charge of the collection of the toys for needy children, was responsible for raising funds for indigent families, and had to write about "the accursed stuff" in the newspaper; "I hate it with an undying hatred," he concludes. Although there is the possibility that Saxon doth protest too much, his letter does reveal quite a discrepancy between his personal feelings about this assignment and the public figure of the benevolent reporter that emerged on the pages of *The Times-Picayune*.

The following year the young reporter was given a monumental assignment, which, again, he did not enjoy. This task was unpleasant for a different reason, however. In the newspaper's coverage of the 1920 mayoral race, Lyle Saxon emerged as the figure behind the exposé of various vices and sources of corruption in city government. Saxon's articles contributed to the defeat of the four-term incumbent, Martin Behrman, but also led to his becoming a target for revenge by certain underworld figures. Dreyer claims that some attempts were even made on the reporter's life at this time.[7]

After these less than halcyon early days on *The Times-Picayune,* Saxon finally began to get involved with various endeavors with which he was greatly pleased. One such feature, which he initiated at *The Times-Picayune*, was the book review page, specifically the "Literature and Less" column.[8] After repeatedly asking his superiors for a column of literary criticism, Saxon was given the job—but in addition to his regular feature work. His managing editor considered the book page, Saxon remarked later, "a sort of reward of merit, so to speak—just a little toy for me to amuse myself with . . . ."[9] The *Times-Picayune* feature writer, busier than ever before, still considered this a virtual coup in his journalistic career. He confides in an article of 1927 that he had enjoyed his previous work on the newspaper "more or less" and recalls how he spent his time interviewing murderesses or "visiting county fairs and writing descriptions of fat cattle" but, he continues, "then I got the book page."[10] Difficult as this extra assignment was for Saxon (after all, as he quips, "women kept on murdering their husbands and cows kept on getting blue ribbons"), the "Literature and Less" column Saxon began was surely a welcome addition to his duties. He may have thought he was in paradise from the first day at the newspaper, but this breakthrough was the beginning of his real pleasure and of his real fame there. For the next few years at *The Times-Picayune,* after about 1920, he would achieve increasing distinction and command respect as an individual writer; he was completing a long apprenticeship and had shed forever the anonymity of staff reporter.

In 1921 Saxon embarked on the most ambitious project of his career. Beginning with the April 24 issue of the newspaper, he wrote a daily story under the title, "At the Gates of Empire." The feature continued throughout the summer, concluding on August 14. The author's prefatory remarks at the beginning of the first chapter are an attempt to clarify the exact nature of the upcoming stories. His clarification, however, is more than slightly confusing itself:

> This is the story of New Orleans, from its beginning to the present day, set forth in a series of episodes, each one dealing with an important period in the city's growth. It is less than history—and more; it is more than fiction—and less. It is fragmentary, but it is continuous. The whole is a narrative; yet each division is a story in itself.[11]

Essentially, then, Saxon informs his readers that they are embarking on a serialized historical novel, and the story eventually grew to novelistic proportions. The manuscript of "At the Gates of Empire," donated to the Louisiana State Library by Saxon's aunts, is over four hundred pages long.[12] In the story, Saxon uses a fictitious family, the Beaumonts, around whom to weave his Louisiana history lessons. He traces the effects of the last two hundred years on this family in particular and on Louisiana in general. The Beaumonts are virtually the only unreal characters in the story, however; and they are continually involved with the most famous and the most extraordinary of the real characters of the day.

Characteristic of this involvement of the various Beaumonts with the important actual personalities is the landing of the first of the family, young Pierre Beaumont, in New Orleans in 1718. His pirogue is met by none other than Bienville himself, who exclaims appropriately: "This city commands the whole river! The very gates of a vast empire!" (10). Pierre, ecstatic at arriving at the new France, "fell upon his knees, and, taking a handful of soil pressed it against his lips" (14). All is not right with the new world, however; for Pierre has left behind his Marie, the girl he loves. "Marie was rich; he was poor," Saxon rather economically tells his readers; and therein, of course, lies a tale of woe which ends with young Beaumont sighing deeply for Marie's "laughing eyes and . . . soft red lips" (13-14). Saxon has this heartbreak last ten years in time but only one chapter in manuscript, for Marie eventually comes to the new world, marries Pierre, and becomes the matriarch of the great Creole family.

As the couple matures and the heirs arrive, Saxon unfolds historical events in a dazzling, if not dizzying, panorama of family scenes. Pierre, having become the wise old patriarch, endowed with Saxon's hindsight of history, often makes remarkable predictions of future events. At one point, for example, he predicts that "stately buildings" will encircle what is now Jackson Square and that "a mighty cathedral [will] arise" nearby (66). Pierre is still alive when New Orleans comes under Spanish control and sees his city prosper and grow complacent toward potential enemies. Shortly after an apt warning about the British threat to New Orleans, he dies melodramatically in the great fire of 1788 (125). Saxon employs his fictional family members well in this scene, for as the old man dies almost in despair at the ongoing ruination of the city he has seen built, the voice of youth, in the person of his great-grandson Jacques, assures him redundantly: "Houses can be rebuilt again!" (123).

The Beaumont house is, predictably, rebuilt, and the family is next depicted by Saxon in 1803, when Jacques, now aged thirty-two, attends the transferral ceremonies in the Place d'Armes. In *Fabulous New Orleans* Saxon comments on the little noted historical fact that the day New Orleans became a part of the United States was a day of mourning among the Creoles in the city. In "At the Gates of Empire," he very effectively portrays this attitude, describing Jacques and his mother weeping as they watch the "foreign" soldiers, speaking a strange language, remove the French flag and carry it to the Cabildo (155). Jacques continues to resent the Americans (he "cordially detested" them) until he meets, and eventually marries, an American girl. In one of Saxon's best scenes, then, the hostility of the Creole for the American is resolved by a "marriage," literally and figuratively, of the two cultures. The Americanization of Jacques is completed when, fighting side by side with Jackson against the British in 1815, he remarks to a fellow soldier from Kentucky, "We are all Americans now!" (191).

Saxon, perhaps growing weary with the pace of his story and of history, speeds more rapidly through the second century of New Orleans life. Beginning about two-thirds through the manuscript of "At the Gates," Saxon's Beaumonts are born, mature, and die at a much quicker pace than their ancestors, coming and going like Franklin's ephemerae. Consequently, most of the latter-day Beaumonts are less fully drawn characters, and some become *in toto* what their forebears were only in part: vehicles to personalize the history. Maurice Beaumont, for example, is a ghost of a character who contracts yellow fever and dies in a scene taking only six lines to relate; his great-great-grandfather Pierre's death scene during the fire, Saxon relates over five pages (cf. 120-24 and 269).

In many cases, however, the author's increased pace serves him well. What he loses in depth of characterization as his history progresses into the second century, he more than compensates for in becoming less heavy-handed and didactic; as his characters' prophecies and pronouncements decrease, Saxon's subtlety and sophistication increase. A case in point is the treatment of Paul Beaumont. After dispensing with the Civil War in a short chapter, Saxon takes his family rapidly toward the turn of the century. In another effective use of the Beaumonts as a microcosm for all New Orleans, he portrays a schism in the family which arises out of their conflicting attitudes toward the post-war boom of the "new" city—beyond the French Quarter. Saxon exemplifies the new New Orleanian in Paul. This young man not only sells the Beaumont jewels to buy property outside the Quarter, but marries a girl who "could not even speak French" and who finds the Quarter quaint and "interesting—like a bygone world" (355-58). Although Saxon spends so little time on these Beaumonts that the characters emerge as somewhat shadowy figures, Paul, at least, does not deliver pat harangues about the rising threat of the British or contrived pronouncements about all of Jackson's fighters being Americans. In Saxon's later representation of a type in the individual, Paul's few actions speak more eloquently than old Pierre Beaumont's many words.

In what is perhaps the artistic climax of "At the Gates," Paul's sister Inez calls on her mother, Isabelle Beaumont, now the aged matriarch of the family. As he describes this confrontation of the new and old Orleanians, Saxon shows an impressive use of certain symbols for the decaying world of Isabelle and the old Creole family she represents. As Inez, the daughter, walks down Royal Street to visit her mother, Saxon writes:

> In Royal Street, the cobblestones were rough and uneven. They were
> in need of repair; they were so rough, in fact, that riding out in the
> family carriage was almost impossible, as one was jolted almost to
> pieces. (378)

The crumbling cobblestones, now an unfit road for the family carriage to travel, function as a nice symbol and set the mood for what the daughter encounters as she approaches the old house. The stench of sewage and decaying animal matter permeates the entire Quarter, and Saxon notes that this smell of death was even noticeable to Inez as she entered the Beaumont courtyard. As she climbs the stairs, bearing her gift (a bouquet of white roses) to Isabelle, Inez notices the dim light from the street falling upon an ancient portrait of Pierre Beaumont. Finally, entering the "half-light" of her mother's room, Inez places the flowers in water and calls, "Maman!" repeatedly. Thinking her mother is sleeping in the old four-poster bed, she approaches, touches the old woman's hand "as it lay upon the coverlet . . . . Then Inez knew" (380).

The death of the oldest Beaumont is thus prepared for and described by Saxon in a manner completely different from the flamboyant and florid death of Old Pierre. The tenderness, subtlety, and restraint of the later passage are in striking contrast to the clumsy, melodramatic benedictions and prophecies that Saxon unmercifully has Pierre deliver as he dies during the raging fire. Saxon's last great Creole figure dies in her sleep in an upstairs room as her daughter, looking at the scene "reflected in the glass door of the armoire," sits by her side and remembers playing in the room as a young girl.

Obviously, it is possible that Saxon may have drawn on details of his own mother's death for this very effective scene. Beginning with the next generation of Beaumonts in the story, however, certain similarities to Saxon's own family surely appear. Virginia Beaumont, for example, is described by her brother as "dead gone on women's rights" (384). Saxon later tells his readers that this Beaumont girl was a suffragist leader and attended sessions of the state legislature demanding various women's rights (388). He could very well have made all these statements, of course, about his own grandmother, Elizabeth Lyle Saxon.

An even closer parallel exists, however, between Virginia Beaumont's nephew Frank and Saxon himself. Frank is the last of the family and, like Saxon, is thirty years old in 1921. A newspaperman, he is given

an assignment to write the history of New Orleans. Here Saxon has progressed to an interesting point: in completing his own story, he arrives at the
present time, during which his fictional counterpart completes a similar
story for his newspaper. What Frank Beaumont feels as he finishes his
assignment surely reflects Saxon's own feelings. The fictional reporter
begins to ponder what lies between the lines he has written and hopes that
he has given a full picture of the old and the new. Saxon then has him
deliver the "punchline" and the *raison d'être* of Frank's and of Saxon's
stories:

> That was the right idea, Frank thought. The old should be preserved,
> but the new encouraged. The two were compatible—it must be so.
> Otherwise there was only decay ahead. (416)

Frank, having stayed up all night writing his story, leaves his office and
observes New Orleans at dawn. In a far less didactic and much more
sophisticated way, Saxon then makes the same point that had struck Frank
at the newspaper office. The light of the rising sun, Saxon concludes,
shone on both the old church spires and on the windows of the new
buildings of the business section; the whole city was bathed in the morning
sunshine, and, with the coming of the new day, "the shadows disappeared"
(418).

Despite the creditable final chapters of "At the Gates of Empire," the
work is no masterpiece. Charles East, former director of the L.S.U. Press,
read the manuscript several years ago and found most of it "embarrassingly
dated."[13] Saxon's own attitude toward the story was reasonable and shows
no inordinate pride. In a foreword to the manuscript, he writes:

> "At the Gates of Empire" has no literary pretensions; it is a simple
> story, simply told. I have tried to make it accurate in detail, and I have
> tried to give a true picture of the life of the men and women of New
> Orleans through the changing years.

Saxon, explaining in this foreword that the story had run serially in
The Times-Picayune, then includes the usual disclaimer about his
fictitious characters. By its content and by its very existence, this foreword
suggests that he attempted at some later time to have "At the Gates of
Empire" published in book form. He may not have tried very hard,

however. Catherine Dillon, a close friend of Saxon since his youth, writes that the author found his first book-length manuscript "very embarrassing."[14]

Surely it is to Saxon's credit that he found certain parts of this romance embarrassing—as perhaps more than one potential publisher has found it over the years. Parts are very poor, and much of the manuscript is tedious reading. The circumstances of the writing were probably such that some excuses can be made for Saxon. He must have grown weary from the first chapter in April to the last installment in August. These daily assignments were, in all probability, like Saxon's book page—desserts in addition to his regular work. As noted above, his scope narrowed considerably as he wrote; perhaps because of this trimming of his sails, however, Saxon shows a marked improvement within his story. His later use of symbols, as in the death scene and the sunrise scene, as well as his growing restraint, are evidences of a kind of maturity developing in the writer during the four-month serialization. This maturation, incidentally, seems as thoroughly spontaneous as it is obvious; surely no Joycean stylistic variance was premeditated as the story unfolded to modern times.

The overall change within the manuscript can best be seen in comparisons of the two death scenes and of the two love scenes discussed above. The bathetic death of Pierre in the midst of the great fire is succeeded by the pathetic scene in the upstairs room on Royal Street. Here, Isabelle's death is anticipated by the smell in the streets, the white roses, and the "half-light" of the room. In the two love scenes, the tritely expressed love of Pierre for the girl he left behind is in sharp contrast to the almost mystical love affair between the newspaperman and his city. In this latter case, perhaps the love of the city was more real to Saxon than the love of a woman. In a scrapbook, he once wrote these lines about New Orleans:

> When one writes of a city dear to him, he is tempted to compare that
> city to a woman. And if, for a moment you will grant that I—as a
> man—am also a lover, I shall try to tell you of the woman to whom I
> offer my love . . . this woman, New Orleans . . . ."[15]

At any rate, the last part of "At the Gates of Empire," written *con amore* and reflecting the steady improvement characteristic of the manuscript, provides the reader with a memorable conclusion. Ponderous as his initial book-length effort surely is, Lyle Saxon proved to his *Times-Picayune* readers and proves in his manuscript that he could in the end manage scenes of love and death and indicates a promise of better things. During four months of 1921, therefore, Louisiana history progressed two centuries on the pages of *The Times-Picayune;* and, at the same time, Lyle Saxon traveled quite a distance himself.

Notwithstanding Saxon's praise, through the fictional Frank Beaumont, of both the new and the old city, there is no doubt that the Vieux Carré charmed him far more than the burgeoning new business district. "As far as I am concerned," he writes in *Fabulous New Orleans,* "the old section must always remain the most interesting, for it was the cradle of the city's history. To me the modern city is—a modern city" (260). It is not surprising, then, that Saxon chose to live in the French Quarter from his first days as a newspaperman in the city. What is surprising, however, is the appalling condition of the old section about the time of World War I. Lillian Hellman describes the city during this time as a very dirty place, "with open sewers and epidemics . . . ."[16] Noteworthy too are the facts that, before 1920, the French Opera House was gone, the St. Louis Hotel had been razed, livestock was kept in the Pontalba Buildings, and Gallatin Street was notorious for its criminal element.

The young newspaperman was surely distressed by this situation when he decided to reside in New Orleans. He evidently resolved from the beginning, however, that he would live in the notorious Quarter and that he would do all he could to transform it. Sometime "very early in his newspaper career,"[17] Saxon rented a house at 612 Royal Street. Frederick Karl seems to assume that Saxon's having a home on Royal is indicative of his inherited wealth, his "plantation background."[18] It should be remembered, however, that Saxon rented or acquired his early French Quarter properties during what were, to put it mildly, buyers' markets in the old section of New Orleans. He was fond of recalling later that he leased this sixteen-room house on Royal Street for sixteen dollars a month.

Saxon's friend Ray Thompson writes that everyone the young reporter knew begged him not to live among the thieves and squalor of the Quarter.[19] Undaunted, however, Saxon leased and restored this Royal property. Muriel Saxon Lambert told me of her visits to this house and recalled that her cousin Lyle was one of the first people to restore a Vieux Carré dwelling. That he was instrumental in the restorations that followed is a foregone conclusion. Robert Cantwell recalled years later the important role Saxon played in saving the Quarter from total ruination, and another writer pinpoints Saxon as the precipitant of the entire movement to save the Vieux Carré.[20] Longtime New Orleans bookseller and publisher Tess Crager told me emphatically that "it was Lyle Saxon and nobody else who saved the Quarter."[21] Through the efforts of Saxon and others, moreover, the Vieux Carré Society was established shortly after World War I, and a city ordinance was passed stating that no further changes could be made to a building in the Quarter without the sanction of the Society. The "cradle of the city's history" was thus safeguarded, and its reporter-resident had played a major role in its salvation.

On the pages of *The Times-Picayune,* Saxon steadily reported improvements which were made in the Quarter. As his own restoration on Royal Street progressed, he began to propose the idea of living in the Vieux Carré to his artist-friends. Robert Tallant, co-editor of *Gumbo Ya-Ya*, writes of Saxon's habit of getting his friends to walk with him through the old streets while he talked with them of the historicity of the place and encouraged them to move there.[22] "Then there began an influx of painters and writers," Tallant continues, "most of them searching for another Greenwich Village, many of them poseurs and fakers, but some genuine workers." Gradually, Tallant concludes, the French Quarter—primarily because of Saxon's influence—became "more an art colony, less an underworld."[23]

Throughout the next several years he would spend in New Orleans, Saxon lived intermittently at the 612 Royal Street house and, on occasion, in one he had bought in 1920, located at 536 Royal. The house at 612 was three stories high, complete with wrought iron balconies and courtyard, and was even "immortalized," for a brief period, in the fiction of Fanny Heaslip Lea.[24] Elsewhere it is described as having been "the Mermaid Tavern of Royal Street," as a "perpetual open house," and as the showplace and guest-house of visiting dignitaries and celebrities.[25] Saxon's many friends and the contacts he made through his work at *The Times-Picayune* make all these descriptions seem quite accurate. Saxon's salon, conducted first in this ancient house and to be continued in other parts of the Quarter, in New York, and at Melrose plantation, was open in earnest by 1920.

One of the first of Saxon's artistic friends to join him in residing in the Quarter was William Spratling. When Spratling arrived in New Orleans to take a position as instructor in architecture at Tulane University, he was advised discretely by older faculty members "that it would be more respectable" if he were to live elsewhere than in the Vieux Carré.[26] Spratling's future would involve an impressive variety of accomplishments, including publishing a book with his friend William Faulkner, mining silver in Mexico, and attaining a national reputation as an artist. During the first few years of his stay in the Quarter, however, he illustrated some of Saxon's newspaper stories and persuaded his friend to write an introduction for his own volume of New Orleans drawings.[27]

As Saxon's salon was forming, Grace King was, of course, the literary lioness of New Orleans. Saxon's friendship with her evidently began during his first days in the city. He attended many of her Thursday afternoon teas and found her works an inspiration and a useful source of information. Saxon's friendship with Grace King continued until her death in 1932, whereupon he delivered a eulogy at a memorial service for her and served as one of her pallbearers.[28] Almost forty years older than Saxon, King struck him as "too straight-laced,"[29] however, and it is doubtful that their friendship was as warm or as comfortable for Saxon as those he found among his cronies in the Quarter.

Surely Saxon's closest friend by the end of 1922 was fellow *Times-Picayune* employee Roark Bradford. More than any other single figure, Bradford would share his friend's triumphs and disappointments until Saxon's death. Mary Rose, Bradford's wife, comments in a letter to Cammie Henry that Lyle was her husband's best friend for the twenty-four years they knew each other.[30] The two met at the newspaper office when both were put on the night shift. Bradford, at that time a bachelor, was feature editor of the newspaper and met with his follow workers in a speakeasy called "The Press Club" as often as in the office.[31] The comradeship among the writers and artists in these days was fondly remembered by Bradford years later. In a letter to Saxon, written after his friend had departed for New York, Bradford laments that the Quarter had become filled with "country boys and gals . . . coming in to be Bohemians" and that immorality "lacks that calm, professional dignity" it once had.[32]

Sometime during the zenith of the dignified immorality of the early 1920s, Saxon and Bradford gave birth to Annie Christmas. This character, a kind of female Mike Fink with some of the physical prowess of Paul Bunyan, was created *ex nihilo* by the two over drinks in the Quarter.[33] Saxon and Bradford were known to create history on occasion, and Saxon was widely notorious for enjoying the perpetration of a hoax. "These two inventive brains, Lyle and Brad," Mary Rose Bradford explains, "made up out of whole cloth the goddamdest funniest stories of the early '20's which have since crept into the folklore of New Orleans."[34] Mary Rose goes on to explain the birth of this folk heroine, Annie Christmas. Running short of fodder for *Times-Picayune* features on New Orleans folk characters, Saxon suggested that he "discover" old manuscripts which dealt with the "ancient" myth of Annie. This decided, he and Roark made up all kinds of stories relating to a legendary river lady. The only problem left was naming her. Saxon suggested "Mary Christmas," Mary Rose recalls, but her husband cautioned: " 'Nobody would believe *that*. Call her Annie Christmas.' Result: folklore."

Not only did Annie Christmas make the pages of the newspaper, but Saxon continued the story, still preserving the illusion of repeating old folk tales, in two of his books.[35] Several years later, an unsuspecting Carl Carmer asked Saxon and Bradford for information regarding tall tales from the New Orleans area for inclusion in his book *The Hurricane's Children.* Fellow *Times-Picayune* reporter Meigs Frost recalls the result: "Saxon and . . . Bradford fed him Annie Christmas raw. He gulped it. He gave Annie Christmas a whole chapter in that book."[36] In a sense, of course, by 1937 when Carmer accepted and perpetuated Annie, she had become legend.

Just as Roark Bradford's friendship would continue throughout the years following 1922, so would a relationship Saxon established the next year. In March 1923, at one of Grace King's "Thursday afternoons at home," Saxon met Cammie Garrett Henry. When the *Times-Picayune* reporter mentioned to Henry that he was to do an assignment soon in Natchitoches, she invited him to visit her at Melrose plantation, some fifteen miles from the town. Cammie Henry, whose husband had acquired the plantation in 1899, restored the grounds and buildings at Melrose and, by the time she met Saxon, had begun her collection of Louisiana lore in the form of scrapbooks.[37]

Saxon first visited Henry at Melrose on April 1, 1923. He was overwhelmed with the peaceful nature and beautiful setting of the place and wrote "Aunt Cammie" three days after he returned to New Orleans, thanking her for the pleasant visit and confessing that the day at Melrose "seemed too good to be true."[38] In the same letter, Saxon vows that "if there is any possible way in the world to arrange it," he plans to come to Melrose in the summer (of 1923), live in one of the cabins, and write a novel. This is the earliest of several early references the author would make to what would eventually become *Children of Strangers* fourteen years later. According to

Saxon's longtime friend Francois Mignon, he looked at one of the slave cabins during this initial visit to Melrose and exclaimed to Cammie Henry on the spot that he could write a book there. Even if such a Cooper-like declaration sounds suspicious, Saxon's statement in the letter does verify the fact that he decided very early to write someday at Melrose. Within the next decade, he was to write part or all of four books there.

Saxon did not let his enthusiasm over the April 1 visit cool before he drew on it for a Sunday feature for *The Times-Picayune.* "Easter Sunday at Aunt Cammie's" appeared in the April 22, 1923, magazine section. Saxon begins this article, full of exorbitant praise for "Aunt Cammie" and Melrose, with the declaration that when he dies and goes to heaven, he will "pass by the halos, the harps, the wings and all the rest of the celestial grandeur" and spend his time instead on Melrose plantation.[39] Remarkably, after only one day at Melrose, what would seem romanticized first impressions turn out to be feelings that Saxon would never really change or temper. His comments that Aunt Cammie "wins you to her at once" and that he never felt so much at home anywhere else reflect as accurately his feelings twenty years later.

Saxon was not able to arrange leaving *The Times-Picayune* to go to Cammie Henry's cabin and write his novel in the summer of 1923. During this year and the next, however, he wrote several short stories, one play, and a few features for the Sunday *Times-Picayune* and, in addition, had an article published for the first time in a medium other than a newspaper. Perhaps inspired by his visit to Melrose, Saxon wrote a good deal of fiction during the next several months after his initial visit there; all this work, however, was evidently still done in addition to his regular newspaper assignments. Following the Melrose article, eleven featured items by Saxon appeared in the *Times-Picayune* magazine. The first of these is in the May 27, 1923, newspaper; the last appeared in July of the next year. Like "At the Gates of Empire," the articles are uneven in quality. It is entirely possible, moreover, that since Saxon was embarrassed by the long serialized story, he did not point with great pride in subsequent years to some of these items either. They do represent, however, an important step for the reporter: they are another departure from straight news assignments and anticipate his turning first to the writing of short fiction upon leaving *The Times-Picayune* in 1926.

Saxon's initial full-length effort in the newspaper's Sunday fiction format is a story called "The One Thing."[40] This story revolves around a stenographer named Emily, who is blind, but is "not mawkishly sentimental about it." Emily may not be, but Saxon is mawkish about the blindness and includes the predictable comments about the girl's never having seen a rainbow or a sunset. The story depicts primarily a relationship Emily develops with a male pen pal who does not know she is blind and who writes her wonderful letters, which her sister reads to her. Emily's chief interest in common with the man is a love of the opera. As Christmas approaches, one letter arrives with "the one thing" that Emily's friend is sure she will love: a pair of opera glasses. Saxon, like almost everyone else in 1923, surely had read his O. Henry; by 1919 over 4,100,000 volumes of O. Henry's stories had been sold. Of course since a great many of O. Henry's tales had been published in the same format—in the Sunday magazine of the *New York World*—Saxon was especially writing in the mode of the "master." F. L. Pattee's description of the formulas followed in the *New York World* stories fits Saxon's in *The Times-Picayune* well,[41] and the notorious ironic surprise ending is apparent in "The One Thing."

Saxon's next Sunday fiction appeared four months later and bears the intriguing title "The Perfume of Her Presence."[42] This story is actually a dramatic monologue with brief stage directions at the beginning and end. One of the two characters, a poet, talks; and the other, Marie, his very dumb blonde companion, listens. In the best tradition of Browning, Saxon's young poet keeps the reader informed of the actions of his sleepy listener by asking questions ("You smile? You do not understand?") as he delivers his harangue to her. The subject of the talk is perfume and its influence on men. Saxon, having warned the reader in the first paragraph that the girl is sleepy, delivers his O. Henry Sunday punch by having the young man finally reach the climax of his tirade only to discover that Marie is "sleeping like a tired child." The couple in this story, as thin, artificial, and exaggerated as Pattee describes many of O. Henry's, nevertheless are reminiscent of more creditable literary relationships as well. The situation between Saxon's young man and woman is somewhat akin to that between Jean Toomer's narrator and Avey in the "Avey" section of *Cane*.[43] Saxon's treatment is light, of course, but the wide gulf is present between the poet-man and pedestrian-woman in both stories, and in both the man ends up talking to himself when the woman falls asleep.

"Blackmail," Saxon's next *Times-Picayune* effort the following spring, involves a situation wherein a cunning woman is rejected as a mistress and, therefore, seeks revenge by blackmailing her former lover.[44] The narrator is directly involved; for he acts as an intermediary between the former lovers, and he eventually discovers the would-be blackmailer's flaw: alcoholism. In her drunkenness, the girl admits previous con games, and the narrator, realizing this is just another, threatens her with exposure and saves his friend. The blackmailer is thus blackmailed in a plot the creator of Red Chief would surely have appreciated.

The fourth *Times-Picayune* story, "The Man Who Hated Women," involves a confirmed misogynist, a reporter named Dangerfield, falling in love and changing his feelings toward women.[45] Passionate as he had been in his woman hating, he loses all ill feelings for the opposite sex because of his angelic wife. Saxon gives his readers more than a modern Benedick, however, and adds to the irony inherent in this situation. The woman Dangerfield marries turns out to be "wanted in Butte, Mont., for theft and for a badger-game in Kansas City." Dangerfield orders her away, leaves his job in the city, and turns up years later in a scene like the one with which Saxon begins the story: delivering diatribes against women among his fellow reporters in a café.

Four of Saxon's stories in the *Times-Picayune* magazine, then, contain a female character who somehow is degraded or ruined in the end. In the first three, Emily, Marie, and the blackmailer, all blondes incidentally, are depicted unfavorably and given no touch of grace by the author. Emily's fault is only blindness, but she is crushed for the sake of an ironic ending; Marie emerges as nothing more than the stereotypical dumb blonde, as she falls asleep during her poetic lover's speech; and the blackmailer is vanquished, undone and denied the enormous sum she has demanded. In "The Man Who Hated Women," Dangerfield's wife, "one of those soft, well-rounded little blondes," is also exposed and fittingly rejected. The reader is tempted to conclude that Saxon, not Dangerfield, was the man who hated women, or at least blonde women. More likely is the possibility that he had found a formula his editor and/or readers had approved and stuck with it.

The fifth story is a surprising departure from the others. It is a suspenseful tale that shows somewhat more art than previously. "The Return" is that by George Durand to Marie, his fiancée of ten years before.[46] The couple had quarreled, and George had forsaken her. Now contrite, he wishes to call on her but is greeted at the door, after an unusually long delay, by her eccentric uncle. This old man, Prosper Marinee, is distracted and will not respond to George's questions about his niece. Saxon herein displays an adept foreshadowing of horror; all sorts of strange and ominous things begin to affect George. He feels a "vague fear" when he enters the house, he notices that several rooms are barren of the grand furniture that once adorned them, he senses a "peculiar odor . . . an odor of animals" in the air, and, strangest of all, he sees no trace of Marie. Finally he hears a sound, like the scampering of tiny feet, emanating from a room overhead. George is then given an amazing explanation by Prosper. The old man has developed a group of cannibalistic rats to devour their fellow creatures and thus rid the city of its vermin problem. Listening horrified, George frantically asks the old man where Marie is. Prosper ignores his questions and explains that some rats can be made so vicious as to attack and kill human beings, to devour them without a trace. "Where is Marie?" George implores and, upon reflection, asks Prosper how he knows his rats can kill a person. "I know—ah, I know" is the answer.

In "The Return" Saxon is quite successful in mounting his horror toward the climactic, grotesque revelation. The story contains certain similarities to well-known tales of horror and suspense. George's "vague fear" upon entering Prosper's house is very similar to the feelings of Poe's narrator, for example, in "The Fall of the House of Usher." The old friend of Roderick Usher at one point, in fact, refers to his feelings about the house as "vague sentiments." Other parallels exist between Poe's famous story and Saxon's "Return"—including the mysteries surrounding the woman of the house, the unusual sounds emanating from unseen sources, and the return of an outsider to a house of horror and decay in each story. Prosper Marinee, moreover, has a good deal in common with Hawthorne's Dr. Rappaccini, for Saxon's character, too, is one who "cares infinitely more for science than for mankind." The story also exemplifies a pattern that Joseph Blotner describes as a "distinctly Faulknerian trait": the use of an intricate plot with mysterious elements, the provision of all necessary facts, and the revelation of the causal relationship of the facts in the end.[47] Saxon's final *Times-Picayune* story from this period is no gem of horror and suspense and is far inferior to the tales that it resembles. It represents amelioration, nevertheless. The difference between "The Return" and the literary trick Saxon plays on poor blind Emily in his first story is at least as great as that between the closing and opening chapters of "At the Gates of Empire." In both instances, Saxon was getting better as he went along; the maturation process is obvious as his apprenticeship was running its natural course very nicely.

The *Times-Picayune* writer was publishing more than just short stories in the Sunday magazines of 1923 and '24. Saxon wrote one play during this period, a one-act effort called "Epitaph," which appeared in the fall of 1923.[48] This play is a rather feeble one consisting of four characters, two of whom are ghosts, and set in a cemetery. After the ghosts, former lovers, reveal in painfully clumsy expository passages that they had a child several years ago, this child and the man she thinks is her father approach to visit the female ghost's grave. The irony of the situation lies in the child's wondering what her mother was really like and why she herself is nothing like her "father." Saxon plays this irony for all it is worth and far more; the reader gets a glimpse of what O. Henry may have been like as a playwright. Saxon's play was produced, at least once, at Le Petit Théâtre du Vieux Carré and was "enthusiastically received."[49] "Epitaph," along with Saxon's earlier dramatic effort in Chicago, "The Peacock," and his stated desire to write plays indicate a continuing interest in drama over the years.[50] Nevertheless, no other plays have survived, and this was a genre in which he was never to succeed. If "Epitaph" provides a clue, drama was certainly not his forte, and if there were other plays, they are perhaps well lost.

Saxon's other major productions of this two-year period are best described as elaborate "features." Subsequent to his article on Melrose came "After All These Years."[51] Here Saxon deals with the true story of a New Orleans couple who remarried in 1923 after being divorced thirty-eight years. The feature is the most mawkish and sentimental of all the *Times-Picayune* pieces. Saxon falls victim, for example, to the temptation to philosophize on how the man and woman must have felt when they were separated and lonely: "Only those who have known love, and all the happiness that love brings can know true loneliness. It is like an acid eating into your brain . . . ." Hopefully, this article, perhaps this simile, is what Saxon had in mind when he confides laughingly in a letter to a friend that the "human-interest rot" is what he does "so outrageously" for *The Times-Picayune.*[52]

In the fall of 1923, Saxon began to publish various features relating to New Orleans and rural Louisiana. His breakthrough into magazine publishing came in November with the appearance of "A Breath from the Vieux Carré" in *House and Garden.* The next two *Times-Picayune* features, "The Mistletoe Trail: Christmas on a Louisiana Plantation" and "Gallatin Street," would appear later, with minor changes, in *Old Louisiana* and *Fabulous New Orleans* respectively. During Mardi Gras in 1924, a

Saxon article on the history of Griswold Jewellers of New Orleans was published.[53]

Significantly, the final *Times-Picayune* feature from this period, like the last serial installment and the last Sunday short story, seems preeminently the best. "The Toil of Worship" is a description of the plans of the good Catholics of rural Canal, Louisiana, to build a new church.[54] The construction will be done by the parishioners themselves from the cypress trees that grow around them. Saxon is obviously impressed with the faith and industry of these people engaged in the proverbial labor of love. The final paragraphs of the article are quite well done. In them Saxon, watching the country folk go to the old church building for mass, uses symbols for their religion and for his own feelings:

> I lay that night upon sheets which smelled of rainwater, dried in the Southern sun, that sweet, undefinable odor that seems to emanate from the sunshine itself. And I . . . woke to the sound of the church bell, calling the faithful to mass.
>
> Outside my window a mockingbird in a flowering plum tree was filling the air with his song. In the road the people were passing by, in Sunday clothes, on their way to church . . . but [the bird], pagan creature, continued to sing, oblivious to everything but the Easter sunshine which poured down upon the world.
>
> And his song mingled with the calling of the bell.

The fragrant sheets, the bird in the flowering tree, the sunshine, and the bird's song excite Saxon's senses, while the people in their Sunday clothes surely have their senses fixed on the service they are summoned to by the tolling bell. This very well-written feature is interesting for what it implies about the author's personal feelings and beliefs. Although the sounds mingle outside the window, the song of the "pagan creature" would always be more attractive to Saxon than "the calling of the bell."

By 1925 the newspaperman's major contributions as a full-time employee of *The Times-Picayune* were over. He wrote no featured items for the Sunday magazine after the summer of 1924. The author was apparently quite ill for several months during this period, owing chiefly to his very demanding workload.[55] At this same time, Saxon's social life in New Orleans had become extremely active. His circle of friends widened considerably during late 1924, 1925, and early 1926, and in these years he made contacts, many with fellow writers, that would last the rest of his life. The number of writers and artists who deemed the Quarter both safe and pleasurable increased dramatically over the early days of Saxon's residence there. By the time the author left New Orleans in 1926, the impressive group who had visited extensively or resided in the city included Sherwood Anderson, William Spratling, Oliver La Farge, Roark Bradford, Edmumd Wilson, William Faulkner, Hamilton Basso, Dorothy Dix, Carl Carmer, Lord Dunsany, and John Dos Passos. To varying extents Saxon knew all these people and many more. In describing the Vieux Carré of the late 1920s, one writer comments that this section of New Orleans "holds more of those who have their heads in the clouds than any similar area in the world, including Greenwich Village . . . ."[56] One of Faulkner's biographers has recently described New Orleans of this era as "a writer's paradise," "an artistic milieu," and as "Paris of the South."[57]

Saxon continued to live variously at 612 and at 536 Royal; the latter property he sold in mid-1925—no doubt in preparation for leaving New Orleans. Whether at one of the Royal houses or at another on St. Peter Street where he apparently spent brief periods during renovations at 612 Royal, Saxon furthered his reputation as "genial host"[58] to the literati of New Orleans. The various free-lance writers, newspapermen, and Tulane University faculty members with whom Saxon socialized called themselves the "Shasta Daisies society."[59] Ben Franklin of Baton Rouge, a Tulane student in 1925, talked with me about various activities of this "society." The group had no trouble, Franklin explained, in getting alcohol in one form or another, and "needle" beer was a favorite beverage.[60] The writers stuck together, were very clannish, and inspired each other in literary activities. Saxon, Franklin recalled, was especially well liked, was unobtrusive, and "didn't have an enemy." Spratling, recalling these same days, writes in his autobiography:

> We were all very close. We saw each other every day, almost every evening. If it wasn't at Lyle Saxon's house, it was at Sherwood and Elizabeth's or my own, and there would be John Dos Passos, or perhaps Carl Sandberg or Carl Van Doren or a great publisher from New York, Horace Liveright or Ben Huebsh, all people we were proud to know.[61]

By the time of the soirees Spratling mentions, Saxon and Sherwood Anderson were well acquainted. The two men had met in 1922, when Anderson would lunch with Saxon almost daily in New Orleans.[62] Although they would perhaps never be as close as in the early days in New Orleans, the two writers remained friends and continued to correspond throughout the years. In a study of selected Saxon-Anderson letters, Cathy Harvey points out that, unlike others, Saxon "reciprocated Anderson's interest with affection and gratitude"; Saxon said he felt like a "puny child" compared to the older writer and claimed he would rather have Anderson's praise than anyone else's.[63]

By 1925 Sherwood and the third Mrs. Anderson, Elizabeth Prall, had set up housekeeping in a Pontalba apartment. Saxon, like Faulkner, was fond of Elizabeth Anderson and wrote in a letter to a friend in New York: "she has done no end of interesting things . . . but you have to draw her out, and when Sherwood is there she never says a word."[64] In the same letter, the author comments that Anderson, just returned from his 1925 lecture tour, had "cleaned up" in the college towns "where the students welcome him with open arms and the faculty asks him, privately, not to put notions in the boys' heads." Saxon then describes one of the Andersons' parties; the guests on this December day, 1925, included "young J. Hamilton Basso," William Spratling, "some strange psychologist," and a Russian Jew and his mistress. The Russian, a devoted socialist, created an uproar at the party, Saxon says, by screaming that Anderson had sold out to the capitalists when the host announced that he had signed a six-thousand-dollar contract with a women's magazine.

Another writer Saxon knew well by the time he left New Orleans was Oliver La Farge. This novelist, whose *Laughing Boy* would appear in 1929 and win him a national reputation, found, according to his biographer, a "creative well of inspiration" for his stories in New Orleans.[65] La Farge joined the Tulane faculty in 1925 and, like Spratling, lived near Saxon in the Quarter rather than in a more sedate part of town. The two writers were evidently confidants—at least concerning literary matters, for in a letter written shortly after the appearance of *Laughing Boy*, La Farge confesses to Saxon that he is having a great deal of difficulty writing again, that since the novel he has "gone sterile."[66]

Still another novelist whose fame lay in the decades ahead came to New Orleans in January of 1925. William Faulkner, staying at first with Elizabeth Anderson and her son at the Pontalba apartment, soon moved into the downstairs rooms of Spratling's house in the Quarter. Elizabeth Kell was at this time a reporter for *The Times-Picayune;* she came to know Faulkner when he was hired as a babysitter by some of her friends.[67] She recalled that Faulkner developed a friendship with Saxon soon after his arrival in New Orleans. David Minter includes Saxon among those who "befriended" Faulkner and from whom the young Mississippian "found help at every turn."[68] Another of Faulkner's biographers mentions that Faulkner would turn up at various parties—such as those at Saxon's apartment—"where everyone would seem to be talking at once in a crowded room, smoking and dipping their drinks from a large bowl of absinthe or pernod poured over a big piece of ice."[69] With the twenty-seven-year-old Faulkner living first at Anderson's and then with Spratling, he and Saxon surely were present at the same party quite soon after the former's arrival in January.

Early the next month, Faulkner's first item appeared in the Sunday *Times-Picayune* magazine.[70] Like Saxon's dozen articles of the previous two years, Faulkner's contributions consist of short stories and features or, to use the more familiar term, "sketches." Like many of Saxon's stories, too, Faulkner's *Times-Picayune* sketches reflect the "Age of O. Henry"; some are, as Blotner says, "surprise-ending formula stories."[71] Frederick Karl calls one of Faulkner's *Times-Picayune* pieces "a shabby piece of fiction, using an O. Henry surprise ending . . . ."[72] No influence of Saxon on Faulkner—either in format or in content—should be inferred in the case of these newspaper sketches, for both writers were of course influenced by the desires of the editors and by the success of the formula stories.

In another sense, however, Saxon may very well have had some influence regarding Faulkner's *Times-Picayune* contributions. Blotner's informants told him that Saxon was pleased when the young man from Mississippi was given a chance to earn some money by writing for the newspaper.[73] As mentioned above, Faulkner and Saxon very likely met at some party a few weeks before the former's initial story was published. Saxon's closest friend, Roark Bradford, moreover, was then Sunday editor and, according to his wife, "passed around among Lyle, Bill Faulkner, Sherwood Anderson, and other Ganymedes of the French Quarter" the small fees he was allowed to pay for Sunday fiction.[74] It seems quite characteristic for Saxon to have encouraged Bradford or someone at the paper to accept work from Faulkner. For whatever reason, the younger man "looked up to" the established reporter;[75] and, according to George W.

Healy, Jr., longtime editor of *The Times-Picayune,* Faulkner often came to the newsroom to talk with Saxon and others.[76]

Even more significant than the possibility that Saxon encouraged the newspaper editors to publish Faulkner's stories is the possibility that he encouraged Faulkner to write them. Faulkner so often alluded to Anderson's influence during their New Orleans days (an influence Saxon acknowledged as well[77]) that perhaps other early influences on Faulkner have been overlooked. Carvel Collins points out, however, that at least the earliest of the *Times-Picayune* pieces "were certainly not the product of Sherwood Anderson's daily example as a writer, because . . . Anderson was not then in New Orleans."[78] From the first days, though, Faulkner did have Saxon as daily example—an especially good example of what *The Times-Picayune* would want. Although it would be ludicrous to suggest that without Saxon's influence Faulkner would not have turned to fiction, it seems similarly inconceivable that the older writer did not have some effect on the writing of these stories and sketches that, as Collins says, "foreshadowed some of [Faulkner's] mature subsequent work."[79] Whatever the inspiration, Faulkner's earliest fiction was the product of a time when he frequently socialized with Saxon, one of the luminaries of the newspaper that published his early sketches.

Curiously enough, Saxon seems to have had no significant involvement with *The Double Dealer,* the other source of Faulkner's New Orleans work. John McClure, fellow *Times-Picayune* employee and Saxon's successor on the book review page, was a steady contributor, as was Hamilton Basso. Most of those associated with the magazine, in fact, were at least casual acquaintances of Saxon. One extensive study of *The Double Dealer,* however, reveals no connection between Saxon and the magazine.[80] No unsigned contribution is identified in this study as Saxon's, and there is no intrinsic evidence to indicate that any of the anonymous pieces are by him. Another discussion of Saxon and *The Double Dealer* indicates that although the author "served on the magazine's staff for seven months," he was an "outsider"—not a close friend of the founder and not a member of an "established" New Orleans family.[81]

For whatever reasons, then, one of the most widely read Orleanians was never read in the other literary centers that received the now-famous little magazine. Saxon's Sunday successes in *The Times-Picayune* may have precluded his interest in *The Double Dealer;* the salaried reporter may not have been enthusiastic to publish in an organ that had not paid its contributors since 1922. Speculation is vain, naturally, but it is conceivable too that he had work rejected. The prestige of *The Double Dealer* is now, of course, well established by its contributors, who read like a regional Who's Who of the 1920s. If Saxon shunned this famous publishing venture of the Quarter because he thought it inferior to the Sunday literature of *The Times-Picayune*, his taste today looks especially and unfortunately shortsighted. To the newspaperman, it should be remembered, however, the difference between a story or sketch for *The Times-Picayune* and for *The Double Dealer* in the 1920s could have been simply the difference between twenty-five dollars and nothing.

One French Quarter publication that did not exclude Saxon, though, was Spratling and Faulkner's *Sherwood Anderson and Other Famous Creoles*, a tongue-in-cheek portrait book of the various habitués and residents of the Vieux Carré, published privately in 1926. In addition to Spratling's caricature of the title character, the book contains Faulkner's notorious parody of Anderson in the foreword and his various witticisms about the lampooned artists of the Quarter. The drawing of Saxon shows him reclining against a pillow reading Strachey's *Eminent Victorians*; one writer has recently described the caricature of Saxon as "a decadent, effete fellow with an imperious look."[82] Faulkner's line below the drawing reads: "The Mauve Decade in St. Peter Street."

Sherwood Anderson and Other Famous Creoles indicates how conditions had changed in the French Quarter since the days Saxon braved the filth and decay and rented his first house on Royal Street. Not only were there so many artists and writers in the Quarter as to furnish fodder for Spratling and Faulkner's satire in 1926, but the "Mauve Decade" had indeed come to the Vieux Carré. Tess Crager told me that to say that Lyle Saxon, primarily alone, changed the face of the Quarter is not an exaggeration, but the "plain truth." By the mid-twenties surely, as Saxon himself once said, Sherwood Anderson was "the idol of the aspiring group" of artists.[83] Anderson, however, had arrived much later than Saxon and himself was drawn to set up residence there before he became the magnetic figure attracting many others. In 1934 Edmund Wilson singled Saxon out for John Peale Bishop to look up in New Orleans since Saxon "knows everybody," and a few years later *Newsweek* paid tribute to Saxon, describing him as "the adviser, comforter, and financial ally of bitter and poverty-pinched young writers" of New Orleans.[84]

During this period from about 1919 to 1926, Saxon was involved in literary activities in more than the advisory capacity mentioned in *Newsweek*. His successes in *The Times-Picayune*, especially his serialized history and the Sunday fiction, might indicate that things could only get better for him at the newspaper. By 1926 he had not only "arrived" as a first-rate New Orleans newspaperman; he was perhaps the highest paid reporter in the city.[85] Another *Times-Picayune* reporter during those days told me that anyone interested in newspaper work in New Orleans in the 1920s "adored" Lyle Saxon.[86] These were the circumstances, then, when one of the most admired writers in the city quit his job and rather suddenly went to New York.

One reason for Saxon's extraordinary move was surely the way he came to feel about many of his assignments with *The Times-Picayune*. From the first days of his return to newspaper work in the South, his workload had been heavy. Moreover, the daily tasks he performed throughout his tenure at the newspaper consisted of many mundane news stories and many inane features. His assignments, for example, included articles on the influence of Spanish architecture on modern buildings, a series about "Unusual Ways of Making a Living" among New Orleans's working masses, several articles on drug abuse in the city, an exposé of prison conditions, and coverage of various motion picture openings at local theaters.[87]

As early as 1918, Saxon in his letters confides his true feelings toward having to write so much under such hectic conditions. In two beautifully written letters to Mercedes Garig, his former mentor at L.S.U., Saxon reveals his reservations about writing for a newspaper and, specifically, about much of the work he had done. In a letter written in the early autumn, composed at his desk at the *New Orleans Item*, Saxon compares newspaper work to acting: "it lasts not one minute longer than the scene is played; and if it is art at all, it is transient art, like a dancer's, and dies when the music stops."[88] Saxon then reacts to Garig's observation that he writes "too freely" and with "too much fluidity." He admits that the charge is true and says his newspaper writing is

> like pouring water out of a pitcher . . . my words run all over the floor, all over the house, all over the world. . . . I think that it is because I write too easily, nothing that I write causes me an effort; consequently, nothing that I write has any lasting value.

Three months later, in a letter written at year's end, Saxon tells Garig of
inadvertently kindling his fire with a section of the newspaper containing a
story he had labored long and hard over. He writes,

> and there I was making a fire with it. And all over New Orleans people
> were doing the same thing. . . . I started to pull the thing out of the
> grate . . . . Then changed my mind and applied the match, thinking,
> "What's the use?"[89]

In late 1919 the author tells his Aunt Maude that he will "probably
keep at this damned game" until he dies, pondering life's futility.[90] After
another six or seven years at the same "damned game," though, Saxon
shows increasing frustration and bitterness over his newspaper work. In a
1926 letter to Sherwood and Elizabeth Anderson, he complains of the "rut"
he finds himself in, adding that he has reached the "depths of prostitution"
and that he has to go to New York if he is ever to "amount to anything."[91]
A few months before, in a letter to former *Times-Picayune* employee Noel
Straus, Saxon parodies his own worst style. He relates a very moving
story about meeting a courageous dwarf named Julia, but says that if he
ever wrote it for the newspaper, the story would "have to be some blah
about 'Miss Julia's body is little, but her heart is big!' You know the sort
of thing I do . . . ."[92] "Newspaper work is fine for the young writer if not
overdone," Saxon said in a 1933 interview, "but I believe it is possible to
write too long and too much on newspapers, with the result that the writer
burns out."[93] This is a rather colossal understatement considering Saxon's
candid revelations to his friends about his own newspaper assignments—
even quite early in his career.

It seems very unlikely, however, that Saxon would have remained at
The Times-Picayune even if his sole assignment had been the Sunday
fiction. Overwork was evidently not the only consideration for leaving.
Surely he was aware that most Sunday magazine stories were, as F. L.
Pattee said in 1922, "as ephemeral as the comic sections which they
neighbor."[94] Saxon evidently submitted other stories to fiction magazines,
unsuccessfully, while he wrote these newspaper pieces. The difference
between the author's *Times-Picayune* stories and his first magazine story,
published in *The Dial*, is striking enough to indicate that surely the writer
knew that one kind of fiction was likely to be more lasting than the other.
Pattee, again commenting on the pulp fiction of the day, remarked that the

newspaper stories were designed to catch the reader, to stun him if necessary, and were always done "in altitudissimo."[95] The conscientious artist,
Pattee continues, is by contrast concerned with "really durable material" and
must strive to be "a serious portrayer of human life . . . ."

Lyle Saxon certainly had the desire to become a serious literary artist
when he left *The Times-Picayune* in 1926. His feelings toward the work he
had done for the last eight years and toward the "art" he had produced were
revealed implicitly in a 1940 interview. When asked about his early days in
New Orleans, he referred to the whole period as an apprenticeship.[96]
Saxon's departure was, in part at least, an escape from the days spent and
from the stories written "in altitudissimo." As surely as he knew the difference between the stories of *The Dial* and of the newspaper, he knew he
could never produce the former within the format of the latter. Instead of
pursuing his early "hard news" reporting, he had gravitated, within the
newspaper, to the book review page, to the serialized romance, and to the
Sunday stories. His affinity for fiction, which had shaped his journalistic
career, could now only lead beyond the newspaper and—at least for a
while—beyond New Orleans.

3

DEPARTURE:
NEW YORK AND MELROSE

SAXON SEEMS TO HAVE BEEN in his prime physically during his early New York days. In his mid-to-late thirties, he enjoyed relatively good health, though Edmund Wilson alludes to Saxon's "old Southern gentleman bladder trouble" during heavy drinking.[1] Those who associated with Saxon at the time often describe him as cultivated, affable, and urbane—though occasionally "rather ostentatious, voluble."[2] Mutual friends of Faulkner and Saxon recalled that Saxon, "a tall, plump, blue-eyed man," was perceived as an "elegant bachelor," as a "charmer and raconteur."[3] More specifically, other friends have described him as having unforgettable pale blue eyes, standing about six-feet-two-inches tall, and frequently dressing in an elegant black linen suit.[4] Many who knew Saxon well have also alluded to his soft, cultured speech, which women found particularly attractive.

Those years immediately following Saxon's leaving *The Times-Picayune* were also the most productive of his literary career. In addition to publishing a book a year from 1927 to 1930, the young author wrote his most important short fiction and many book reviews and features for various magazines and newspapers during this time. This chapter will focus on the shorter productions of these years; the next will examine the four books Saxon wrote for the Century Company.

The title of the present chapter is, admittedly, an oversimplification, for Saxon's departure from New Orleans did not result in his spending specified and consecutive time periods in New York and at Melrose plantation. Beginning actually in about 1924, Saxon was, as Bernard De Voto once called him, "an itinerant bird," living and writing variously in New Orleans, Baton Rouge, Melrose, and New York.[5] Wherever he was during these years, however, Saxon continued to move from journalism toward fiction, to establish more friendships with the prominent literati of the day, and to secure a reputation for himself as a distinguished man of letters.

Among the several conditions in late 1925 and early 1926 that led Lyle Saxon to leave New Orleans was evidently an untenable situation that had evolved between the writer and a married woman, Olive Boullemet Lyons. Well known for her beauty and charm, Olive Lyons was the wife of a prominent and wealthy New Orleans pharmaceutical merchant and a resident of the Vieux Carré. Saxon had described the Lyonses' French Quarter home in his 1923 article in *House and Garden*.[6] Olive Lyons was well acquainted with the various writers and artists of the Quarter. A published poet, she served on the Advisory Council of *The Double Dealer* in 1921 and was a contributor to that magazine as well. Saxon's 1925 diary contains frequent mention of her, and one entry is particularly interesting:

> Driving with Olive in afternoon and a rather serious conversation in my apartment where we came late. Alone at night—I thought more about the situation—lucky perhaps that I am soon going away.[7]

Whatever trip Saxon alludes to in the diary—probably his move to New York—he did not go away for any length of time for over a year after this diary entry. In the interim, the relationship with Olive continued.

Exactly what this relationship was is somewhat difficult to determine. Those friends of Saxon whom Harvey interviewed indicated that he was in love with one woman, and "that woman was Olive Boullemet Lyons"; yet these same informants were divided as to whether or not Lyons and Saxon were lovers.[8] Saxon's cousin recalled to me that the author kept a photograph of Olive Lyons at his bedside in the St. Peter Street apartment and that he often remarked to her that Olive was the only woman he had ever known who possessed both striking beauty and great intellect.[9] One friend of Saxon with whom I talked in Louisiana acknowledged that the author was in love with the woman but doubted that the friendship was actually a romance;[10] others, like Tess Crager, assumed that he did have a love affair with Lyons. Another of my informants declined to name the woman Saxon loved in New Orleans in the 1920s, but indicated that an unfortunate love affair was influential in his leaving for New York.[11] An unrequited love is mentioned in Dreyer's essay, wherein the cause of Saxon's "broken heart" is likewise nameless.[12] Regardless of whether or not the relationship between Saxon and this woman was consummated sexually, their association in New Orleans had become, by 1926, a favorite subject for the local school for scandal.[13]

The question of Saxon's actually having an affair with Olive Lyons is of somewhat more than tangential significance here. Not only would such an affair be a significant factor in his decision to leave Louisiana, but, of course, it indicates the author's heterosexuality, which some of Saxon's friends strongly denied. In fact, several informants who talked with me about this and other love affairs of Saxon took his heterosexuality as much for granted as others took his homosexuality. During the author's youth, as noted in an earlier chapter, he seems to have dated several young women and to have had at least one heterosexual love affair in Texas. His boyhood friend George Favrot, however, may well have been an early homosexual contact. Harris Downey told me that the two young men were lovers and that, despite many other homosexual affairs, Favrot was the only close contact in Saxon's life. In speaking of the author's homosexuality, Downey pointed out that it was never a significant part of anything Saxon wrote. This seems an accurate enough observation as far as the subjects, themes, and major characters in Saxon's works are concerned.

Many others I spoke with, some of whom knew Saxon late in his life, supported the view that the writer was homosexual.[14] Because of the many discrepancies and contradictions concerning this aspect of Saxon's life, I conclude that what Joseph Henry and others have told me is probably accurate: that he was bisexual. Several of Saxon's letters and diary entries also indicate the author's intimate relationships with both men and women.[15] Those I talked with about this matter, however, mentioned repeatedly that Saxon's homosexual affairs were discrete, never a problem for his heterosexual friends, and not a significant part of his literary life.

In addition to the situation involving Olive Lyons, an important factor in Saxon's leaving New Orleans was the warming of his relationship with Cammie Henry at Melrose. As noted in Chapter 2, he had visited the plantation in April 1923. By 1925 his visits were almost regular weekend jaunts, and he surely longed for the day and the circumstances that would permit his going there to write. He made extended visits to the plantation in February and in April of 1925. Saxon's visit to Melrose in April was both restful and stimulating. In his diary he speaks variously of being "at peace" and of getting "much peace and rest" at the plantation.[16] On April 10 he comments that he was able to write again there for the first time in several

months. These comments indicate that Saxon was beginning to look upon
Melrose not only as a haven from the hectic social life of the Quarter, but as
a place where he could compose the kind of stories he really wanted to
write.

Perhaps on this trip to the plantation, or during another in 1925,
Saxon wrote "Cane River." This story, published in the March 1926 issue
of *The Dial*, appeared while Saxon was still employed at *The Times-
Picayune* and was surely another significant reason for his leaving the
newspaper to write fiction. "Cane River" anticipates Saxon's novel,
Children of Strangers, not only in setting, but in the use of "Yucca"
plantation—a fictional representation of Melrose—and of Mr. Guy, the
patriarch of Yucca who appears later in the novel. The essential difference
in subject matter is that the novel is concerned with mulattoes, while the
earlier story focuses on the lives of the blacks.

"Cane River" is narrated by a Yucca plantation black and is the story
of Susie, who came to the Cane River country as a girl. Susie was a "bad
one," and an "untamed savage" black, who was called "Trick-nigger" by the
others.[17] The men liked Susie all the better for her wildness, Saxon's
narrator explains, and she liked the black men well—especially a trapper
named Big Brown.   Not long after Big Brown began courting Susie,
when she was fourteen and "her popularity was at its height" (208), the
girl became pregnant and Brown disappeared. Babe Johnson, a Yucca
plantation hand, married Susie. A month later the girl gave birth to Big
Brown's child.

Although the early days of this marriage were peaceful, the narrator
explains, the blacks of Cane River had no reason to believe that Susie had
reformed. She played the blues on the mouth organ, for example, and
"folks that belong to the church have no business playing the blues" (210).
Real trouble erupted on Cane River when Big Brown returned and resumed
his affair with the all-too-willing Susie. The pair flaunted their sin before
Babe, who eventually challenged Brown to a fight. Miserably defeated by
the larger man in this encounter, Babe began to contemplate revenge. The
final break between Susie and decent black society occurred when she
proudly wore a string of red beads her lover had given her. This act of
marital defiance resulted in her being "read out" in the African Baptist
Church.

The remainder of the story concerns Babe's effort to save face, to
regain the affections of his wife, and to vanquish Big Brown. By following

the trapper Brown, Babe manages to catch his enemy in one of his own large bear traps. This occurs in a secluded gully far into the swamp, and no one but the hidden Babe is around to hear Brown's vain cries for help. Once Big Brown's leg is caught, Babe simply waits until he dies from the wound. In an effectively ironic scene, he frees Brown's horse from where it is tied, fearing that "the poor thing would starve" (217). "When [Babe] crept to the gully next morning," Saxon writes, "he saw long streams of red ants in the grass, going towards the trap" (218). Thinking his victim dead, Babe seemingly has complete revenge. In the interim, however, Babe's horse has returned to the plantation. Susie, already filled with vague fears that something has happened to Brown, sets off into the direction from which the riderless horse has come. When Babe returns to the trap to inspect Big Brown's corpse, he discovers that Susie, now wildly deranged, has found the body of her lover in the swamp. His efforts to explain his motives to her and to comfort her are in vain, and she runs away wildly "deeper into the woods" (221).

Several aspects of "Cane River" are reminiscent of Saxon's later works. As mentioned above, the setting of this local color story is the most obvious parallel between this and *Children of Strangers*. Present too in both works are Saxon's references to the "codes" that existed within and among the three groups on Cane River: the whites, the blacks, and the mulattoes. These codes are manifested in "Cane River" in Mr. Guy's "hands off" philosophy regarding trouble among the blacks themselves and in Brown and Babe's civility toward each other despite their conflicts over Susie (209, 212). Even when Babe is planning his death stalk of Brown and asks Mr. Guy for permission to leave his work, the planter, "remembering the Cane River code, merely nodded assent" (214). The various groups, in the story and in the novel, manifest a certain knowledge of the codes; the whites, blacks, and mulattoes know what action or inaction is expected of them in a given situation. In his behavior regarding Susie, moreover, Babe Johnson anticipates a character in *Children of Strangers*. In the novel Numa happily marries Famie Vidal after she has become pregnant with another man's child. In another parallel situation, Famie and Susie both eventually become outcasts within their mulatto and black worlds respectively, and each is displaced from the church in which she grew to maturity. Finally, Saxon's concern with superstitions in "Cane River" is a common element between this and a great deal of his later work. Aunt Dicey and Susie, when she senses something terrible has happened to Big

Brown, note certain ominous signs—such as a single leaf on a Chinaberry tree and the screech of an owl (219).[18] As one writer has aptly noted, Saxon "builds upon a natural background of negro superstition and fatalism" in "Cane River" to heighten the mystery and horror of his story.[19] In this sense readers will be reminded of Jean Toomer's *Cane,* especially the often anthologized "Blood-Burning Moon."[20]

With one important exception, "Cane River" is a very well-constructed story. At least one reader noticed very early, however, that the choice of a narrator is perhaps ill-advised. One of the judges for the O. Henry Memorial Award pointed out that there was no need for the story to be narrated "as by a plantation Negro, or any Negro."[21] Not only does this narrative plan serve no real purpose; it is not particularly successful. The style appears to be more sophisticated than that of a Yucca plantation black, Saxon's poetic license notwithstanding. More importantly, perhaps, the story contains at least one somewhat condescending comment that is not very credible coming supposedly from one of the blacks. Saxon writes that so many of the young black men have been in prison for a year or two "for bigamy, or a shooting scrape, or for some other minor offence" that prison "is rather like sending a boy off to college" (207). The irony in this comparison, apparent to Saxon's readers and to the author himself, would probably not have been humorous to the plantation black who tells the story; in fact, the comparison would not likely occur to him. Since the narrative is really from an omniscient point of view by the end of the story, Saxon would have done well to have abandoned his attempt to relate the events through the uneducated black character. In short, while there is much to admire in Saxon's vision in "Cane River," his narrative voice does not ring true.

Readers will surely notice far more virtues than flaws in the story of Susie and Babe, however. Impressive is the manner, for example, in which the outcome of "Cane River" is neatly, consistently, and yet unobtrusively foreshadowed throughout. Babe desires above all—above even saving his own reputation as a man—the subduing of Susie. Immediately before he encounters Susie at the scene of Brown's torment, Babe dreams of the day when "he could return to his mules again, a peaceful man" (220). He will never find peace and security in his cabin with Susie, however, for, as Saxon writes, she was a wild woman, a savage, "with her wild woolly hair, that she disdained to straighten with 'ointment' as the other girls did . . ." (208). The reader is told at one point that Susie would sometimes laugh out in her sleep at night "like a crazy woman" (212). Saxon thus aptly prepares for Susie's wild, uncontrollable grief at the end when she "seemed incapable of controlling her eyes" and burst with loud "witless" laughter (221).

The author also uses certain devices almost as refrains to remind the reader of Susie's wildness. The red beads she flaunts are obviously a symbol of her open defiance of the code of behavior expected of a decent black Baptist wife. These beads are as symbolically appropriate for Susie as Faith Brown's pink ribbons are for her. Not unlike Hawthorne's use of the ribbons, Saxon's symbol is skillfully employed to link Susie's infidelity and Babe's revenge. While Babe Johnson waits for his prey to die, the cuckolded husband lies in a stream and watches "the leaves that drifted by in the slow-moving current: long green leaves, that were like little snakes; round red berries, like Susie's red beads" (218).

Used far more often is another symbol involving Susie: her playing upon the mouth organ. Saxon's use of this device seems intended first to remind readers of Susie's infidelity and of her wildness. At one point the old blacks of Cane River are scandalized as Big Brown calls on Susie while her husband is away, lolls on her front porch at her feet, and listens as Susie plays the blues for him on the mouth organ. "Across the narrow river," Saxon writes, "the wailing strains came, whining with slow, suggestive undulation" (214). After her rejection from the church, the narrator explains, Susie simply sat on her gallery on Sundays, "wearing the red beads, and with the baby on her knee—Big Brown's baby—and played on her mouth organ. Played the blues, mind you, over and over . . ." (213). The mouth organ and, specifically, the blues music Susie plays on it are linked not only to the girl's irreverent wildness but also, by implication at least, to her madness. In the final scene of the story, when Susie finds Brown's body, she has the mouth organ with her "still clenched in her hand, her eyes rolling wildly" (220). Just as Saxon uses her sensual music earlier to symbolize her moral wildness, he now employs the discordant playing to indicate her emotional wildness. After encountering Brown and upon being confronted by Babe, Susie plays "a tuneless and discordant strain" on the harmonica, and, Saxon concludes,

> In the clearing, Babe stood stupidly. From far off, an imperfect thread
> of melody was carried back to him—fainter and fainter—the same
> whimpering strain, over and over and over . . . . (221)

The wild "Trick-nigger" who had played the blues repeatedly to the passing churchgoers in her defiance now plays this imperfect melody to the deep woods in her desperation.

Saxon seems not to have been so much concerned with any thematic burden in "Cane River" as he was with the depiction of life—savage and brutal as it sometimes could be—among the blacks of the Cane River country. In fact, his characterizations are so true to life that in a letter to a friend Saxon once registered shock that after completing his story, he had "discovered a real 'Susie'!"[22] He writes further:

> How nature does follow art, as Oscar [Wilde] used to say. Her name is Nina, and she lives out on Little River . . . . She is skinny and scrawny, with huge lips, and a wild face, and she plays the harmonica!

In another letter, written perhaps a month later to Olive Lyons, Saxon mentions that "Cane River" has been rejected by *Cosmopolitan* apparently because the magazine preferred "something 'ending on a happy note.' "[23] Saxon obviously did not consider lightening his conclusion, however; for he says of *Cosmopolitan:* "may they rot in Hell!"

With regard to the ending of "Cane River," readers may be tempted to conclude, as Aunt Dicey does in the story, that Susie undergoes a fall because she rejects and ridicules the moral code of the good members of the African Baptist Church. When Aunt Dicey is scolding Susie about wearing the beads, for example, she warns the girl: "Gawd gonna strike yo' down" (218). Perhaps God does strike Susie down, but Saxon does not exactly reward Babe Johnson, who, although a murderer, is not in violation of the Cane River code of protecting his home and marital bed. The inequities of crime and punishment in the story can be explained by the fact that the Cane River codes are not Saxon's and, of course, are not universal. While Susie's defeat implies that one who flaunts accepted behavior will be struck down, Babe's defeat suggests that one cannot impose accepted and expected behavior on another person—or at least on a wild person. This is, it would seem, true naturalistic fare; Babe cannot silence Susie's music, and her blues becomes repeated, discordant sound.

Readers may well find elements of genuine pathos in Saxon's story as well. Despite the cold premeditation with which Babe goes about his plan to kill Brown, the husband will likely evoke readers' sympathies. Surely, he is no noble Ulysses vanquishing the would-be suitors of his fair

Penelope, but he is at least sincere in his desire to be, as Saxon says at one point, "master of his own cabin" (220). More importantly, perhaps, readers are told that even though Susie was "a bad one," Babe loved her and knew that Big Brown did not. In his innocence, then, Babe sets out to commit an act that he thinks will ensure his happiness, remove the object of Susie's attentions, and tame a wild thing into loving him and into living blissfully within the codes of Cane River. Babe is doomed to defeat, however; and the impossibility of his living with Susie within these codes is implied in the first sentence of Saxon's story: "Susie was not a native of Cane River country" (207). The description of her wildness follows immediately and anticipates well the imperfect, repetitive strains of the mouth organ with which Saxon ends his story.

The New York publication of "Cane River" must have held great significance for the author. Sherwood Anderson wrote him praising the story, and Saxon's response indicates just how much the story—and Anderson's praise—meant. Saxon writes in a letter dated March 3, 1926, that even though he considers himself "hard boiled," he was moved to tears over Anderson's kind words about "Cane River."[24] He must have been greatly pleased with some of the other words of praise his story elicited from various literary friends in Louisiana. Dorothy Dix wrote him almost immediately after the story appeared in *The Dial* and congratulated him for writing about blacks not in relation to whites as "everybody" else had done, but in regard to their own lives among themselves as a people.[25] Roark Bradford assured his friend that he knew as soon as he read "Cane River" that Saxon would be one of the literary "finds" of 1926.[26] Perhaps Saxon was most excited over a note that came from Grace King, who wrote:

> I am enthusiastic about your story. It seems to me to be perfect . . . .
> I congratulate you but more do I congratulate the Dial for recognizing
> its force and beauty. *You have arrived.*[27]

This accolade, reminiscent of Emerson's greeting Whitman at the beginning of the great career, is almost tantamount to the passing of the mantle. In the next four years, Saxon would succeed King as the foremost chronicler of Louisiana lore.

The real significance of "Cane River" in light of Saxon's literary career is not, however, that his fellow Orleanians were convinced that he had arrived as a literary artist of a high order. Far more important is that this story demonstrated to Saxon himself that a highly respected New York literary magazine liked his work. One distinguishing characteristic of "Cane River" that is almost never present in Saxon's *Times-Picayune* stories is restraint. The highly charged tale of murder, revenge, and insanity is presented not sensationally, but with repose and dignity; and the restrained atmosphere of the *Dial* story seems as premeditated as the sensational atmosphere of the newspaper stories had been. Pattee once pointed out that O. Henry, Saxon's early model and the master of pulp fiction, lacked repose and that art is, by contrast, serene.[28] Saxon was certainly well aware that his own newspaper fiction, like that of the *New York World* writer, lacked repose, and the author unquestionably desired to create more enduring works of art. In a letter written in late 1925, after *The Dial* had accepted "Cane River," Saxon laments to a friend that he can never write "the real truth" in a newspaper story.[29] "Cane River" is thus a turning point in Saxon's career; it is "the real truth" expressed with serenity.

Having made the intellectual move to writing fiction worthy of the literary magazines of New York, the time was now ripe for Saxon to make a geographical move as well. Although he took this step in the fall of 1926, he had seriously contemplated doing so several months earlier. In a letter from Sherwood Anderson, written probably in November of 1925, the older writer tells his friend Saxon to contact O. K. Liveright (Anderson's literary agent) and Anita Loos when he gets to New York.[30] Even earlier in 1925, Saxon had written in his diary that he had begun preparations for "leaving New Orleans for good."[31] These preparations evidently involved the selling of the property at 536 Royal.[32] About the time of this move toward at least temporary financial independence, however, Saxon was, according to one account, delayed almost a year in his plans because of an extended illness, or series of illnesses, which put him in the hospital and kept him in a sickbed for a long period of time.[33]

Perhaps still not strong physically and considerably depleted financially, Saxon finally moved to the publishing center to peddle his literary wares. The earliest Saxon letter from New York is dated October 18, 1926, and is written to his Aunt Elizabeth Chambers. In this letter the author speaks of his visit to the Sherwood Andersons in Virginia en route and then says of New York:

> ... there's something in the air that seems to pep me up ... but I am
> quite sure that I'll never become a typical New Yorker that believes that

> New York is the only town in the world . . . It doesn't impress me as
> much as it oppresses me.[34]

Saxon was to be as true to his first impressions of the big city as he was to those of Melrose after his first visit there. Tess Crager commented in an interview that the author often said that he was always homesick when in New York. Saxon once wrote to Olive Lyons: "And while I know one million people here [in New York], I have no close friends."[35]

Although Saxon initially stayed with his friend Noel Straus on 54th Street, he moved to 3 Christopher Street in Greenwich Village a few weeks after he arrived. He was to maintain this fourth-floor apartment until 1932. During this period Saxon would often spend five or six months of the year in New York—usually from late summer until around Christmas. The first several letters that he wrote to Olive Lyons from the Christopher Street apartment are a rich source of information about his first days in the city. In one of the earliest letters to her, he explains that the "den of Vice" in which he lives is called Greenwich Village, and "I live in the lousiest part of it" over a "sort of anarchist bookstore" in a one-room attic apartment.[36]

Understandably, the author met some interesting characters in such a setting, and his descriptions of them in the letters to Olive show his good humor. In the January 7, 1927, letter to Olive, he writes that the occupants of the other six apartments in his building include a woman nicknamed "Slats," two men he has never seen emerge, and a "hard-boiled virgin" who shares the fourth floor. Saxon describes one day when Slats came to his apartment and told him the full story of her life—complete with a description of her current sexual activities—in the span of five minutes. The author follows the account of Slats with this statement:

> Such is life in the big city. It is a pity that I couldn't have come here
> ten years ago when such carryings-on would have given me a kick.
> Now I'm only sympathetic and cordial about it, but don't share the
> youthful enthusiasm about "living life"—having been living it for
> many years with small success.

At age thirty-five, Lyle Saxon was evidently not a true Bohemian in this Bohemian world.

By early 1927, though, the author had met and was already socializing with several prominent writers, many of whom lived near him in the

Village. He wrote to Olive that the names on the mailboxes in his neighbor-
hood were like the lists on magazine covers saying "In this number . . . ."
One friend, Edmund Wilson, was able to get tickets for most first-night
dramatic performances in New York, and the two saw a great many plays.
Wilson wrote to Hamilton Basso about taking Saxon to a rehearsal of an
expressionist play—"the worst I ever saw."[37] In his January 7 letter to
Olive, Saxon comments on some "stupid stuff" by Belasco that he has seen,
mentions being impressed but not moved by performances of *The Emperor
Jones* and *Beyond the Horizon*, and points out that because a crusade is
currently under way against so-called filth in the theater "all the dirty plays
are drawing capacity audiences." Saxon tells Olive that one New York
friend had taken him to a really bad show to retaliate "for some of the drinks
I gave him in New Orleans."

In a serious mood, however, Saxon discusses seeing Chekhov's
Three Sisters, starring Eva LeGallienne; he was very impressed with the
actress's performance and with the play:

> But honestly, Olive, never, never have I seen such marvelous acting or
> such a marvelous play. I didn't think I had it in me to be so deeply
> moved by anything. And it brought home to me very forcibly that Mr.
> Chekov, writing in 1901 or thereabouts, had said about all there was to
> say about futility, and his stuff makes these boys—such as Ernest
> Hemenway, for instance, appear as babies trying to make words with
> alphabet blocks . . . .

Saxon's reaction is understandable from one who had read the Russians as
a boy. It shows too a preference for the "classic" European drama on the
New York stage over the "dirty," "sensational" plays the author says he
witnessed the large audiences relishing. The criticism of "Hemenway"
indicates a general disdain of contemporary American writers—at least
compared to Chekhov.

Saxon's letters to Olive Lyons, often candid and almost always
delightful, are often written over a pseudonym. The first part of this
January 7, 1927 letter, for example, is in the voice of "Abe Buzzard" and is
addressed to "sister Sadie"—that is, Olive. The origin of this private joke
between the two lies in a newspaper clipping that is attached to one of
Saxon's letters to Olive, now at Tulane University. The clipping describes
a real-life Abe Buzzard who, released from a Pennsylvania prison at age

seventy-two, plans to become a prison evangelist.[38]   Here Saxon, in the
voice of "Abe," tells his sister Sadie that he is going to make "a cleen breast
of it (although it has been a long time since I had a cleen breast, to tell the
truth, having been in jail mostly and not being convenient to no bath-
room) . . . ." Saxon (Abe) explains further: "I have decided to make my
peece with God . . . . You see it's like this, Sadie, I've been a bad man, I
have and I shore have been punished good and plenty for it." He is pleased
to hear that his sister moves in high society in New Orleans, but, he
continues, "that don't supprise me none as we Buzzards was always high
flyers." Now Abe gets to the point; he tells Sadie he is going to preach—
"having got the tip from a Baptist preecher who is a good friend of mine. (I
met him in jail where he was serving a term for bigamy, poor boob)." So
Abe looks forward to his preaching career and, quite confidently, plans to
"knock Billy Sunday for a home run . . . ." Saxon's Abe Buzzard sounds
like he would fit right in with the Misfit, Tom T. Shiftlet, Haze Motes, or
other O'Connor classics.[39]

   After almost two years of Abe and Sadie's correspondence, Saxon
adroitly uses Abe's voice to describe the cold weather and perilous conditions on the streets of New York. In the same long letter of January 7,
1927, containing his drama reviews and descriptions of his Village neigh-
bors, Saxon tells Olive a story to make the point that "[the] streets ain't
safe." Having broken his only coffee cup, Abe reads a department store ad
for "a whole teaset" on sale for $1.19. So he decides to take advantage of
this extraordinary bargain, even under the dangerous wintry conditions of a
cold New York day. Saxon, as Abe, explains:

> So down I went [to the department store]. Yes'm. That's just what I
> did. After fighting and clawing and bamming my way through the
> crowd at the bargain basement, I finally laid down my one nineteen and
> got a imitation willow-ware teaset, same being . . . all very nice, only
> called "seconds" because of smeared patterns in the china or something.
> Well, home I started, carrying same under my arm. I forgot to tell you
> that I live just where five streets come together in a way that nature
> itself can't endure . . . and automobiles and trucks and things coming
> from every way at once, and a big wide triangle-shaped place to cross.
> And here I was carrying chiny and crockery and the streets coated with
> ice two inches thick, and me slipping and sliding around in every
> direction. Well, as you have guessed long ere this, *I didn't make it.* A

taxi came raring after me, and I begins to fly up into the air, let out a yelp and throw the package containing teaset high into air. It lit sometime after I done so, and made a different kind of noise, whereas I said "Oompt" and "Goddam" the teaset goes "Bling" and "Crash." A pretty girl in a fur coat says: "My god the man has killed himself," and the snooty fellow that was with her says: "Oh, I hardly think so." And just then the teaset, which had been falling all this time, hits him on the foot and he begins jumping around and yelling, while the girl laughs and is much pleased. All of which cheered me up a little, and I rose, rubbing my seat and resumed my way home, where I found my whole Body a Mass of Black and Blue, and not one single piece of the said chiny whole. Not one piece. So one dollar and nineteen cents had gone plum to hell and I was just that much nearer to the poor house and not one single thing (except my bruises) to show for it. No Sadie, the streets ain't safe, leastways not for folks like me.

Saxon's Abe Buzzard narratives are rich indeed. His humor is never better anywhere else in the letters—or in his fiction for that matter. Abe's yarn of his mishap with the teaset could not have been told much more deftly by V. K. Ratliff or Simon Wheeler. In actuality, Saxon was an insecure, struggling, transplanted New Yorker when Abe's teaset tale was written; Olive at the time was struggling courageously against breast cancer. Their relationship was a complex one with emotions—expressed or suppressed—surely quite charged. Yet even after all these years and despite the private jokes and topical references, the Abe and Sadie letters somehow wear well and furnish pleasure. They are like those five streets that come together in a way that nature itself can't endure.

Near the end of this same letter, with now a worried Saxon speaking seriously to Olive, the author reveals how very financially insecure and precarious these early days in New York had become:

I'm working very hard. Hours and hours every day at the typewriter; somedays I only go out to meals and then back here again. I'm getting a lot done, but whether it is good or not, I can't say. My money will last through April—or maybe May, so if I don't sell something by that time, I'll have to find a job in a shoe-shining parlor.

Although Saxon fails to mention his aunts to Olive, he evidently was forced to provide a good deal of support for them and for his invalid grandfather by this time. One letter from Saxon's Aunt Elizabeth assures him that although she and Aunt Maude and Grandfather are having a hard time financially, they can manage without his help.[40] It seems safe to conclude that Aunt Lizzie wants Saxon to read between the lines, however, especially when she also tells her nephew that she wants him to keep what money he has because she knows that it "flies oh so soon (especially with you) . . . ."

Perhaps I should mention here, incidentally, that many have evidently inferred that Saxon knew no financial hardship at any point in his life. Faulkner's biographers seem to assume, based substantially on interviews with contemporaries of Saxon and Faulkner, that Saxon's hereditary wealth, his French Quarter properties, and his "best-selling" books enabled him to live in a comfortable, even affluent manner. His prodigality and his generosity in the early New York days would quite understandably result in Faulkner's friends remembering Saxon thusly. In one 1985 study, moreover, the writer mentions that Saxon had moved to New York because of the success of *Father Mississippi*, which was actually published a year after he moved there.[41] Cathy Harvey is quite right, it seems to me, when she points out that Saxon "was obliged to leave for New York to sell the completed manuscripts" of the relatively few short stories he had finished during his last days in Louisiana.[42]

By February of 1927 Saxon's financial situation was reaching a crisis. "I'm still just one jump ahead of the poorhouse," he confided to Olive, "as my income from writing does not meet the outgo from living . . . and my 'capital' is steadily diminishing."[43] After four months in New York, without his steady and substantial *Times-Picayune* salary and having to contribute to the Chamberses, Saxon's situation was beginning to grow serious. His anxiety is obvious in another passage of this February letter to Olive: "God knows what the summer will bring about. Unless, of course, I manage to land in one of the more popular magazines." Saxon's statement here is doubly ironic; for his fortune was about to change for the better, and apparently he was never again to be in quite this serious a financial state with so few options. He did manage to "land" soon in *The New Republic* and other magazines, and what the summer brought about was the aftermath of the most dramatic and devastating flooding of the Mississippi River in modern history: the natural catastrophe that gave Saxon his first great literary opportunity and led to his first book.

Saxon's *New Republic* article, published on March 23, 1927, is called "Voodoo."[44] He would later incorporate this sketch of a visit to a black New Orleans voodoo ceremony into *Fabulous New Orleans,* and I will discuss the piece in some detail in connection with that book. The publication in which "Voodoo" appeared is interesting, however, in light of Saxon's Southern background. Edmund Wilson had gotten the article published for him, and Saxon was less than enthusiastic about his fellow Louisianans' encountering his work in a magazine that "advertises itself to be 'a thorn in the side of complacency.' "[45] He asked Olive not to show her copy around too freely because he did not think *The New Republic* would do him any good in "our fair Southland." Saxon's suspicions were probably accurate. Roark Bradford wrote his friend shortly after the appearance of "Voodoo" to apologize for not having been able to read it since the only store he knew of that carried *The New Republic* in New Orleans had sold out and "the Library never takes such a scandalous magazine."[46]

During this same month, Saxon achieved much wider notice by his winning a place among the *O. Henry Memorial Award Prize Stories of 1926*, edited by Professor Blanche Williams of Hunter College and others. Saxon's "Cane River" was chosen, along with stories by fifteen other writers, from a group of two thousand stories. The same volume contains selections by Wilbur Daniel Steele, Sherwood Anderson, Booth Tarkington, and Saxon's longtime friend and fellow Louisianan Ada Jack Carver. The introductory remarks compliment Saxon's story as being of "three-star quality," especially in the presentation of "the more repellent details," and brands Saxon as a distinctive literary discovery of 1926.[47]

Two months after the O. Henry volume appeared, Saxon published "Fame" in the short-lived *New Orleans Life* magazine.[48] This story, the only item the author published outside New York from the time he left *The Times-Picayune* until 1930, is unlike most of Saxon's other published works of the period. It is unquestionably an artistic regression from "Cane River" and is little different from the Sunday *Times-Picayune* surprise-ending stories. It is to be hoped that he had written it during one of his earliest retreats to Melrose and did not regard it seriously. The main character of the story is a New Orleans newspaperman whose country cousin has achieved fame for her writing. Cousin Luella Slattery, a resident of a small town in Louisiana (very like Natchitoches or Cloutierville), is viewed enviously by the literate but pompous journalist. The reporter visits Luella to see what her story, called "A Message to Women," is all about. He discovers, however (and here is Saxon's Sunday punch again), that Luella's published "story" is a homespun testimonial about a certain all-purpose tonic; this published commercial is her "message to women." The newspaperman, who had expected to encounter another Kate Chopin, thus gets considerably less than he was hoping for. So does the reader.

About the time "Fame" was published in New Orleans, the 1927 flood waters were raging. In Louisiana the Mississippi River poured over its banks; New Orleans itself was seriously threatened. In New York the editors of *The Century Magazine* became convinced that the American reading public would be interested in firsthand accounts of the tragedy. Lyle Saxon was thus in the right place at the right time to be dispatched to his homeland to report on the disaster areas for the magazine.

Although some accounts contend that Saxon was at work on *Father Mississippi* before the spring floods of 1927,[49] he was actually commissioned by the Century Company during the height of the disaster. His assignment was first to do a series of articles for the magazine, to be followed by a book-length study of the river, its lore, and its history. In a letter to Olive Lyons on May 4, he discusses the flood, commenting wryly that his Aunt Maude is probably "enjoying the whole thing . . . ordering the refugees around and having a grand time," but makes no mention of his arrangement with Century. In the next letter, three days later, however, Saxon tells Olive that the publishers want the flood articles and a book about the river and that they are financing a trip down the Mississippi for him to observe the situation.[50]

From the dates the author mentions in this letter (and assuming that he kept to the schedule that he plans there), most of his fieldwork was done from about May 12 until the end of the month. During this time, much of which he spent actually assisting rescue squads aiding refugees, he acquired a profound sense of respect for the river and assumed an attitude of sobriety about the flood that was perhaps lacking when he was in New York joking about his aunt's role in the rescue work. The three articles Saxon wrote for *The Century Magazine* appeared in late summer and are vivid portraits of a tragedy poignantly drawn by a sensitive and sympathetic observer.[51] The voice throughout the flood stories is not that of a New York reporter dispatched to an assignment, but that of an impassioned Louisianan who has seen his homeland in ruin.

The three *Century* stories were later incorporated into *Father Missis-sippi* as separate chapters. The actual writing of these articles, as well as of the majority of the book, was done at Melrose plantation. Sometime during the middle of 1927, circumstances at Melrose evolved so that Saxon could have there, available whenever he desired, a place of his own to write. The cabin that he had especially liked during his first visit to Melrose (and in which, he supposedly remarked, he could write a novel) became vacant that summer with the death of a Henry family servant who had lived in it for all of his hundred and three years. Saxon knew Cammie Henry would not displace the old man from his home, and when the author had first seen the cabin in 1923 and had met its ancient inhabitant, then aged ninety-eight, he must have wondered how much longer he would have to wait to be able to write there. According to Francois Mignon, Henry informed Saxon of the availability of the cabin in a telegram consisting of this terse message: "Aunt Jane and Uncle Israel have gone to last reward. Yucca House is ready. Come to Melrose and write."[52]

Saxon did indeed go from the flooded areas to "Yucca House," as the cabin was known, to write about the river. This cabin, much older than the main house at Melrose, was constructed about 1750 and, according to Joseph Henry, was used until the Civil War as the slave hospital. During the remainder of his life, Saxon would work on at least part of all the eight books he wrote and edited in this ancient cabin. Other artists would come and go, staying in various other structures as well as in the main house (as Saxon himself had done), but after 1927 Yucca House at Melrose was Lyle Saxon's personal retreat.

Almost from the beginning the author had mixed feelings about his days in the cabin. The former Orleanian was often given to mocking various aspects of his rural life. In a letter written probably less than a year after Yucca became available to him, Saxon jokingly remarks to Olive:

> The mosquitos were so thick in my cabin that I just managed to squeeze
> in at the door, but then of course I've taken on weight and there is more
> flesh for the mosquitos to enjoy. How I love to make God's creatures
> happy, for am I not the least of His wonders? Here in the country one
> is so conscious of His Maker.[53]

The next year, evidently bothered by the Henrys' young daughter, Saxon comments to Olive that although the girl has finally gone off to summer camp, "God is much too cruel to let her stay there."[54] A diary he kept during some of his later work in the cabin reveals too his loneliness and boredom. After a trip into town, for example, Saxon thanks "Mr. God" that he does not have to live permanently in Natchitoches or any other small town and, in a later entry, rejoices when Roark and Mary Rose Bradford visit him from New Orleans—with an ample supply of big city whiskey.[55] The peace and calm Saxon felt while alone in Yucca House, however, were often restorative and conducive to his writing, as the author frequently mentions. Throughout his diaries and letters from the 1920s until his death, Saxon exhibits an ambivalence about life at Melrose, at times viewing New Orleans or New York life as stimulating and Melrose life as dull and, in other moods of course, detesting the hectic pace of the big city and longing for the country pleasures at Yucca. Presumably, then, he variously thought of the cabin as his paradise or his prison, an escape and yet an exile.

By the end of August 1927, probably with the manuscript of his first book in hand, Saxon returned to Greenwich Village. He may well have stopped again in Virginia to see Sherwood Anderson, who had invited him to visit "after the Mississippi River thing is off your hands."[56] Saxon had by this time acquired something of a national reputation because of his *Century* stories. On August 31, he wrote Olive complaining of all the manuscripts he was beginning to receive from "one thousand amateur writers of the fair Southland . . . ."[57] Since none of the "thousand" sent return postage, Saxon continues, "I shall kindle the First Fire of Fall with inspired words." Despite the recognition from his stories and his somewhat triumphant return to the city, he continued to be anxious about his dwindling bank account; royalties from *Father Mississippi* were still about seven months away. Saxon too did not miss Louisiana any less than before. He resumed his writing efforts at 3 Christopher Street, then, still hungry and homesick.

Regardless of Saxon's letter to Olive, filled with despair and depression upon the return, the most anxious and insecure of his New York days were surely behind him. The remainder of 1927 and the next year brought not only more publications and more money, but additional friendships for the author. The first achievement came only two weeks after he wrote Olive. Saxon's story "The Centaur Plays Croquet" was included in the first *American Caravan*, an impressive anthology of American writing published intermittently from 1927 until 1936. The editors of this first *Caravan* were Van Wyck Brooks, poet and playwright Alfred Kreymborg, Lewis

Mumford, and Paul Rosenfeld, literary and music critic for *The Dial*. Saxon mentions in a letter of January 7, 1927, that he had met Kreymborg and Rosenfeld, a close friend of Sherwood Anderson, and that he liked both men "immensely";[58] it is very possible that he had met Brooks and Mumford as well. In addition to Saxon's friendship with at least two of the editors, his ally Edmund Wilson had a story in the anthology. Wilson, Anderson, or any one of the editors Saxon knew, then, could have been instrumental in the publication of "The Centaur."

The 1927 *American Caravan* is a distinguished anthology indeed, and Saxon's story appeared in good company. Several genres are represented, and the various writers whose work is found in the *Caravan* include Wilson, Hemingway, Dos Passos, Malcolm Cowley, William Carlos Williams, Mark Van Doren, Archibald MacLeish, Gertrude Stein, Babette Deutsch, Louise Bogan, Brooks Atkinson, Allen Tate, Robert Penn Warren, Hart Crane, and Eugene O'Neill. *The New York Times* scorched the anthology, however, as "amorphous" and "embryonic" and "a manifesto of the extreme left wing of American Letters."[59] The reviewer for *The Dial* was essentially favorable toward the overall aim of the *Caravan*, but unimpressed with the individual items, suggesting, for example, that the story by Edmund Wilson "would be better in almost any wastepaper basket . . . ."[60]

Saxon's opinion of Wilson's story or of the volume as a whole is unknown, but he was surely happy to have his story included. "The Centaur Plays Croquet" had been written sometime before the end of 1925 and had been accepted for publication before the *Caravan* only to be, as the author once remarked, "snatched back again at the last minute."[61] Saxon confides in a letter to Olive that he is quite happy the story, "that poor thing," is finally to find a publisher; "I'm delighted," he writes, "that he's gone from me at last."[62] Saxon's seeming attitude of good riddance toward "The Centaur" here is misleading, however; for he was very proud of this work. In 1925 he wrote to Caroline Dormon, for example, that he felt the story "has some lovely cadences in it . . . like real poetry . . . ."[63] Two friends of the author with whom I spoke stressed Saxon's affinity for the story, and his obituary in *The New Orleans States-Item* claims that the author viewed "The Centaur" as his best effort.[64]

The story itself is as odd as the incongruous image conveyed in the title. The narrative plan, for example, is unconventional, quite befitting the events narrated. The story consists of six sworn testimonies by individuals who witnessed various aspects of "The Strange Case of Mrs. John David

Calander of Mimosa, Louisiana, and the Fabulous Monster Which She Kept as a Pet . . . ."[65] The first testimony, by one Matthew A. Fleming, M.A., Ph.D., member of "the American Association of Sciences," and chairman of the Department of Ancient Languages at the University of Mimosa, provides readers with the essential events of the story. Fleming has evidently solicited and assembled the other five testimonies in the case and presents them, as would be expected of a scientist, in an objective light to enable readers to induce their own conclusions about Ada Calander and her pet.[66]

Saxon's Dr. Fleming informs readers that Ada, abandoned at a Catholic orphanage as an infant, grew to maturity and married a Mimosa lawyer and faithful Baptist, John David Calander.[67] After the honeymoon in New Orleans, the couple began to go their separate ways, with John David spending much time at his office and Ada, curiously enough, wandering all day through the swamps and woods and writing strange poetry for *Harper's Magazine*. "In June, 1884, when Ada Calander was 20 years old," Dr. Fleming reports, "she brought a strange pet home with her . . ."(349). This pet was, Fleming points out, either a centaur or, according to another witness whom the scientist spoke with, "an unusually intelligent horse which the perverse and unhappy woman had disguised in some way to resemble a man."

The relationship between Ada and "Horace," as her pet was called, came to be a very close one. Saxon has his scientist-narrator quote "an extremely indiscreet" prose poem, titled "The Centaur Plays Croquet," which he says he found among Ada's papers after her death. In this poem, Saxon shows an impressive adeptness with symbols in his character's description of the croquet game between the centaur and herself. The sexual implications inherent in Ada's poem, which the author aptly represents as shocking to Dr. Fleming, can be seen in the following excerpt:

> Come, my Centaur, let us have a game of croquet! The colored balls lie like painted flowers on the lawn and the wickets stand in order as do the events of my life. . . . Sadly you stand, slowly swaying your tail, and holding the mallet poised; while I, with tiny black lace parasol tilted against the sun, lift mincingly my skirt and strike the ball with an affected scream of excitement—strike daintily, for fear of splitting my polonaise of striped silk. (348-49)

Significantly, the mallet is linked with the centaur in the poem and the wicket with Ada. The phallic and vaginal counterparts in the game, combined with the ecstatic striking of the ball by Ada and the lifting of her skirt, indicate that the *New York Times* reviewer of the *Caravan* might have been thinking of "The Centaur" when he complained that some of the stories showed "a very strong leaning . . . to the unsavory, not to say bawdy."[68]

Returning to how the lady met her strange companion, Dr. Fleming, now relying on the testimony of a Calander family servant, explains that Ada had found Horace in "the deepest part of the swamp" (351-52). After the meeting, Mrs. Calander had spent long days in the woods on picnics with Horace, had taught him to converse in French, and had dressed him in a silk shirt, which covered the animal part of his torso. Ada, at this same time ceasing all physical relations with her husband, used Mr. Calander's shirts, vests, collars, and ties to dress Horace's human parts. Thusly arrayed, the pet spent most of his time in the house with his "mistress."

This situation, hellish for the poor husband and idyllic for Ada, suddenly changed, Fleming continues, when Horace took up with a wild mare and began living in the pasture. Frantically, Ada set about to regain her lover. The mare came to be adored by Horace, who had shed his clothes upon first encountering her. After Ada had prepared a special bowl of oats for the mare, however, the animal "fell sick and died, miserably and in great pain. So it was, that Horace came back to live in the house once more" (357). Ada had thus vanquished her rival and regained her companion.

The presence of Horace in the house, Dr. Fleming explains, led to all sorts of wild rumors and to outraged attitudes among the good citizens of Mimosa. When a group headed by the mayor and the Baptist preacher stormed the plantation to put a stop to the strange and unholy situation, Ada fled on Horace's back. In agony, John David Calander committed suicide, and, after a trip to New Orleans with the centaur, Ada returned to the plantation. Shortly thereafter, the scientist explains, she was seen "weeping over a new-made grave under a magnolia tree" (358). Horace was never seen again.

The final part of Dr. Fleming's long testimony describes his visiting Ada, "in the interest of [his] scientific work." He was accompanied on this venture by his daughter Mildred-Virginia, "a scholar and a student as well" (359). This visit occurred in 1905, twenty years after the previously related events. The man of science minced no words in this investigation, for he asked Ada specifically if she had once had a centaur for a pet; but "Ah, I do

not remember . . ." is the simple response (360). Ada Calander later, however, in a conversation about Mildred-Virginia's dislike of men, slipped
with: "Ah, my dear, wait until the right horse comes along!" (361).
Realizing what she had said, Fleming continues, Ada ordered the scientists
away. Upon leaving, the pair discovered under a tree in Ada's yard a grave
marked "In Memory of My Beloved Horace . . . His soul goes whinnying
down the wind" (361). Fleming's only remaining disclosures are that a few
months after these events, Ada Calander died, her property was sold to
some businessmen (who promptly constructed the Mimosa Country Club
on the site of the plantation), and the gravestone of Horace was lost or
thrown away.

The five testimonies that complete Saxon's story add no new information but expand on events alluded to briefly by Dr. Fleming. A nun,
Mother St. Abraham, confirms that Ada was of unknown parentage but
denies that she was the child of a nun and refutes the possibility that Catholicism led to Ada's strange behavior. Mrs. James Branch then provides
testimony about her own well-intentioned visit to Ada, which resulted in her
being ordered out by Mrs. Calander. Amelie Boudousquie of New Orleans
next testifies as to having seen Ada and Horace at the French Opera House.
At this point, Saxon's J. J. McBryde, the local Baptist minister, describes
the raid on Ada by the shocked and enraged citizens of Mimosa. Finally,
Adolph Wunsch, an old stonecutter, provides testimony regarding the
extraordinary purchase of gravestones by John David Calander for himself
and his wife—while both were in perfect health.

"The Centaur Plays Croquet" is a very well-written story. Possibly
as a result of revisions over the period from the original composition to the
appearance in the Caravan, the details in each narrative are rich sources of
irony and satiric humor. The various testimonies come from all the witnesses for the prosecution, while the defense rests in peace. Each testimony
is doubly interesting in light of who is testifying, for Saxon does an impressive job of matching, and of contrasting, his tellers with their tales. The testimony of Dr. Fleming is characteristic of a man of science. Fleming,
whose name was perhaps chosen to suggest Sandford or Alexander
Fleming, presents the evidence objectively. He carefully points out that
while some contended that Ada had a centaur for a pet, others explained the
beast as no more than a disguised horse. As mentioned above, his visit to
the Calander plantation in 1905 was in the interest of science, and his final
statement is that he has done his best "to point out the facts" in the case

(362). Characteristic of a scholar is Fleming's concern with accuracy and detail. He even refers readers, for example, to the specific volumes and months in which Ada's poems appeared in *Harper's Magazine*.[69] At times he seems almost to speak in footnotes.

Another characteristic of Dr. Fleming's testimony is the manner in which he painstakingly presents facts in the precise order in which they occurred. At one point he even chides himself for getting slightly out of order in his narrative (359). Fleming's tendency to get ahead of himself enables Saxon, through the good doctor, to titillate readers and nicely to foreshadow the entrance of the centaur into the story (on the sixth page of Fleming's narrative). The author has his scientist-narrator remark ominously that as a girl Ada and her governess cavorted in the woods on strange adventures and that the girl had an unusual interest in mythology (345). Young Ada's copy of Burton's *Anatomy of Melancholy*, which Fleming has before him as he writes, was well read, covered with marginalia, and contained a drawing of a centaur on the flyleaf.[70] Saxon's Dr. Fleming also comments on Ada's especial enjoyment of Mardi Gras on her honeymoon. The bride, he explains further, appeared "to enjoy particularly the *mythological quality* of the festivities . . . the nymphs, mermaids, satyrs . . ." (347).[71] In these preliminary remarks, Saxon's meticulous narrator has thus aptly foreshadowed the affinity for Horace, and Saxon has aptly whetted readers' appetites by the time he finally has Dr. Fleming introduce the fantastic pet.

The account by the nun is likewise especially meaningful when the teller is compared to the tale. The rumor that Ada was the child of one of the Holy Sisters was started, the nun says, "by those Black Protestants . . ." (362). This narrator goes on to point out that Ada's adult behavior was a result not of her Catholic girlhood, but of her subsequent years in the Episcopalian home of her foster parents. The nun reminds readers further, in a kind of absolvent climax, that Ada's husband was, after all, a Baptist; and with this flat statement the Sister rests her case. Saxon's nun so guiltlessly and guilelessly protests her own and her church's innocence in causing Ada's downfall that her testimony is one of the richest sources of irony in "The Centaur."

Ironic too is the testimony of Ada's neighbor, Mrs. James Branch.[72] Saxon masterfully has this good woman's words reveal just how good and well intentioned she was in the case of Ada. After explaining that she had never cared for those who hold themselves better than other people, Mrs. Branch explains how she decided, out of duty, to visit Ada but found that "she certainly was an affected woman . . ." (363). Among "the things about [Ada] that I didn't like," Mrs. Branch continues, "she refused point-blank to join the Ladies-Aid . . . ." This affront, of course reason enough to Saxon's narrator never to accept Mrs. Calander, did not preclude another visit. Mrs. Branch admits, surely feeling she was going the scriptural second mile, that despite being offended, "I felt it my duty as a Christian to forgive and forget." Upon calling on Ada again, however, the good neighbor once more was insulted, and this visit was the last. In Mrs. Branch's gospel, I feel sure, two miles are a literal limit to travel, and two visits to Ada are quite enough.

Saxon exploits this same kind of irony in the next testimonial, by the fine Creole lady Amelie Boudousquie. This lady and her mother, a Beaumont (Saxon's fictional family in "At the Gates of Empire"), encounter Ada and a strange companion, with the lower part of his body covered by a black curtain, at the opera in New Orleans. Although the sight struck Miss Boudousquie as odd, she did not seek to ask Ada about the man, "being a true Creole lady . . ." (365). Despite this narrator's disclaimers about not wanting to pry, she reveals how she and her mother waited under a darkened arcade in Toulouse Street for a considerable time in order to get another glimpse of Ada's companion. In fact, her entire testimony is an account of the extent to which she and her "true Creole" mother go to satiate their hunger for scandal.[73]

Especially devastating to the teller is the testimony of the good Baptist minister of the town. Saxon has the Reverend McBryde relate how he became convinced that Ada was guilty of "outrageous behavior" as a result of the rumors about her; "Where there's smoke, there's bound to be fire!" he concludes with less than a full measure of Christian trust.[74] McBryde, gradually revealing himself to be a pompous bigot, says he decided to call on Ada and was admitted to her drawing room by an "impudent nigger" (367). Here he found an "obscene" picture of Europa and the bull and "an indecent statue" of a centaur with a nude woman on his back. McBryde then relates how he demanded from Mrs. Calander an explanation for this filth, only to be glared at "with those mocking, hypocritical, *Catholic* eyes of hers." When the preacher returned to the house with his deputation of good citizens, intending Ada no bodily harm but meaning "to throw the fear of God into her heart," he reveals how the group destroyed the painting and the statue and gave Ada's black manservant a thorough beating as well—"to teach him not to interfere with Southern justice" (368). McBryde's testimony ends with this statement: "If more men would take the stand that I do, there would be less laxity in Louisiana." The preacher's final, nicely alliterative four-word phrase (which might have served a local politician well for a campaign slogan in the 1920s) is quite a euphemism. Saxon's readers are left to ponder the manifestations of less laxity: more of that for which McBryde has taken his stand—religious intolerance, invasion of privacy, censorship, and racial violence.

Saxon ends the story with the testimony of the stonecutter, Adolph Wunsch. This narrator provides readers with an account of Mr. Calander's purchase of "costly" gravestones for himself and his wife. Since this occurred immediately prior to his own suicide, the tormented husband might well have been planning a murder as well. The stonecutter remarks that even though Calander's purchase was unusual, "I was in need of money just then ... I only thanked God for his foolishness, and wished that more men would order their tombstones in advance" (369). Saxon seems in this testimony to have chosen his narrator's name especially well. Not only does "Wunsch" use a form of the verb *wish* in the passage quoted above, his testimony provides readers with the details preceding Calander's suicide, the fulfillment of his death wish.[75] At the close of his narrative, the old man recalls the words he was ordered to carve upon the two stones purchased by Calander. On the husband's, Wunsch carved: "He did his best to understand, and failing, died"; on Ada's: "She was carried away by her hobby; but for all her strangeness, she was a charming woman" (369). Probably Saxon knew many readers would recall the eccentric relationship with the centaur and, when reading "hobby" in Ada's epitaph, think of "hobbyhorse" (or "hobby Horace"). At any rate, the stonecutter, by recalling his work, is able to provide the story with an epitaph as well—an apt role for a tombstone maker.

Although none of Saxon's stereotyped narrators emerges as a full-fledged character, the author manages them well and accomplishes no small task in telling the strange case of Ada from six different points of view. The real strength of the narrative lies in the author's creation of ironies resulting from the gaps between the speakers' words and deeds. Fleming's pedantic testimony, itself humorously "scientific" and "scholarly," provides enough information regarding the following five testimonies to heighten the comic and ironic elements in each. Readers know in advance of McBryde's narrative, for example, that the preacher tried to save Ada from the pagan beast; then when the nature of this Baptist beast becomes apparent, a rich irony results.

"The Centaur" may not emerge as so much of a thematic success as a narrative one, however. It is indeed, as one writer remarked, "entirely different in mood" from anything else Saxon published.[76] Saxon's fantasy seems suggestive of many ideas. Certainly, as my discussion of the testimonies indicates, it is a satirical story with the satire directed not at Ada's folly, but at pedantry, at Catholic intolerance, at good country people, at Creole pettiness and spinster gossip, at Baptist intolerance, racial prejudice, and censorship of art, and even perhaps at a man's wish (Wunsch) to make a dollar under any circumstances. The satire is often indirect, with each of Saxon's witnesses placing the noose around her or his own neck.

The key to the story thematically, however, seems to lie in what Saxon had in mind in the Ada-Horace relationship. The question surrounding the nature of Horace himself, with some "competent witnesses" seeing him as a centaur and others as a horse, is not as important to answer as readers might first suppose. What is important is that Ada virtually eschews her marriage bed to enter into a sensual, bestial relationship with this creature.[77] Centaur or horse (and "Horace," as a near-homonym, is a clue), Ada's love of the creature is tantamount to an acceptance of the mythological or the pagan and to a rejection of the accepted modes of Christian behavior characteristic of Mimosa, Louisiana, in 1884. There are, after all, codes and conventions in this fictional town, just as on Cane River.

Repeatedly Saxon juxtaposes pagan and Christian elements in the story. Fleming tells of Ada's early turning from Catholicism to heathen myth; he later links Mr. Calander with "true Christian fortitude" and implies Ada's sexual rejection of him. Mrs. Branch, after commenting that she is a Christian woman, concludes that centaurs exist only in the "diseased imaginations of insane and heathen peoples." Most notable, however, are Ada's own words on the relationship of ancient myth and the Christian religion. In her poem quoted by Fleming, she writes:

> What a Godlike brute you are, my Centaur! Still . . . you have no
> soul, you fabulous man, you glorious beast, born two thousand years
> too late . . . or is it I who have mislaid my era? (350)

Ada's ambivalence toward the pagan world here is interesting when compared to her conversation with McBryde. The preacher chides her for believing in an "impossible, abnormal, and perverse" creature like a centaur, only to be asked by the lady if angels are normal and if they, with their birds' wings, "lie down to rest, as humans do, or . . . roost, like chickens, in the trees" (368). To Ada, a centaur is as real, indeed more real, than an angel; and Saxon's sympathies seem to lie with the lady.

When the author has Ada forswear her marriage bed and make the ultimate commitment to sensuality with the beast, when she and the centaur play croquet, Saxon's heroine clearly chooses the pagan over the Christian; she embraces ancient myth and rejects the ethos of the rural, early twentieth-century South. The rest of the story is, then, a rich Horatian satire directed at intolerance of this choice (and, again, the centaur is aptly named). The citizens of Mimosa simply expected Ada Calander to become a good, docile wife, entertain them cordially when they called, join the Ladies-Aid, and behave like a good Christian woman ought to behave. She should have mimicked their lives as they mimicked each other in their little town so nicely named. Saxon's chief point seems to be that in condemning what Ada has done or is even rumored to have done—in destroying the deviant from their idea of the good—the good citizens of Mimosa belie their own claims to goodness and mock their own best attempts at Christian charity.

For whatever specific reasons, the author was, as I have already mentioned, proud of "The Centaur." Worthy of pride are several elements in the story: the erotically laced prose poem, the gradual revelation of Ada's propensity toward pagan myth, and the use of the multiple narratives. The six testimonies regarding the strange case of Ada even build an atmosphere of verisimilitude not unlike that surrounding the strange case of Mrs. Veal. The story is not without shortcomings, though. Readers could easily argue that Saxon loads his dice in favor of his pagan heroine. Ada's tortured husband, for example, whose only fault seems to be that he is a Baptist, must endure the most cruel and unusual kind of perfidy from his mate; and, after all, the intolerant townspeople are scandalized, among other things, by a horse being kept in the drawing room.

It should be remembered above all, however, that the story is fantasy and fun and that pointing out such flaws is like contending that a diamond could not be as big as the Ritz Hotel. Saxon's satire succeeds admirably. His depiction of reactions to a woman's embracing a tradition different from the Judeo-Christian one she is expected to embrace is an important one and, surely, a meaningful one to students of American fiction. The author's overall picture of the code-breaker and his self-incriminating portraits of the small-minded, small-town folks scandalized by the code-breaker seem to be ably accomplished and to be understandable sources of pride for Saxon. He seems to have enjoyed the exposé immensely. In fact, Saxon remarked to his friend Noel Straus that he would like to write another story "in somewhat the same vein as 'The Centaur.' "[78] The author explained that this story would be "about a woman who presents her visiting card, and upon it is engraved: 'Mrs. John Culpepper Randolph, Adultress' . . . sort of a scarlet-letter theme brought up to date."

What is true of so much of Saxon's work seems particularly true of "The Centaur Plays Croquet": although not without flaws, the story certainly is good enough to be worthy of new attention. To phrase it alternately, the story is far too good to have disappeared completely. Saxon himself once expressed a fear that "The Centaur" would be buried in the huge tome, the *Caravan*, and buried it has remained for over sixty years.[79] Unlike many of the other stories in the anthology, Saxon's "Centaur" is in direct line with what the editors said they wanted. In the preface to the *Caravan*, Brooks and the others express a desire to publish intermediary forms of literature which have often been rejected by "passive and recessive" literary magazines.[80] "The Centaur," turned down previously by other editors, is an unconventional story in format as well as in content. Despite Saxon's friendships with the *Caravan* editors, his story was evidently not chosen on politics alone.

Gilbert Seldes admits in his *Dial* review of the *Caravan* that he has not been able to read all the contents of the book, yet he then complains that the writers included submitted fiction in conventional form and that no one wrote stories concerned with social satire.[81] Evidently Seldes had not read Saxon's story before writing his review; for "The Centaur" seems not only representative of what the *Caravan* editors desired, but is also a splendid example of what the *Dial* reviewer finds lacking. Regrettably, as Seldes's comments suggest, Saxon's fears were well founded: among the many works by brighter literary lights, his centaur was buried from the beginning.

Following closely the author's accomplishment in the *Caravan* was the appearance in October 1927, of "The Long Furrow."[82] This finely wrought story concerns the relationship between a white man, who is slowly dying of tuberculosis, and a black field hand on a plantation. "The Long Furrow," incorporated as Chapter 16 of *Children of Strangers*, is an integral part of the novel and will be discussed in some detail later in connection with the book. Noteworthy here, however, is that Henry Tyler, the black man in the story, is an individualized, fully developed character in no way suggestive of one of the common black stereotypes in the fiction of the day. Hewitt H. Howland, editor of *The Century Magazine,* was quite moved by the story. In the letter he wrote to Saxon accepting it for publication, Howland compliments "its subtlty [sic] and its restraint, its beauty and its color, its humanness and its sympathy."[83] This encouragement was extremely meaningful to Saxon, but so was the compensation; he confided to Olive that Howland's letter with the check from Century came just as he was looking at the gas connection "with friendly interest."[84]

While the *Century Magazine* containing Saxon's story was on the newsstands, *Father Mississippi* appeared in the bookstores. Almost exactly a year after leaving New Orleans, Saxon's initial book was published, but this event did not bring him unqualified joy. One reason is that the author was consistently more proud of his fiction than of his nonfiction. He wrote to Caroline Dormon that when he discovered the Century editors were "jazzing up" "The Long Furrow," making rather substantial changes, he "went right down and raised hell."[85] Saxon told Century that they could "make all the errors and corrections that they pleased" on *Father Mississippi*, but that "when they started monkeying with a short story, . . . I was ready to howl." Hewitt Howland apologized, Saxon explained, "and said that he would restore every kidnapped comma and semi-colon." Two days later Saxon confided to Olive that he looked forward to the appearance of "The Long Furrow," but not of *Father Mississippi*.[86] On the day the book appeared Saxon wrote to his Aunt Elizabeth:

> "Father Mississippi" is published today. Just down the street from here
> is a bookstore—and the window is filled with copies of the book.
> Makes me feel queer to see it there. It doesn't seem possible that all
> those messy pages that I sweated over last summer should evolve at last
> into anything as tangible as a book—and people should actually pay
> good money for it. . . . All I can say is that I hope I can make some
> money out of it all.[87]

In this same letter, Saxon repeatedly complains of having to go to various teas and dinners in his honor. The new Century author may exaggerate to his aunt that "all this fuss means nothing," but it seems accurate to conclude that Saxon's first published book did not strike him as his greatest literary accomplishment to date. The examination of *Father Mississippi* in the next chapter, including a look at its many flaws, indicates again Saxon's sound literary judgment—even of his own work.

Saxon continued in the limelight during the last two months of 1927. In November his "Cane River" was again reprinted. This time the story was selected by Edward J. O'Brien for inclusion in *The Best Short Stories of 1927*. *The New York Times* praised O'Brien as a qualified judge of short fiction, and the tales selected in 1927 bear out that praise.[88] As in the *Caravan*, Saxon's story is among good fiction; represented in the anthology are Hemingway, Owen Wister, Sherwood Anderson, Roark Bradford, DuBose Heyward, Oliver La Farge, and J. P. Marquand. The next month, on December 3, 1927, a Saxon article appeared in *The Publishers' Weekly*. That the author was not too proud to peddle, indirectly at least, is evident from this piece. His predictable thesis in "Make This a Book Christmas" is that readers could give no better present than a nice book to a loved one. Not exactly as a disinterested observer, Saxon points out that there are many good books—"this year particularly"—to choose from.[89] He never names *Father Mississippi*; but selling the new Century volume, at five dollars a copy, must have been what Saxon was doing between the lines.

Just as Saxon's social life in New Orleans was an active one even during his long workdays at *The Times-Picayune*, the New York social calendar was, almost from the beginning, about as full. Soon after arriving he met Zona Gale and Carl Van Doren; in his early letters to Olive, Saxon describes meeting and socializing with Elinor Wylie and William Rose Benét, whom he liked "immensely."[90] Wylie, whom Saxon says in one letter was "sort of queen of the roost," hosted regular Sunday evening parties for the literati. At one of these parties in February 1927, Saxon met Ford Madox Ford, Heywood Broun, and Theodore Dreiser, who furnished some whiskey that was so bad it made at least one indulging guest violently ill. Drinking was heavy at these gatherings, Saxon tells Olive, and Wylie's parties he describes as a kind of "Who's Who Among Writers" in New York.

Saxon occasionally stayed with Sherwood Anderson in Virginia on his way to New York during these years, but the two saw much less of each other than in old French Quarter days. Saxon must have been buoyed up tremendously by Anderson's help and encouragement in the late 1920s. Apparently in a letter or when he visited the Andersons, Saxon had asked for advice about revising "Cane River" or had expressed frustration at how long the story had taken him to write. At any rate, probably in August of 1927, Anderson wrote this encouraging response:

I have been reading your story again. It is quite perfect. You are wrong
in thinking anything need be done to it. My own notion is that so
perfect a short story doesn't appear once in ten years.

For God sake Lyle don't be discouraged that such work doesn't
come fast. Suppose you are another ten years making a half dozen such
tales. What does it matter. Plenty of people grinding out the other sort
fast enough. Anything any good has to come slowly. Some women
have a lot of children and none of them any good. Writing such tales is
a good deal like having children. You have to become pregnant. Then
carry the thing around inside you while it grows. . . . You are on the
right track. Hang on and be patient. And forgive me for being so damn
fatherly about it.[91]

Later Anderson was instrumental in getting Saxon's "Cane River" and a few
other stories translated into German by Karl Lerbs, who had translated his
own *Poor White* and other works.[92] The stories were published in
Germany, and, although Saxon laughingly remarked that the "armful of
German banknotes" he received from Lerbs amounted to only eighteen
dollars,[93] his old friend Anderson had made him an internationally
published author.

Saxon was, of course, only one among the many Southern writers
and artists who migrated north during these years. Orleanian William
Spratling had a New York apartment down the street from Saxon, and
Mississippian Stark Young was well established in the city by this time.
Before Saxon gave up his apartment on Christopher Street in 1932, moreover, Thomas Wolfe, Carl Carmer, Julia Peterkin, William Faulkner, and
many others had come to New York. In one of Thomas Wolfe's pocket
notebooks, kept between October 1929 and January 1930, the novelist lists
Lyle Saxon, DuBose Heyward, William Rose Benét, and eight other writers
he has recently met in New York; Wolfe heads the list of names with "The
literary life—I know these 'uns."[94] At a luncheon at the Biltmore in 1929,
Saxon himself quipped: "When someone asks me if I have seen such and
such a Southerner recently, I reply, 'No, I haven't been in New York
recently.' "[95]

Just as the author had kept in touch, more or less, with most of his
literary friends of the Vieux Carré, he and Faulkner had renewed their
friendship at least once before the novelist came to New York in the fall of
1928.[96] According to Faulkner's biographers, Saxon "served as local

hosteler"; his apartment served as a "clearinghouse" for Southerners coming to New York and as a meeting place for the "Southern Protective Association."[97] This was the phrase Saxon and the other Southerners used to describe themselves since they took care of each other's needs in the big city; as one writer has said, the name described "their own habit of mutual aid."[98] Faulkner's immediate need was a place to stay, and he remained for a few days with Saxon at 3 Christopher Street upon his arrival in New York. Saxon at this time was at work on *Fabulous New Orleans*, and Faulkner was revising *The Sound and the Fury*. Blotner, citing artist Owen Crump, explains why the Mississippian remained only a short time at Saxon's:

> Lyle Saxon had been hospitable as ever . . . so hospitable—"Father Superior of the group," one called him—that Faulkner found the atmosphere hectic. A pot of Southern drip coffee was always on the stove and served with ceremony. People knocked on his door day and night, and there was usually a crowd there. Faulkner had to get a place by himself where he could concentrate.[99]

This comment is interesting in light of Saxon's having left Noel Straus's apartment shortly after arriving in New York because of the noise and confusion there. At this time Saxon commented that all he desired was to be left alone so that he could write; "and it is necessary," Saxon concluded, "to live alone in order to do that."[100]

Understandably, then, no rift ensued after Faulkner's hasty departure from 3 Christopher Street. On the contrary, the two men evidently continued their friendship throughout the months they were both in New York. Faulkner and Saxon sometimes dined together, according to Carl Carmer, who occasionally joined them.[101] As had been the case in New Orleans, the two writers, traveling in the same social circle, surely crossed paths on numerous occasions. Faulkner had moved from Saxon's apartment to stay with Owen Crump, whom he had met at Saxon's. Crump recalled the day in December 1928, when Faulkner decided to return to Mississippi to write. Having received an advance of two hundred dollars, Faulkner had his pocket picked in the Village. Two hours before his train was to leave, Faulkner and Crump set out to collect enough donations from friends to pay for the novelist's trip home.[102] Ben Wasson writes that Saxon and Spratling "felt that Bill should have an extra amount of money for his train ride south, and they scrounged around and fattened his new wallet."[103] Saxon was thus among the donors who enabled Faulkner to return to Oxford, where he began *Sanctuary* the next month.

Not long after Saxon and the others bought his ticket home, Faulkner wrote his famous short story "A Rose for Emily."[104] Various aspects of this story are interesting here because of certain parallels to Saxon's "The Centaur Plays Croquet." Emily Grierson and Saxon's Ada Calander are both in opposition to the traditions and codes of behavior "we" expect of them. Faulkner once said that Emily "had broken all the laws of her tradition, her background . . . ."[105] Ada, of course, had done the same thing. Both women, moreover, were admired by their creators. Ada was Saxon's favorite heroine,[106] and Faulkner's portrait is, of course, a rose for his fictional lady. Both characters also were willing to take drastic steps to hold on to what they loved. In Saxon's fantasy Ada poisons her competition to regain Horace, and Emily buys the rat poison to retain Homer.

Most notable, however, are parallels between the two stories involving visits to each lady by the well-meaning and/or scandalized citizens of Mimosa and of Jefferson. The Baptist minister visits Ada only to be insulted and to encounter blasphemy. The Baptist preacher in Jefferson, forced by the ladies to call on Emily, "would never divulge what happened during that interview, but . . . refused to go back again." The similarity between the visits of Dr. Fleming and Mildred-Virginia in "The Centaur" and of the "deputation" that calls on Emily is likewise noteworthy. As the Flemings approach the Calander house, Saxon's narrator notes that the roses were drowned in masses of weeds and that the steps were rotted away (359); Faulkner's words about the "stubborn and coquettish decay" of the Grierson house would aptly apply. Upon entering Ada's house, the Flemings were met by "an aged Negro"; the Aldermen, of course, were led to Emily's parlor by Tobe. After noting that Ada, then aged forty-one, looked like a woman of seventy, Dr. Fleming points out that "the floor was deep in dust, the dust being particularly noticeable" (360). When Faulkner's deputation entered Emily's house, they noticed a smell of dust and disuse, "and when they sat down, a faint dust rose sluggishly about their thighs . . . ." Finally, the less than cordial receptions of the visitors are similar in the two stories. Ada asked Fleming, he notes, "to state my business and be gone; and . . . offered us neither chairs nor refreshment . . . ." After a few moments, Ada ordered the "instant departure" of the Flemings, ejecting them "without further ado" (360-61). Emily

Grierson similarly "did not ask [the Aldermen] to sit" and, after a brief time, ordered Tobe: "Show these gentlemen out."

Whether or not these parallels between the two stories are coincidental is an interesting question. Any suggestion of another possible source for Faulkner's "A Rose for Emily" should perhaps be offered with trepidation. After all, sources such as Poe, Dickens, Cable, and others have already been suggested. Well known too is the possibility of the real-life inspiration of the story based on the courtship of an Oxford woman by Captain Jack Barron; and Faulkner's own previous creations, especially Miss Zilphia Gant, are in a sense Emily's literary ancestors as well. In view of all these possibilities, any contention that "The Centaur" was an inspiration for Emily's story seems farfetched—especially since Faulkner's tale, if all the theories are valid, is one of the most inspired he ever wrote.

On the other hand, it seems likely that Faulkner was at least aware of or perhaps quite familiar with Saxon's "Centaur" by the time he wrote "A Rose for Emily," indicating the parallels between the two stories may be more than coincidental. Initially, it should be remembered that the two writers had spent considerable time together in New York a few months before the later story was written, and it seems likely that Faulkner would have been aware of Saxon's recently published work. Faulkner owned a copy of Saxon's *Father Mississippi*, published within a few months of the *American Caravan* containing "The Centaur Plays Croquet"; and, in fact, Michael Grimwood has suggested that Faulkner drew on *Father Mississippi* as a source for "Old Man" and "Mississippi."[107] Blotner suggests another of Saxon's books (presumably *Fabulous New Orleans*) as an inspiration for one aspect of Faulkner's "Red Leaves."[108] Some of the *American Caravan* anthologies were surely known to Faulkner as well. He submitted a story of his own to the *Caravan* in early 1930, and he had a thorough knowledge of one of Robert Penn Warren's stories that appeared in *The American Caravan IV*.[109] In his discussion of *Father Mississippi* and Faulkner's pieces dealing with the Mississippi River, Grimwood suggests that Saxon, a "noted raconteur . . . undoubtedly shared his recent flood experiences" with his New York friends and that "Faulkner probably heard tales that Saxon had not committed to print."[110] It seems just as safe to speculate, as Grimwood does regarding *Father Mississippi*, that Faulkner also read the tales Saxon did commit to print.

Whatever the Mississippian's knowledge or opinion of "The Centaur" might have been, Saxon greatly admired "A Rose for Emily."

Several of his friends commented on how much he enjoyed the story of Emily Grierson, and Harris Downey told me that Saxon owned a privately printed copy of "A Rose for Emily."[111] If Saxon suspected, or knew, that his own "Centaur" had in some way inspired Faulkner's story, his affinity for "Rose" would surely have been heightened. Even if Saxon suspected no influence whatsoever, though, when the creator of Ada Calander read about Emily Grierson, he must have felt at least the shock of recognition.

During the last quarter of 1928, the period of Faulkner's visit to New York, Saxon certainly had stories besides "The Centaur" on his mind. Marianne Moore had accepted "Lizzie Balize" for *The Dial* in June; this story, which later became Chapter 19 of *Children of Strangers*, appeared first in the October *Dial*.[112] The same month, Saxon's "Have a Good Time While You Can" was published in *The Century Magazine*.[113] This article constitutes, with some elaboration, the first part of *Fabulous New Orleans*, which the Century Company issued on October 26, 1928, exactly one year after *Father Mississippi*.

The connections with Century brought Saxon increased renown the rest of the time he maintained the Christopher Street apartment. In August 1929, the company published "The Gay Dangerfields," which later became the second chapter of *Old Louisiana*.[114] This book appeared on October 25, the author's third in two years. In October of 1930, the fourth book written by Saxon and published by Century was completed. This biography, *Lafitte the Pirate,* one of Saxon's most lucrative in itself and by the various offshoots from it, was the final work the author did with Century.

As Saxon's arrangements with his first publishers and with *The Dial* tapered off, however, his connections with the *Herald Tribune* and with various New York magazines increased. Several of his next published pieces were features much like those he had done in *The Times-Picayune*. "Mardi Gras" is somewhat of an introduction to the carnival for *Herald Tribune* readers and adds nothing to the account in *Fabulous New Orleans*.[115] Neither is anything noteworthy regarding Mardi Gras conveyed in Saxon's "The South Parades," which appeared in the August 1930 *Theatre Arts Monthly*. Saxon here even plagiarizes himself as he repeats some of the phrases from his *Herald Tribune* feature.[116] Between these two Mardi Gras articles, Saxon published "Easter on the Plantation" in the Sunday *Herald Tribune*.[117] This sketch was written several years before and, like the carnival features, was a presentation of Louisiana subject matter for the New York audience. The piece contains a description of an

Easter worship service among the blacks of Cane River and was to be adapted for the last chapter of *Children of Strangers*. Two other features written during these years involve various aspects of the Lafitte story. Both of these appeared in October 1930—one in a New Orleans magazine and the other in the *Herald Tribune*.[118] As Saxon had done with the first three books, he thereby managed to get the subject of his latest biography before the public's eye immediately prior to publication.

During his days on Christopher Street, Saxon also wrote reviews. Between 1929 and 1931, six book reviews by the author appeared in prominent New York newspapers and journals. All six reveal Saxon as a somewhat gentle reviewer. He managed to find something good in each book he evaluated, and his positive comments far outweigh the negative. Five of Saxon's critiques are of books long since forgotten; the other is of *The Sound and the Fury*. The author's opinions of the five books now relatively obscure are interesting over forty years later and, in some cases of course, render Saxon less than a prophet.[119] *The Magic Island* by W. B. Seabrook, according to the reviewer, is "certain to be discussed," and Stark Young's *River House* is called "a novel of first rank." A little back scratching was possibly involved in some of these reviews. Edward Larocque Tinker, whose *Old New Orleans* is recommended heartily by Saxon, would in later years favorably review three of Saxon's books. In the next few years too, Saxon would exchange reviews with Hamilton Basso and Roark Bradford, and a collusion is probable in some such cases. Stark Young, as a matter of fact, reviewed *Old Louisiana* quite favorably in *The New Republic* three days before Saxon's praise of Young's *River House*.

This kind of literary nepotism may seem cause enough to be suspicious of Saxon's very favorable review of *The Sound and the Fury*. Frederick Karl, in fact, contends that Saxon's *Herald Tribune* review is "so full of favorable comments it must be viewed as *parti pris*."[120] This seems to me an unfair evaluation of the review; for, among Saxon's dozens of book reviews, it is as unique as was Faulkner's book among that fall's group of novels. Admittedly, all six of Saxon's New York reviews are favorable, indicating success for each of the books. His accurate prophecy about the greatness of *The Sound and the Fury*, it could be argued, is no more than a manifestation of the law of averages; and one out of six is not even a good batting average. It should be pointed out, though, that nowhere else in a review, before or after the one of Faulkner's novel, does Saxon indulge in such enthusiastic praise.[121] Unlike most of the other books Saxon evaluated, moreover, *The Sound and the Fury* did not contain subject matter he was almost expected to praise—such as accounts of old steamboat days on the Mississippi or of the land pirates on the Natchez Trace.[122] It also seems unfair, actually illogical, to suspect Saxon of an ulterior motive in the case of Faulkner's novel. The younger novelist not only would never reciprocate in praise of a Saxon book, but, compared to Young, Basso, Bradford, and the others of this "mutual review society," Faulkner probably seemed already the least likely ever to do Saxon a good turn in print. Saxon's review seems eminently sincere to me, and it places him almost literally at the front of the long line of those who have been confused, yet deeply moved by the book.

In the first sentence of his review, Saxon contends that Faulkner has "gained in power" with each of his four novels and that this book is one of "extraordinary effect."[123] He states further that *The Sound and the Fury* is "as merciless as anything that I know of which has come out of Russia." This comparison is interesting in light of Saxon's statement to Olive Lyons in January of 1927 that "Hemenway" and "these boys" are like babies compared to Chekhov. Saxon next attempts to recount the Compsons' story, section by section, as so many have done since. The Quentin section, given slight treatment in his summary, was evidently very confusing to Saxon, but even this part of the novel has seemingly communicated without being understood. The reviewer describes the prose of the Benjy section as "pitifully moving" and calls Dilsey "a magnificent figure." Saxon's last paragraph seems worth quoting in its entirety:

> It will be interesting to see what readers and critics think of this novel by William Faulkner. Many, I am sure will call the author mad. But if Faulkner is mad, then James Joyce is equally so; if Faulkner is obsessed with futility and insanity, so is Fyodor Dostoevsky. It is true that "The Sound and the Fury" is insane and monstrous and terrible, but so is the life that it mirrors. It is difficult to read, but I could not put it down. I believe, simply and sincerely, that this is a great book.

This is the kind of praise that led Joseph Blotner to describe Saxon's review as the best of those early ones following the October 7 publication and which resulted in Minter's citing it first among the "favorable" *Sound and Fury* reviews.[124]

Saxon's speculation, less than a week after the publication of Faulkner's book, about others' reactions to *The Sound and the Fury* is especially interesting. Many would, of course, call the author mad. Jay B. Hubbell, in *Who Are the Major American Writers?*, notes that during the years in which Faulkner's best books appeared, the majority of literary critics were "either puzzled, angered, or disgusted by what they found in them."[125] Hubbell also mentions the "fortunate" fact that in the case of each major American writer, there have been "a few discerning critics who recognized his genius long before the general public was aware of his significance." Lyle Saxon was surely among those few who, very early, saw more than madness and futility in Faulkner.

As a matter of fact, three years before Saxon's *Herald Tribune* review appeared, he had read parts of the manuscript of *Mosquitoes* when Faulkner visited New Orleans one weekend. Saxon wrote Sherwood Anderson remarking how "*very* good" he found the new book by "Bill Falkner (Faulkner?)."[126] By the time Saxon reviewed *The Sound and the Fury*, he knew which spelling to use, and the question mark was removed. Although the closest and most significant association between the two writers ended by late 1929, Saxon certainly seems to have played his important minor role in Faulkner's life. As Karl has said, "Saxon deserves a place in Faulkner's life for several reasons. He was a part of that crowd . . . who aided Faulkner at critical points when he was about to make a decision."[127]

Not long after the last of his *Herald Tribune* reviews, Saxon gave up his apartment in the Village, and his New York days were, essentially, over. The author of course, even from 1926 to 1932, moved around so often that the label "New York days" is more facile than accurate. It should be reiterated that, in addition to New York and Melrose, he spent a great deal of time with his aunts in Baton Rouge and with friends in New Orleans. All his travels and his several homes notwithstanding, however, certain facts of Saxon's life during the first six years away from *The Times-Picayune* make Melrose and New York of primary importance at this particular stage of his career. In the Louisiana retreat he discovered a good place to write. At the same time, in New York, by his connections with Century and elsewhere, he discovered publishing opportunities. In the Village, he made new friends and met fellow artists—some already successful and others struggling, as was Saxon himself initially. Many of the successful ones aided him, and, when Saxon was in a position to help others, he seems to have done so without exception. Carvel Collins told me recently that in talking with Faulkner's friends over the years, he had consistently heard compliments and positive comments about Lyle Saxon.[128]

Along with a handful of other writers and artists of the 1920s and '30s, Saxon was in the fortunate position of having been a part of the literary coteries of the Vieux Carré and of Greenwich Village. One of the earliest French Quarter residents of the New Orleans group, he soon achieved a central position among the New York literati as well. By 1931, after all four Century books were published, he was described as "a much-sought speaker, giving talks at meetings of the National Arts Club, the Author's Club, the P.E.N. . . . ."[129] The northern environment surely gave him a new, and of course wider, perspective from which to view Louisiana. In some senses, the North only impressed him by its similarities to the South. He once remarked to Rachel Field during a tour of old New England homes that the people of the two parts of the country had much in common and that the only difference was that "in New England people in the end just dried up, whereas in the South they simply fell apart."[130]

A good deal of insight into Saxon's decisions to leave Louisiana and to return in 1932 can be gained from a passage in "Fame." One of the characters in this story, which Saxon probably wrote in 1925, is a newspaper reporter who is disillusioned with his work. The autobiographical elements in this description of the character are obvious:

> He . . . had wanted to write, and he had gone to New Orleans, after his
> four years at the State university, to get a newspaper job. Ten years of
> it. He had a good position now, but the writing dream was as far away
> as ever. He had tried, but the thing failed, somehow. A good news-
> paperman, yes, but limited. He realized that.[131]

Saxon's own desire to write outside the confines of the newspaper office had taken him to New York. By the time he left, he was no longer a writer "limited" in scope by journalistic bounds. By 1932, having published numerous works of various genres, Saxon would leave the marketplace in which he had peddled his wares and return to Louisiana; there he could pursue further "the writing dream."

TRAVELS:
THE LOUISIANA "EATIN' BOOKS," 1927-1930

DURING A THREE-YEAR PERIOD at the end of the 1920s, Lyle Saxon wrote four books. All were published by Century, and all are, essentially, biographies: the "life stories" of a river, a city, a state, and a legendary buccaneer. *Father Mississippi* (1927), *Fabulous New Orleans* (1928), *Old Louisiana* (1929), and *Lafitte the Pirate* (1930) provided Saxon with steady income from the times of their publications until his death. No one of these volumes made the author a rich man; neither did the combined royalties give him any kind of financial independence. The books did sell well at various times, however, and were incorporated into other media, such as radio dramas and motion pictures. According to Tess Crager, Joe Gilmore, Saxon's butler and longtime friend, came to call the four Century volumes "our eatin' books."

"Uneven" seems a particularly appropriate word to describe the quality of Saxon's "eatin' books." At worst they are potboilers that emphasize grotesque and sensational elements from the history or the pseudo-history of Louisiana. At best they are vivid regional surveys that exhibit variously a genuine pathos or a delightful whimsicality on the part of the observer. Saxon never wrote or, according to his friends, never said anything which would indicate he took any inordinate pride in these works. In fact, his public statements, letters, and diaries indicate that he viewed as a "serious writer" one who wrote fiction—not journalistic or historical works. Even during the writing of his four Century volumes, he never lost sight of his dream to write fiction; he once called his nonfiction "stepping stones" toward that end.[1]

The author's head could very easily have been turned since the Louisiana books led to his being widely hailed as his state's foremost historian and identified as "the new chronicler of the South."[2] Actually Saxon's histories, as he knew better than anyone, added little or nothing to what Gayarré, Castellanos, Chambers, King, and dozens of others had already written about Louisiana. They are not well-documented, scholarly, or even well-organized historical surveys. Without further comment on the historicity, I will concentrate here on the journalistic and fictional aspects of the books: on the contemporary events about which Saxon reported and on the stories that he apparently created *ex nihilo* in the four volumes. This emphasis seems appropriate not only because these are generally the liveliest parts of the books, but also because of the author's repeatedly stated preference for fiction over history. Readers of the "eatin' books," incidentally, cannot always easily distinguish between fictive and factual elements and are made to feel that at times Saxon himself lacked either the ability or the desire to make this distinction.

Beginning with an incontrovertible fact, however, Saxon first wrote for Century his accounts of the mammoth and destructive Mississippi River floods of 1927. Estimates of the flood damage range from 250 to 300 million dollars, and over three hundred people died in the tragedy. In the early spring, of course, stories relating to the floods occupied the headlines of virtually all the major newspapers in America. By the end of May, however, the accounts of the disaster, as one writer later remarked in *The New York Times*, were "pushed off the front pages by Lindbergh's flight . . . ."[3] In the summer of 1927 Lyle Saxon's articles in *The Century Magazine* reminded his readers of the tragedy and of the ongoing hardships and difficulties for residents of the valley. When *Father Mississippi* appeared in October, the power of the river and the desperate need for further efforts at controlling it were indeed timely topics for consideration.

Saxon's personal involvement with the raging waters and with rescue efforts had occupied his time during the height of the floods. He had participated in the Coast Guard rescues during the latter part of May. His concern during the rest of the spring and the summer was with the articulation of his experiences and the writing of the river's long story. When he first returned from the flooded areas, he wrote Sherwood Anderson: "I got back to Baton Rouge, sore in every part of my anatomy, and blistered and burned beyond recognition from the sun and water."[4] He added that everyone seems to be writing about the flood, yet "nobody seems to be able to get it wet enough or muddy enough to please me."

Saxon's spring experiences served him well in his summer's writing; he knew all too well how wet it was. Yet, as would be the case with all four Century books, he struggled through the composition process. He had to write a tremendous amount in a short time to meet Century's fall publication deadline. Having to write at least two thousand words a day, Saxon told Anderson, "is worrying me sick." Various letters to and from the author during the summer indicate that he spent some time in Baton Rouge and in New Orleans, but he seems to have done the bulk of his writing at Melrose. Drawing on Cammie Henry's voluminous scrapbooks (sources that Saxon acknowledges in *Father Mississippi*), he worked hard for three months on his chronicle of the river.

By the end of August 1927, the author had finished writing the book, or, as he wrote to Caroline Dormon, "the horrible Father Mississippi thing is done at last. . . ."[5] On his way back to New York, rather ironically, Saxon arrived in Louisville, Kentucky, the same time as Lindbergh, the man who had preempted the flood stories in the press. With tongue in cheek, Saxon complains in a letter to Olive Lyons that since he and the aviator were in Louisville simultaneously, "I came near sleeping out in the park—as he seemed to occupy all available hotel rooms." Eventually making his way north, Saxon gives an account of the status of his book in his next letter to Olive. From the middle to the end of August, he explains, he was busily making revisions, having the whole manuscript typed, and examining the first proofs.[6] From the time he sketched notes while on the rescue boats to the late-summer days when he reviewed these proofs, Saxon had spent a hectic three months. The book reflects the author's haste toward publication.

Saxon's introduction to *Father Mississippi* contains a disclaimer, pointing out that this account of the river is not a history "in the strict sense of the word" (v). Instead, the author continues, the book is "like a scrapbook in which I have collected men's thoughts, my own thoughts, and the thoughts and experiences of other men." This explanation seems as confusing and redundant as it is apologetic and, ironically enough, foreshadows the confusion and redundancy throughout the coming pages. In his introductory remarks, too, Saxon tells his readers that they will be addressed directly only at the beginning and at the end of the book. The former section is that in which Saxon's alleged plantation boyhood is described, and the other personal part of the book is the account of the 1927 flood. The three middle sections of the five-part *Father Mississippi* contain a hodgepodge of historical, legendary, and scientific information about the river. This overall plan does indeed result in a finished product that could be described as a "scrapbook," with the emphasis on the first syllable.

Part One of *Father Mississippi*, called "Plantation," begins with the account, discussed in my initial chapter, of the "small boy" who views the mighty river. The point of view then shifts to the first person, and readers are told what the boy recalls about life on the idyllic plantation near the Mississippi. The final chapter of Part One, entitled "Crevasse," describes the evacuation and the inundation of the old family home through the eyes of the frightened and bewildered boy. This nicely written chapter is a creditable initiation story. The boy experiences a nagging suspicion, then a terrifying certainty, that the rising waters he hears his elders discussing have a direct bearing on the security of his home.

Several paragraphs of "Crevasse" describe vividly the exodus of the family, the mules, horses, cows, and chickens as the water surges over its banks and onto the fields. A particularly effective scene is one in which Saxon's narrator recalls seeing a painting lying on the ground. The portrait of his great-aunt had been carried from the plantation, along with other family treasures. The familiar face in the painting, the narrator recalls, "seemed strangely unreal" out of its place in the great hallway and outdoors in the midst of such a tumult (57). The "dark, tragic eyes" of the woman in the picture stared upward in the moonlight when a stampeding mule

> crashed into the portrait that was lying on the grass. I saw the forefoot of the animal go through the painted face, and when he pulled it out again there was only a gaping hole, with the white clover showing through, and the gold frame glinting in the moonlight. (57)

A few hours later, with the rising sun, the boy and his family view the ruination the night has brought. Saxon's description of the scene is memorable:

> . . . we saw that the plantation-house was askew; the whole building slanted down sharply to one side; one of the chimneys had fallen. The flower garden and the shrubs had disappeared. Only the trees remained, standing with water half way up to their trunks, each tree making a fan-shaped ripple in the current. Between us and the ruined house was an unbroken stretch of muddy water. (58)

From the beginning, the "Plantation" section of Saxon's book was one of the most widely discussed parts. Almost every reviewer who mentioned this initial section accepted the first-person narrative literally and assumed that the vivid memories were Saxon's. As I have already pointed out, such an assumption is surely erroneous. Even if not autobiographical, though, the "Plantation" section is so well done that, with only a few exceptions, the rest of *Father Mississippi* is woefully anticlimactic. John McClure lavishly praised the initial chapters of Saxon's book and even ventured the opinion that they constituted "the finest interpretation of plantation life yet done in American literature."[7] Surely many readers would not share the opinion of Saxon's friend McClure, but "Crevasse" would appear in anthologies in later years and was even selected for a radio dramatization almost twenty-five years after the publication of *Father Mississippi*.[8]

The second major division of the book, "In the Beginning," deals with the history of the river. Saxon discusses the Indians who lived along the Mississippi, traces early explorations, such as those led by De Soto, Marquette, and La Salle, and describes the founding of Natchitoches and of New Orleans. Beginning with this section of the book, the author includes extensive quotations from various documents: diaries, newspaper accounts, court records, scientific treatises, and other sources. In one case, for example, Saxon quotes, over the course of nine pages, the diary of Father Hennepin, the priest who accompanied La Salle's expedition (92-101). As interesting as parts of the priest's account are, many readers surely were bothered by such an extensive use of this and other sources. Cleveland B. Chase remarked in *The New York Times* that many of Saxon's quoted reports of the early explorers were already accessible to the reading public and that they added very little to the interest of *Father Mississippi*.[9] Chase's criticism seems justifiable in light of Saxon's pronounced dependence on such sources; his use of large blocks of material is certainly excessive.

Saxon ends his second section strongly, however, with the interesting account of the visit of a group of Illinois Indians to Paris in 1725. The author explains that the story has been told before but proceeds, as in many other cases in the book, to tell it again. Here and elsewhere, readers will perhaps be reminded of times when they are about to be told an old joke, are warned by the teller that they have probably already heard it, then are told the joke anyway—heartily enjoying it once again. Many of Saxon's shorter tales, though twice or more told, hold up very well in *Father Mississippi*. In fact, he follows well Mark Twain's advice on how to tell a funny

story, and his reputation as a raconteur was apparently much deserved. The
high point of Saxon's version of the Indian story in *Father Mississippi* is
the eventual marriage of a Frenchman, Captain Dubois, and one of the Indian women. Back in Illinois, however, the new Madame Dubois successfully leads her tribe in an uprising against the French soldiers and the fort
her husband commands. Saxon ends his account by adding a personal note:

> And the last picture of our Indian princess shows her stripping herself
> of her trailing French dress, her corsets, her religion—all at once. With
> one loud yell she tossed aside her crucifix and embraced again her
> heathen gods. Naked and happy, she returned to the wilderness.
>   And I for one hope that she lived happily ever after! (121)

This seems an understandable attitude from the creator of the wild Susie and
the scandalous Ada Calander. Saxon's last sentence in the passage quoted
above, incidentally, was omitted when this section of *Father Mississippi*
was twice anthologized in later years.

Saxon continues to trace and to rehash various historical events
linked to the river and to the Mississippi Valley in the third part of his book.
The trial of the notorious Molly Glass makes up a good portion of this
section. Molly, a free quadroon who married a white man, was convicted
and executed in 1781 in New Orleans for cruelly mistreating her servants
and for murdering one slave girl. "In view of our present knowledge of
abnormal psychology," Saxon writes, "it would appear that Molly Glass
was a sadist . . ." (144). It would appear that Saxon draws a safe inference
here. The author tediously quotes long passages from court records of
Molly's trial. He seems to have been considerably more excited by what he
wrote of this case than most readers, even lawyers, would be by what they
read of it. The trial of Molly Glass is at best of tangential relevance in a
book, even a scrapbook, about the Mississippi River. Even less pertinent is
the other major constituent of this part of the book: the extensive excerpts
from the diary of "A Woman Pioneer." Martha Martin's previously unpublished diary, which Saxon had access to through her grandson, recounts
various events of her life during the early nineteenth century. Saxon's editing is poor, for although some parts of the sixteen-page quotation from this
diary are interesting, others are quite mundane and grow tedious. John
McClure's contention that the story of Molly Glass, Martin's diary, and all
the other "interludes" in *Father Mississippi* "add fascination to the whole"

seems a kindly view but a difficult one to maintain.[10] Chase's review contains the probably accurate indictment that Saxon seems to have "laid hand upon whatever material concerning the Mississippi Valley he could gather" in his hurry to complete a book-length study of the river while the floods were still on the public mind.[11]

Saxon's fourth division, "Old Steamboat Days," adds nothing new or distinctive of a historical nature. The author seems to have written this section not so much inspired as intimidated by Mark Twain's *Life on the Mississippi*. Saxon's account of the grand steamboating days on the river in fact lacks life. Significantly, when the author quotes one of Mark Twain's descriptions of steamboat racing, he comments that he has selected the quotation because in this passage Clemens "waxes lyric" (214). In "Old Steamboat Days" Saxon seldom does.

The final section of *Father Mississippi*, called "1927," is distinctive for two reasons: it contains the three articles written for *The Century Magazine*, and it ends with Saxon's eloquent plea for steps to be taken to prevent a repetition of the river tragedy of 1927. The three chapters from which the book grew are obviously more skillfully done than much of the rest of *Father Mississippi;* in fact, because of these articles Saxon's fifth section of the book stands out almost like a well thumb. "Episode: Down on the Levee" is a vivid, present-tense account of the early stages of the flood. Saxon describes the scene as he, one other white man, and several blacks wait together, huddled on the levee top, for the Coast Guard rescue boat to return. One old black man dies, and a young girl gives birth in the hours before the boat carries them all away. The account is framed by the plaintive questions of one man who has become separated from his wife. Unknown to him, the woman has drowned.

"Episode: Acadians in the Flood" and the other *Century* article, "And the Waters Receded," are also vivid and memorable. Comparisons of the former article and the notebook in which Saxon jotted down impressions to be elaborated on in "Episode" reveal close parallels and indicate that the former newspaperman stuck closely to the facts in his account for *Century*.[12] In his most dramatic passages vividly chronicling life-and-death struggles, Saxon certainly "gets it wet enough." It is this last section of *Father Mississippi* that apparently influenced Faulkner in the writing of "Old Man" and "Mississippi." Michael Grimwood has demonstrated convincingly that *Father Mississippi* "provided the general background and several specific scenes" for the two later works by Faulkner.[13]

Finally in connection with Saxon's first book, the passages in "1927" in which the author becomes a crusading journalist are persuasive and eloquent. Saxon on the danger of new floods sounds almost like Defoe on the danger of new plagues. The author reminds his readers that in this last great flood the levees "fell to pieces faster than the wires could twang the news to the papers" (298). The great river, he continues, seems almost human at such times, "something human with a kind of Frankenstein-humanness." The author displays a perceptive, and prophetic, view that the people who were not actually flooded out themselves, even including those in New Orleans, would soon forget the potential danger of currently outmoded flood control devices. He effectively chides his readers by pointing out that "recollections of 1918 are not deterring the world from arming diligently for the next war, and the valley cannot help wondering if this flood to end floods will result in nothing but patched levees" (279).

Reviews of *Father Mississippi* were mixed, and some concentrated more on debating the proposed flood legislation before Congress than on evaluating Saxon's book.[14] Attitudes toward the former issues certainly influenced some reviewers' feelings about *Father Mississippi*. While one Orleanian remarked that a copy of the book should be in the hands of every Congressman, Arthur Kellogg commented in *The Survey* that "like most Southerners, Mr. Saxon sees the flood foreshortened—a great stream of water running over his doorstep." The reviews that avoided the issues beyond *Father Mississippi* itself were generally favorable, however. The book was praised in the *Wisconsin Library Bulletin* as well as in *The Mississippi Valley Historical Review*. The *New York Herald Tribune* reviewer, in fact, contended that the account of the flood had "a Defoe ring" about it and that the whole book was the work of an artist. *The Bookman*, too, hailed Saxon as a chronicler who depicted the 1927 flood as it really was.

Negative comments among the reviewers generally grew out of the tediousness of Saxon's long volume.[15] One writer, in *The Saturday Review of Literature*, commented wryly that *Father Mississippi* "is no book to begin if one has a train to catch." More specifically, the adverse comments in the published reviews almost all alluded to, predictably enough, the lack of organization in Saxon's "scrapbook." One Southern journal seemed reluctant to admit to the hodgepodge found in the middle sections and says somewhat euphemistically that the book is "like a club sandwich" with widely varying "interior ingredients." Chase's observation is perhaps the most telling on this issue: "The fact that in the short introduction [Saxon] speaks of the volume as a 'scrapbook' is scarcely enough to excuse the lamentable lack of unity in the material grouped together." The reason for this "lamentable" defect in the book is easily attributable, of course, to the hasty composition. Saxon himself admitted in 1937 that he wrote *Father Mississippi* as he had written his newspaper assignments—"in a hurry."

Despite encouragement and congratulations from some of his friends, the author was evidently disappointed in his initial book-length effort almost from the beginning. Perhaps to buoy him up, Sherwood Anderson wrote a characteristic letter of encouragement in which he told his friend that he loved the whole book and that Saxon could come to southwest Virginia and do a regional history of that area next; "We'll run the weeklies and live on Century," Anderson added.[16] From what Saxon reveals in a letter to Olive Lyons, however, he was not immediately enthusiastic to write another such book. Here the author calls some of the chapters in *Father Mississippi* "moronic" and describes the book in a mocking, telegraphic way; "Out October 31st. Five dollars net. Will anyone buy it. Answer, No."[17] Several years after the publication of the volume, Saxon revealed that he had even been very disappointed at the "superbly ugly appearance" of the book—"bound in drab brown cloth, with an asthmatic steamboat stamped on its cover."[18]

All the complaints and disappointments regarding his 1927 volume notwithstanding, Saxon was busily engaged the following spring on his second project for Century. Although he sounds positive in a May 1928 letter to Olive Lyons, telling her "The New Orleans book goes on apace," he quickly adds, "It's damned dull" and says: "Who ever told me I could write? God done it, and there ain't a word of truth in it." In two other letters to Olive, also written that spring, he confides that each one of the "hundreds of pages" spread out before him, is "worse than the last one" and that working on *Fabulous New Orleans* has put him "in a red and horrible hell . . . plain hell, that's all."[19] Saxon also reveals in the letters that even though he was expected to finish the book by the end of May, he realistically saw June 15 as the finishing date. Evidently Saxon did not meet this later deadline either, for several years afterward he revealed that he fought with the Century Company the whole summer about the title *Fabulous New Orleans*; "they hated it," he wrote, "and wanted to change it . . . ."[20]

On October 26, 1928, Saxon's New Orleans book appeared, however, under the title he desired. *Fabulous New Orleans* was illustrated by

Edward H. Suydam and was one of a series of regional books published at that time by Century.[21] Saxon dedicated his book to Grace King. Like Sherwood Anderson, King had encouraged him in virtually all of his literary endeavors and was, of course, an especially apt dedicatee for a history of New Orleans. One chronicler of Louisiana writers remarks that Grace King "captured the laurels of Gayarré."[22] She had known George Washington Cable, moreover, and surely was to Saxon a link with the literary greats of Louisiana's past.

Just as he does in the introduction to the first book, Saxon apologizes for the historicity of *Fabulous New Orleans*. He explains that the book is "rather like a Mardi Gras parade—a series of impressions" (vii). He goes on to disclaim again that he has attempted to write history "in its strict sense . . . ." Such statements naturally permit Saxon to record the impression of the carnival with which he begins. They also enable him to depart at will and quite without warning from the historical facts before him.

The first of four major divisions of *Fabulous New Orleans* deals with the "small boy" and his impressions of Mardi Gras. Curiously enough, Saxon repeats what he had done, somewhat clumsily, in *Father Mississippi:* he begins in the third person, referring to "the boy" and "his grandfather," and shifts to the first person to continue this account. The passage had appeared before in *The Century Magazine* and was refurbished somewhat to introduce readers to the fabulous city. These chapters are evidently loosely autobiographical; at least Saxon would remark over the years that he based the account on what had happened to him once in New Orleans as a boy.

What happens to the child in *Fabulous New Orleans*—whether faithfully recalled, substantially embellished, or totally fabricated by Saxon—makes for anything but dull reading. Upon arriving in the city for the carnival, the boy is turned over to Robert, a black manservant employed by his grandfather's friend. Robert is told to show the boy around the city and to give him a good time. As one writer has noted, the "time" the pair had was "hardly the kind the Parent-Teacher Association could approve . . . ."[23] The black man takes the boy to see the Zulu King, shows him a Rampart Street bordello, and carries him to a party that erupts into a knife fight and a general melee. Saxon's opening to *Fabulous New Orleans* is brisk and memorable; it is perhaps a boy's quickest and most thorough initiation to the seamy side of a city until young Lucius Priest goes to Memphis with Boon and Ned as his guides.

Saxon does a creditable job early in *Fabulous New Orleans* with what is, again, an initiation story. The boy, for example, learns that "the beautiful masked women who rode upon the floats" are, upon closer examination, "strangely masculine in body . . ." (41). Even the magnificent papier-mâché figures are not quite perfect upon close scrutiny when the parade passes by. Other discoveries recounted in the story are not under-stood or are misinterpreted by the boy, yet are rich sources of humor for readers. On Iberville Street, for example, the boy encounters some "friendly girls" who were "a little fat, it seemed to me, and their lips were very red; but they all smiled and held their kimonos around them, and they all kept crying out for the passers-by to come in and see them" (43). When one lady tells the boy to bring his father by to see her, "being a polite child," he naturally replies: "You must come see us sometime!" (44). Many "peculiar" aspects of this street are perplexing to Saxon's young boy—much like the Memphis "boarding house" is puzzling to Lucius and much like one of Anderson's best-known boys wants to know why.

Another noteworthy aspect of this initial part of *Fabulous New Orleans* is the vivid depiction of the carnival. Saxon represents Mardi Gras in an almost mystical light, and his descriptions of its effects on the boy, and on the man, are very well done. The author at one point calls the night parade a "dream festival" and confesses:

> Even now, twenty-five years later, I cannot look upon one of [the parades] unmoved; but to the small boy they were more real than reality . . . . This was no man-made thing that came out of the dark-ness; it was magic. (59-60)

One review specifically praised Saxon's depicting through the child's eyes those wonders that "even the sombre bells of Ash Wednesday cannot banish from memory."[24]

As in *Father Mississippi,* the middle portion of Saxon's second book deals with the historical background to his subject. Just as the dull realities seem to oppress readers greeted first by the plantation story in the earlier book, these historical chapters dispel the carnival magic Saxon conjures up initially in *Fabulous New Orleans.* It is as if the somber school bells have rung, and readers must now sit down for class. De Soto, La Salle, John Law, and others are again dragged across the stage by the author, yet the historian's heart seems still with the Canal Street revelers. In this second section, called "French Town and Spanish City," Saxon traces the history of the city up to the coming of the Americans. As some of the reviewers aptly noted, readers will find that most of this part of *Fabulous New Orleans* had already been recorded by King, Martin, Gayarré, Fortier, Castellanos, and Cable—all of whom are listed in Saxon's bibliography. His attitude toward his source materials was consistently a casual one, and he was certainly liberal in his use of the various earlier accounts of the city. An attempt to delineate where Saxon acquired what historical anecdote or which matter of interpretation does not seem worthwhile—indeed, does not seem possible.

Perhaps fearing that his book would add nothing new or that it would strike readers as "damned dull," Saxon seems to have begun consciously in this second section to concentrate on the bizarre, unusual, and sensational aspects of Louisiana history. He elaborates, for example, on some of the most colorful trials in the state's history in a chapter called "Crime and Punishment." He often cannot resist reconstructing, or even constructing, the juicy stories behind these trials and points out, perhaps wistfully in the midst of his history, that one of them "offers a theme for a great novel" (126). Saxon also details the punishments commensurate with various heinous crimes. He enlightens his readers on the manner in which executioners once hanged a murderer in the Place d'Armes, broke the arms, legs, thighs, and back of the corpse, stretched the body on the wheel, and exhibited it at the city gate (126).

After this grisly passage, readers of *Fabulous New Orleans* rather incredulously discover that Saxon's next chapter is entitled "A Ghastly Execution." Whether the punishment described here, wherein the criminals were nailed alive in coffins and then sawed in two, is more or less "ghastly" than that detailed above is, perhaps, a matter for debate. What is noteworthy is this chapter, however, is that Saxon continues to exploit the sensationalism and gore in Louisiana's past and seems, at one point, to be almost proud of his state's many cases of torturous punishment. Many Americans, he explains, feel that the atrocities of the French penal colonies have no parallel in this country's history; but there are incidents here "which rival any of the revelations of cruelty elsewhere" (129).

"Gaudy Days," the third section of *Fabulous New Orleans,* is aptly named. Saxon relates some gaudy tales of the quadroon balls, the famous "Duelling Oaks," the "haunted" Lalaurie mansion, and the notorious Marie Laveau, the voodoo queen. Here Saxon warms up considerably. He seems increasingly comfortable with these less than stodgy aspects of Louisiana history. His sense of humor is keen while describing the quadroon balls, which were held in a building quite close to the St. Louis Cathedral. Saxon quips that in one of the structures "men knelt in order to pray forgiveness for sins, committed in the other" (178). His whimsical tone continues in this section when he describes the polite young ladies of society "who were chaperoned within an inch of their lives . . ." and when he remarks that "even a Frenchman" would have had difficulty sleeping in all the beds Lafayette supposedly occupied in New Orleans (179; 204-5). Saxon seems to relish, moreover, the tales of Madame Lalaurie, the Orleanian who in the early nineteenth century was discovered to have tortured her slaves. Like Molly Glass in *Father Mississippi,* Madame Lalaurie is identified as a sadist by psychologist Saxon (217).

In "These Times," the final section of *Fabulous New Orleans*, Saxon seems to have included whatever subjects he had a mind to discuss— regardless of their relationship to "these times." He chose, for example, to include at this point "Gallatin Street," originally written in 1924 for *The Times-Picayune*. This chapter relates actually to old times among the criminal element in the city. Saxon also included here another previously published piece, his first-person account of a black voodoo ceremony. "Voodoo," which had appeared in *The New Republic* in 1927, deals with the narrator's being taken to see the reigning voodoo queen by a black man named Robert. The wild rites and activities (stimulated by alcohol and other drugs) that Saxon writes of having "witnessed" at this ceremony are interesting, but very probably are more fiction than fact. Edmund Wilson was impressed with Saxon's "excellent" account of "his voodoo party";[25] however, one study of voodoo has noted that Saxon's "eyewitness" narrative is suspiciously similar to those of Castellanos and others and that whatever truth was behind such events was considerably embellished with legend.[26] Saxon tells the story as the whole truth, however, and represents the blacks' ceremony as a grisly taboo at which any white man would be horrified. The narrator in "Voodoo" comes to scoff but does not remain to pray. He goes to the ceremony with a condescending attitude, but, shocked and unnerved by what he witnesses, he leaves considerably shaken and humbled.

Several parallels exist between Saxon's first two Century books; many of these elements, incidentally, would preoccupy the author in years to come. In both *Father Mississippi* and *Fabulous New Orleans*, for example, Saxon shows a certain interest in etymological and linguistic matters.

In the earlier book he discusses the origins of the name of the great river and of certain New Orleans family names (68-70; 111-12). He returns to this latter subject in *Fabulous New Orleans* (96). He also informs readers of both books about the background to the naming of the streets of New Orleans (*FM* 109-10; *FNO* 82, 284).

The similarity of the cases of Molly Glass and of Madame Lalaurie indicates another significant parallel and a dominant interest of Saxon's: trials and especially fantastic trials wherein all sorts of heinous crimes come to light and reveal the accused to be sadistic or in some other sense "abnormal." Actually, this seems more than a preoccupation with legal or criminological subjects. Cathy Harvey's examination of Saxon's Melrose library, and specifically of the rather expensive books he ordered in the mid-1930s, leads her to conclude that Saxon was "clearly obsessed" with books dealing with "criminology, demonology, and the supernatural, as well as with social and sexual aberation."[27]

Something else that *Father Mississippi* and *Fabulous New Orleans* have in common, unfortunately, is a general lack of organization and several very obvious flaws. The second book is as much of a "club sandwich" as the first with an even greater variety of ingredients stacked between the bread. The material in *Fabulous New Orleans*, the *New Republic* reviewer noted, appears "disjointed . . . as though each part were written without thought of the whole." This indictment is a sound one, for examples of illogical ordering of chapters abound.[28] The *New York Times* reviewer even commented that the lack of unity indicates that the author "did not set out to write a book," but simply drew together previous publications and sketched impressions.[29]

Some of the flaws in *Fabulous New Orleans* are lamentable essentially because as detractive as they are, they would surely have been easily corrected. The "Robert" of the first and last parts of the book, for example, may or may not be the same black man. Most readers will still remember the manservant who showed the small boy Mardi Gras by the time they get to the end of *Fabulous New Orleans*. It would seem fitting to know, therefore, if this later Robert who now leads the man to the voodoo queen is the same person; and all Saxon had to do was say so or, if not, change the name to avoid confusion. Many minor flaws, moreover, could have been corrected by a few simple omissions. Reviewers noted that the book was repetitious in spots, and it surely is. Saxon twice quotes the same 1726 census (83, 93), he duplicates his discussion of the origins of New Orleans street names (82, 284), and he defines certain words, such as *banquettes*, in two different places (150, 269). Another example of his careless repetition is quite unfortunate because it spoils a good one-liner. He explains at one point that although there were laws in eighteenth-century Louisiana prohibiting white men from living with black women, "we all know something of prohibitions" (180). This smiling reference to the constitutional amendment is enjoyable until readers encounter a mere eight pages later the statement that in the old days duels were prohibited, "but we all know the American reaction to prohibitions of any kind" (188). "We all" know, too, the reaction to a one-liner used once too often.

More than any other single characteristic of *Fabulous New Orleans*, the sensational element seems predominant. Just as Saxon borrowed his facts from many historians, he adapted many of his gory, racy, or grotesque tales from several earlier Louisiana authors. One such source was George Washington Cable, two of whose books are listed in Saxon's bibliography. Cable describes the contents of his *Strange True Stories of Louisiana* as "wild stories of wild times in Louisiana," and this phrase fits much of *Fabulous New Orleans* as well.[30] The earlier Orleanian also dealt with the Lalaurie mansion story and with various sensational trials. Saxon had received advice to treat such subject matter, moreover, even before he contracted for *Fabulous New Orleans*. In a letter discussing *Father Mississippi*, Sherwood Anderson told Saxon that if he did a subsequent book on New Orleans, he should "make it all tales of people as the sadist [Molly Glass] in this book . . . ."[31] Anderson's recipe for the second volume, consisting of "murderers, axe killers, generals, governers [sic]—all kind of nice wicked people," was substantially followed by Saxon. Like Cable before them, both Anderson and Saxon had a newspaperman's sense of the sensational, an awareness of the public's thirst for things "prohibited."

Saxon was surely pleased with many contemporary reactions to his book, regardless of whether or not *Fabulous New Orleans* itself fully gratified him. General statements of praise in the reviews outnumber the negative comments, such as those regarding the lack of unity in the book.[32] *The Nation* congratulated the author for avoiding a mood of "retrospective regret" by showing a love of old and of new New Orleans. *The Booklist* called *Fabulous New Orleans* "fascinating," and Josiah Titzell, in the *Herald Tribune*, applauded the "frankness and distinction" with which the volume was done. The *New York Times* reviewer pointed out that everyone familiar with the Louisiana city would come to cherish *Fabulous New Orleans*.

The statements Saxon received from some of his friends and fellow writers must also have been encouraging.[33] Mississippian Evans Wall, who would dedicate his novel to Saxon in 1929, flattered the older author by saying that no one else in America could have written *Fabulous New Orleans*. Bernard De Voto wrote Saxon, too, praising both of the Century volumes. In this letter De Voto calls *Father Mississippi* "part of the permanent literature of America" and says he envies Saxon's knowledge of "that vastly American experience" that enabled him to write *Fabulous New Orleans*. Carl Carmer assured Saxon that the success of the second Century volume showed that a beautifully written book would always "come into its own." By the end of 1928 Saxon was honored at a reception in the city whose history he had written. Evidently the author of *Fabulous New Orleans* was not without honor even in his own country, for, according to one account, present at this reception were "many lesser literary lights" and Grace King herself.[34]

Saxon's first two "eatin' books" secured for him an enviable position in publishing circles in New York. Since the author had produced two "hot" items in a year, his name became a valuable commodity to hopeful writers as a potential endorser. The advance publicity representative for Houghton Mifflin wrote Saxon in the spring of 1929, for example, soliciting a recommendation for a first novel by a young author.[35] The novelist himself had suggested that Saxon be used to recommend his book. Oliver La Farge, Saxon's old friend from the Vieux Carré, was the budding novelist, and *Laughing Boy* was the volume Saxon was asked to endorse. As mentioned above, Saxon was honored on the dedication page of a novel by Evans Wall in the summer of 1929, and Century actually published this book on Saxon's recommendation.[36] In the same letter wherein he discusses his role in the appearance of Wall's novel, Saxon jokingly tells Olive Lyons: "Total strangers continue to write to me, recalling how well we knew each other in Kansas City in 1912 . . . ." The circumstances described in this letter in 1929 would be repeated and would become a pattern in Saxon's literary life. Time after time young authors would solicit and receive his help, and Saxon would often downplay, even laugh away, the part he played in helping them. Virtually all of the author's friends I talked with recalled his congeniality and sincere desire to help other writers and his unwillingness to take credit for the successes he helped them secure.

With Saxon's own star still rising, the third Century volume, a study of plantation life called *Old Louisiana*, appeared in October 1929.

This book was not so spontaneous a product as the previous two. Saxon's letters and diaries reveal he had long been at work on a manuscript with the tentative title "Plantation People," and he surely used a good deal of this material for *Old Louisiana*. In the introduction to his third Century book, he claims the volume had been "in preparation" for five years (vii). In a 1933 interview, moreover, Saxon indicated that he originally planned to write books on Louisiana, on New Orleans, and then on the Mississippi River.[37] The flood and the book that grew out of it preempted the plantation study, of course, and Century probably suggested the volume on New Orleans as a part of the series on famous American cities; thus the order of this trilogy was reversed. Before *Father Mississippi* appeared, Saxon evidently had not done a great deal on what would become *Old Louisiana*, and he stretched the truth somewhat when he claimed a five-year composition period.

In 1929, at any rate, he turned his full attention to his book about Louisiana plantations. Artist Edward Suydam toured the state that year with Saxon in order that each might sketch the old homes they encountered. The trip was a thousand-mile, meandering journey on which the two men visited and lodged with those whom Saxon had earlier identified as "my array of old lady friends in the country."[38] Much of the material he gathered on this tour was then ordered and transposed into book form at Melrose and at Baton Rouge. Thomas Atkinson recalled to me his meeting Saxon at the home of the author's aunts. This meeting occurred in mid-1929 when Saxon was quite well known for *Fabulous New Orleans* and when, Atkinson explained, he was working "sporadically" on *Old Louisiana*. Saxon actually preferred to sit and talk and mix drinks, Atkinson recalled, but finally met his deadlines and finished the book.

Saxon evidently had as difficult a time composing the parts of the book at Melrose as he had those in Baton Rouge. He reveals, quite characteristically, in a letter written to Olive Lyons in June that he was "going through unshirted hell with this damned thing about plantations."[39] Even the title of the book was a problem; neither Saxon nor Century could think of an appropriate one. The author's suggestions of "Mississippi River Plantations" and "Splendor and Rust" were rejected. Although he had fought for the title of his previous book, Saxon confided to Olive that he "meekly" agreed to the one suggested by Century, which was eventually used for his third volume.[40]

Old Louisiana has certain elements in common with Saxon's two earlier books, and readers of all three perhaps sensed the author was following a formula. This volume was dedicated, as was *Fabulous New Orleans*, to a woman whom Saxon admired: Cammie Henry, whose library the author had again researched. For the third time, Saxon assumes a somewhat apologetic stance in his introduction. Following his "scrapbook" and "series of impressions" comparisons in the first two books, Saxon explains that *Old Louisiana* is "a book of footnotes to history" (vii). He then follows the same plan as in *Father Mississippi* and *Fabulous New Orleans*: he introduces "the boy" and his grandfather in the initial chapter and shifts to a first-person reminiscence with the second. The technique again seems awkward; obviously neither Saxon nor Century had felt this kind of beginning was broken, though, so there was no reason to fix it in *Old Louisiana*.

The boy in Chapter 1 of Saxon's plantation book overhears his grandfather and a friend discussing three families who have "gone to pieces" and wonders what this phrase implies. Specifically, the Dangerfield, Meadows, and Blake clans are mentioned as having declined drastically from the glorious days before the Civil War, and Saxon then describes over the next three chapters exactly what happened to these once-proud Southern families. "The Gay Dangerfields," the second chapter of *Old Louisiana*, appeared originally in *The Century Magazine*. This story deals with the eccentricities of the matriarch of this clan, Kate Dangerfield. This lady, always clad in a black riding habit and smoking a cigarette, was the mother of six children, who were the narrator's boyhood playmates. Nine hunting dogs and an "army" of cats seemed omnipresent in her house and were always ravenously hungry. The narrator points out that this menagerie would show up to beg food at mealtime and that going to the Dangerfield dinner table "was like going to war" (12). The unusual nature of this household is also apparent when Saxon's narrator describes Kate's knocking a cat off the table with a buggy whip and reciting poetry from after supper until 1:00 in the morning (13-14). Saxon's ludicrous account is climaxed with the description of Kate's remedy for fleas in the bedroom where a shocked guest from New Orleans was to sleep. Kate Dangerfield, aided by all her children and several servants, dragged "a large, dirty, and very angry ram" up to the guest room and tied the animal to the bed (16). The theory was that the fleas would leave the bed and infest the wool of the ram. Whether or not this novel pest control plan worked was unknown, the narrator comments, for the guest remembered an important engagement in New Orleans and "left suddenly in the afternoon."

The second and third examples of old Louisiana families that went to pieces contain humorous elements as well, but are generally not as rollicking and are more somber in tone than the saga of Kate. Tim Meadows's financial ineptness is the source of the humor in the second chapter. The head of the once-affluent Meadows family lost well over a million dollars in a few years, the narrator explains, but remained undaunted in his efforts to discover El Dorado. The *New York Times* reviewer remarked aptly that Tim's clan went to pieces "in a wealth of grand schemes reminiscent of Mark Twain's Colonel Sellers."[41] Saxon's readers are given example after example of Meadows's quixotic schemes to regain the family fortune and finally see Tim order a fantastic knitting machine with which he plans to make socks for the nation. After his wife manages to make "one very curious looking sock," the machine breaks, and Tim, enraged, destroys it (29-30). He was later sued by a friend for failure to repay the seventy-five dollars he had borrowed to buy the machine. Saxon observes rather soberly that the Meadows family, once worth several million dollars, "began with everything and ended with nothing. It was all pathetic and, at the same time, ridiculous—a humorous tragedy without even death to give it dignity" (21).

The Blake family, eccentric and "ridiculous" as the others in a sense, was likewise the victim of time and decay, quite literally here since the old house now is in ruins. The narrator was a schoolmate of Tennis Blake, whose family was "aristocratic, romantic, and poverty-stricken" (31). Tennis, his sister Elaine, and their "two maiden aunts" once lived in a plantation very near the Mississippi River. Many of their evenings, the narrator points out, were taken up with Elaine's recitations (in which she was coached by the aunt who had studied elocution) and with analyzing the girl's poems. Saxon chose well the surname for this family blessed with such a gifted poet. The descriptions of the aunts' analyses of the child's verses are richly humorous, for the elderly ladies, convinced that the eleven-year-old girl is a budding genius, painfully scrutinize each line she writes for its true meanings. Saxon thus adroitly satirizes the overly ingenious explication of innocent poetry.[42]

As in the story of the Meadowses, however, Saxon chooses to end his comic family portrait on a somber note. The narrator and his boyhood friend Tennis Blake return to the long-abandoned plantation years after the aunts have died. The course of the river has changed and has almost inundated the entire plantation. The narrator and Tennis walk in silence through the decaying house, and, Saxon writes, "then, suddenly—as though I had heard a bell tolling—the feeling of doom was upon me . . ." (46). Saxon's ending is quite effective here; this intimation of mortality that comes with going home again is reminiscent of E. B. White's beautiful conclusion in "Once More to the Lake: 1942" or of Carrie Watts's last trip to Bountiful.

Unfortunately, these vivid first few chapters of *Old Louisiana* promise far more than Saxon delivers over the next three hundred pages. I think they constitute his best opening and seem quite appropriate pictures of the decaying world that was "old" Louisiana. They are very humorous and very human accounts of a way of life depicted not so much as gone with the wind as "gone to pieces." Whether or not Saxon personally knew the clans he describes, or any such eccentrics, he successfully deals with their individual and family vicissitudes in an admirably restrained manner. He is not overly sentimental or maudlin about the doom that came to these families, and, in a book by a Southerner about the dear departed glory of the South, this seems no small accomplishment. Saxon is in the good company of Faulkner here—though that fraternity was still small in 1929, with more moonlight and magnolias and scores of cavaliers and cottonfields in the Southern fiction soon to come.

In the second division of *Old Louisiana,* readers encounter much the same historical background as in the first two books. For the third time Saxon begins with De Soto, La Salle, and company; for the third time he shows John Law's bubble bursting. He also quotes a lengthy contemporary account of Bienville's exploits (58-76) and a seventeen-page section of a Nicholls family history, which includes a picture of life in New Orleans in the early 1800s (103-20). Saxon secured this latter document from the grandson of the Nicholls who wrote the memoir. A friend of Saxon's once commented that readers probably wonder how he succeeds in securing personal letters, diaries, and memoirs; the answer is that by his charm he can "call on perfect strangers, and come away with the family love letters."[43]

Framing the Nicholls document in this section are two accounts of unusual trials. Again Saxon indulges his fetish and follows the successful formula of the earlier Century volumes. One of these trials, in which two slaves are convicted of murdering their master, leads to the kind of grotesque punishment the author seems so fond of describing, for one of the slaves was hanged and mutilated (93). "The Strange Story of Pauline," Saxon's second sensational account, involves the trial of a mulatto slave, Pauline, who was accused and convicted of torturing her white mistress.

Saxon was probably delighted at having found this story of crime and punishment because it is the converse of the situations involving Molly Glass and Madame Lalaurie. As in the two earlier books, this historical section is uneven in quality. Herschel Brickell's remark in his review of *Old Louisiana* that every historical incident and episode the book contains is of interest and of value seems a very kind view indeed.[44]

The next section of *Old Louisiana* is called "Leisurely Times" and contains a wide variety of materials all loosely relating to life in Louisiana in the nineteenth century. Saxon quotes at length from the 1850 diary of Lestant Prudhomme, a young Creole gentleman who lived near Natchitoches (170-229). After quoting much of this account directly, without editorial comment, Saxon interweaves more of it throughout another chapter and resorts to extensive quotations from various Natchitoches newspapers in a third chapter. The result is that readers, almost on their own with these documents for ninety pages, may get the feeling that their once-amicable narrator, who offered his hand in the opening section, has now left them alone in a rare book room. Actually the disappearance of the narrator and the extensive use of the diary and the newspapers seem indicative of two things: Saxon's growing weary and his overuse of the voluminous Louisiana materials on hand in Cammie Henry's library because, as the old saying goes, they were there.

For his final section of *Old Louisiana*, the author managed to resurrect one of the titles Century had rejected. "Splendor and Rust" contains a "tour" of the old plantation homes Saxon and Suydam had themselves visited. Many of these descriptions are terribly outdated and make for tedious reading. Saxon too makes somewhat of a mess of his narrative at this point in the book, for he cannot seem to decide whether he wants to adopt a Whitmanesque stance, becoming a camerado to readers, or to remain more aloof. He begins in the former vein, telling readers: "Get your bags together and let us go . . . . We shall follow the river all day" (293-94). "We" continue to investigate the houses together as friends until four or five pages into the chapter when "we" cease to be addressed and encounter increasingly impersonal statements such as, "A few miles beyond . . . one finds the old Convent" (300). Throughout the entire final section of *Old Louisiana*, Saxon cannot seem to choose between singing the song of the open road with his readers or going about his tour in a more prosaic manner. He tries feebly at the end, perhaps remembering his Whitman, to regain the original mood when he writes: "Here's my hand. Are we still friends?" (366). "We" may not be friends by this time, however, for the journey through these pages of *Old Louisiana* seems far greater than a thousand miles.

Saxon alternates the chapters that describe the plantations with something old and something new. Three of his digressions from "our" tour are resurrections of old *Times-Picayune* pieces and are typical of his Sunday fiction of the early 1920s.[45] What is new among the narrative elements in this section is a refreshing and irreverent account of a folk tale that Saxon says he heard repeatedly during his tour of the houses. The story deals with a beautiful Indian girl who committed suicide out of grief for her lover. The wide disparity of details in regard to this story—each detail having been offered to Saxon as truth by the various storytellers—prompts the author to retell it containing all variables. Saxon describes, for example, the way in which the maiden mounted "her fiery mustang, Arab steed, or mule," rode to a cliff, and jumped to her death "in the placid (or stormy) waters below" (333). The precise geography of this tragedy is difficult to locate, for, as Saxon concludes,

> She jumped from a cliff near the Gulf of Mexico; she jumped in the Teche country; she jumped near Opelousas; and she jumped at Baton Rouge . . . and she jumped again at Natchez, Mississippi. She also jumped into Red River, near Alexandria, and she jumped into Cane River . . . . My theory is that she jumped in all of those places and in many others. I think she did it for a living, and that the rest of the story was publicity, spread by some primitive advertising man. (333)

Saxon's humor is quite successful here, again reminiscent of Clemens's points about the importance of comic manner as well as matter. This section of *Old Louisiana* is comparable to the bright early chapters. Saxon and his readers are friends again, finally having fun again; but the book is not finished. Regretfully, "we" must go on tour again in the next chapter and see a few more once-stately mansions; and after the visit to the last plantation, our friend is gone, the tour is over, and the book is rather unceremoniously finished.

Despite the unfortunately disorganized manner with which Saxon ends—or stops—*Old Louisiana*, the flaws in the book are far fewer than those in the earlier volumes. The several repetitious phrases and passages that mar *Father Mississippi* and *Fabulous New Orleans* are not a significant problem in the third book. There are only a couple of instances where Saxon's left hand seems not to know what his right hand had done in *Old Louisiana*.[46] Reviewing Saxon's plantation book in the *Herald Tribune*, Henry Steele Commager quite appropriately stated that this third Century volume had the same virtues and the same defects as *Fabulous New Orleans*.[47] I agree that the latest book had the same kinds of defects; *Old Louisiana* surely did not have the same number of defects, though, and represented Saxon's best book-length effort to date. It is almost as loosely organized as the others; Saxon still nods. His meandering narrative in this case, however, seems less objectionable—perhaps because the history of a way of life may wander more than that of a river or of a city. What I believe really distinguishes this book from the others is that, despite the title, *Old Louisiana* is far less high-toned old Louisiana history and far more good fun with a great raconteur winking as he wills.

Praise of *Old Louisiana* was not long in coming and was more pronounced than that of the other books.[48] Stark Young remarked that although the reader may have to be a Southerner to know the book is "true," anyone will find that it is "delightful." John McClure, in *The Times-Picayune*, called the book "gracious and delicate"; another reviewer found it "absorbing." In an Asheville newspaper Professor Howard Mumford Jones described *Old Louisiana* as charming and contended that it was "one of the striking volumes to come out of the South this year."

Certain contemporary reviews of Saxon's book seem especially interesting now. The first, by R. L. Duffus in *The New York Times*, contends that *Old Louisiana* "is nothing so serious as a history of Louisiana or a careful study of a social or economic system. But it is good entertainment and it has a flavor."[49] The flavor is, of course, highly nostalgic and romantic, and this is perhaps one reason the book was favorably, even wistfully, reviewed in New York in the last few months of 1929. In December *The Saturday Review of Literature* praised *Old Louisiana* and made explicit a feeling that surely lay behind other comments about the book. Herschel Brickell remarked in this review that Saxon's volume would be a nice present for anyone interested in Americana, the South, beautiful homes, "or, for that matter, who is interested in anything except the closing prices of the thirty leading stocks."[50] Saxon's book about the grand old plantation days had appeared in the New York bookstores on October 25, 1929, the day after Black Thursday and within a few days of the great crash on Wall Street.

Although hard times were imminent for millions in early 1930, Lyle Saxon evidently continued to prosper by his arrangements with Century. He spent much of the year doing research for what would be his fourth volume with the company and his third with illustrator Suydam. Jean Lafitte was the subject of this next book, and again Saxon began by using Cammie Henry's library. Henry surely aided him in his work in a variety of ways. One letter survives, for example, in which J. Frank Dobie responds to her request for new information on the pirate.[51] What Saxon's patroness found out from Dobie proved useful, for in this letter the Texas professor mentions the Lafitte materials at Galveston, which Saxon later visited to examine several manuscripts. The author, already familiar with Lafitte's haunts in New Orleans, also made trips with Suydam to Barataria in preparation for the book.

By the summer of 1930 Saxon was ready to write. Much of the composition of *Lafitte the Pirate* was done in Baton Rouge. Saxon's aunts had moved from St. Louis Street to 257 Napoleon Street in early 1927, and in this house, which Saxon called a "Victorian retreat," he labored over his manuscript. Harris Downey, then a young instructor at L.S.U., recalled that he watched Saxon write *Lafitte* during that summer. "He had all his notes accumulated when he came to Baton Rouge," Downey told me. Saxon's friend also remembered that the author did most of his writing in the morning and early afternoon, sat with a glass of lemonade on the porch later in the day, and drank whiskey at night. I am not certain why Saxon composed most of *Lafitte* in Baton Rouge instead of at Yucca House, perhaps because of his grandfather's failing health. He did take several of Henry's scrapbooks with him to his aunts' house. He wrote his patroness while in the midst of his work and in this letter comments that he thinks what he has written thus far "is fairly good, and seems a little better than when I read it all over from the beginning; it moves rapidly, and that is one good thing at least."[52] He describes his simplified life to her summarily: "I go nowhere and see no one; my eyes hurt and I'm grouchy and cross and drink coca-cola every hour of the day and night."

Whatever he drank, Saxon wrote all that summer and, according to his September 14, 1930, letter to Caroline Dormon, sent the last chapter of his manuscript to Century in early September.[53] Once again, Saxon seems frustrated by the composition of his book and dissatisfied with the end result. In this same letter to Dormon he says he is "a complete nit-wit, a snarling nervous wreck" after writing *Lafitte*. He mentions that Century thinks the book is the best he has done; "but that only makes me realize . . . that they know nothing at all about such things." Saxon's dissatisfaction with his fourth nonfiction work seems genuine—not some manifestation of false humility or guarded hopes; for in the next sentence, he writes to Dormon: "I wonder if I'll ever write a novel . . . ."

Century's preference for *Lafitte the Pirate* is mildly surprising, perhaps, because this book represents to some extent a departure from the formula the author had followed with his first three. *Lafitte* is filled with illustrations and bears a physical resemblance to the others. As was the case with *Fabulous New Orleans* and *Old Louisiana*, moreover, Saxon dedicated his book to a woman who had influenced and aided him: Mercedes Garig, his friend and mentor at L.S.U. Here the resemblances end, however. The text of *Lafitte* is continuous, not divided into four or five major sections, and does not contain first-person narratives at the beginning or end. The result is a more unified book than before. Saxon does not apologize for this volume as he does for the others. The author's intention, he notes in his foreword, was "to present a truthful picture" of Lafitte "from contemporary documents and letters, and from the crumbling files of century-old newspapers."[54] Instead of a scrapbook, impressions of a passing parade, or footnotes to history, Saxon's readers are here to expect history. The author's simile to describe the difficulty of attempting a factual narrative about such a figure as Lafitte is particularly appropriate:

> It was rather like trying to put together a jig-saw puzzle, a portrait of a man which had been cut into a thousand fragments, and further complicated because upon the reverse side of the portrait was another picture similar in coloring; the second picture was that of a mythical pirate. (ix)

Throughout the book Saxon tries valiantly to avoid turning over the fictitious sides of his puzzle pieces; he succeeds admirably.

Rather than fabricate the boyhood and early years of Jean and of Pierre Lafitte, as other writers had done, Saxon begins his picture of the brothers with the earliest known facts. He first describes their days as blacksmiths in New Orleans. He then traces their initial ventures in smuggling and their removal to Barataria. Jean Lafitte's stronghold was to be on Grande Isle, one of the three large islands among the many *chênières* of Barataria. The Saxon Collection at Tulane University contains some of the author's notes made on Grande Isle when he and Suydam visited there. As in the accounts of the 1927 flood in *Father Mississippi*, the parallels between the sketchy notes and the finished prose are quite close.[55]

Saxon's tracing of Lafitte's activities prior to 1815 is smoothly accomplished and enables him, in part, to pursue some of his favorite subjects again. In 1812 the buccaneer was arrested and tried for smuggling. Saxon, having examined the documents of the trial, quotes charges, testimonies, and depositions at length (81-89). He also manages to excerpt a long portion of the diary of an old woman who once encountered Lafitte personally and to quote the two famous rewards of 1813—one offered by Governor Claiborne for Lafitte and the other offered by the pirate for the arrest of the governor (96-99; 101-03). Saxon is careful to represent Jean Lafitte's love life in a restrained manner, thus avoiding such romanticized tales as Lafitte's being ennobled and redeemed by the love of a virtuous woman. He recounts a simple and tender story, told to him by a descendant of Pierre Lafitte, of the mulatto mistress Catherine Villars, by whom Jean had a child (116-18). The *New York Times* reviewer praised specifically Saxon's treatment of the brothers' mistresses, noting that the women "move through the pages with shadowy but compelling illusiveness . . . ."[56]

Saxon spends little time on the events leading up to and including the Battle of New Orleans. He summarizes the offer of the British to Lafitte, the destruction of Barataria by the Americans, and the pirate's extraordinary decision to aid Andrew Jackson. Throughout all these events, he displays a dogged determination not to lapse into romance and consistently points out that Jean's decisions and actions were geared to what he thought most advantageous for the men he led. The manner in which Saxon's narrative progresses to and past the battle itself may leave readers more surprised than were the redcoats. "It is not my intention to describe the Battle of New Orleans," Saxon writes (179); and he does not do so. Jean Lafitte's specific actions in the heat of battle are, of course, unknown, and it is possible that Saxon felt he could not indulge in a picture of the pirate's deeds in the service of Old Hickory without turning over the more colorful but less factual sides of the puzzle. Another explanation for this curious deemphasis in the book may be that Saxon had read so much about the most famous battle in the history of his state that he could not bear to describe it himself. This seems to be the attitude behind this comment he makes in a letter to Cammie Henry wherein he describes his laboring over the manuscript:

I've just finished the part about Lafitte's offer by the British, and the attack on his stronghold . . . . The Battle of New Orleans begins this afternoon, God help me; but I'll make hash of that in a hurry, as you know how it bores me.[57]

An even greater temptation to fantasize Lafitte, more so than with regard to the battle, comes in Saxon's last few chapters. Again he successfully resists. The pirate's exploits after the War of 1812 in and around Galveston and his eventual disappearance in 1821 have been fodder for all sorts of fantastic stories. Saxon carefully presents the last documented reference to Lafitte and depicts the three pirate ships sailing away from Galveston for the last time out to sea: "Out of life, into dim legend" (256). This passage is quite well done and, as one reviewer noted, perhaps should be the end of the book.[58] Saxon sometimes fails to recognize his own best exit lines, however, and *Lafitte the Pirate* goes on for three more chapters. Although surely anticlimactic, these final chapters vivify the picture of Lafitte as dim legend. They recount what newspapers, novelists, and poets have made of the buccaneer. Saxon points out some of the more fantastically erroneous details of various works about Lafitte by Ingraham, George A. Pierce, and others. The author never quite rants here; the tone of Saxon's indictment is similar to that of Mark Twain in "Fenimore Cooper's Literary Offenses." After quoting Pierce's description of Lafitte's boldly conquering a British vessel, with a dagger in his clenched teeth, for example, Saxon comments: "And if that isn't a pretty bit of invention, I'd like to see one. However, Mr. Pierce is only warming up. He can do better without half trying" (279). Finally, Saxon smiles away his fellow Louisianans' gold fever as he relates some outrageous and feverish attempts to find Lafitte's buried treasure. This entire last section of Saxon's *Lafitte* is a kind of "Billy in the Darbies," and the ironies between Melville's poem and tale are similar to what readers of Saxon's book feel when confronted with Lafitte as full-blown legend.

Saxon's final effort for Century, *Lafitte the Pirate*, can be compared in several ways to the three previous books. Although the author does not make his usual disclaimer about this book as history, *Lafitte* is not much more scholarly or well documented than the earlier ones. Saxon is again quite indiscriminate and casual in his use of previously published sources, drawing variously again on Grace King, Gayarré, and others. His use of primary material, most of which he found at the Rosenberg Library in

Galveston, is admirable, but herein is a problem of the book too. Saxon's documentation is so poor that readers, upon encountering, for example, an interesting statement by Andrew Jackson, are often left wondering when and where such a statement was made (184-85). Evidently Saxon did not always know the sources of the materials he used, for in his manuscript he sometimes pasted unlabeled, yellowed newspaper clippings. On the other hand, however, *Lafitte the Pirate* represents amelioration in that it is a far more cohesive book than the others. The stylistic flaws such as repetition and the awkward incorporation of long quoted material are not characteristic of *Lafitte*.

A major distinction of Saxon's fourth book is his resistance to telling a new and unfounded aspect of the Lafitte story, to adding to the dim legend as almost each author before him had done. He managed somehow to write in an essentially objective light concerning this famous Louisiana hero. Typical of his determination to avoid an apologia or a romanticization is the comment he makes when discussing Lafitte's days as a Spanish spy: "I will not attempt to justify, nor even explain his decision; I can only make the flat statement that he became a spy" (209). The subject of Saxon's biography, of course, had been described before in many ways, but seldom by "flat statements."

Reactions to *Lafitte the Pirate* were positive, and the reviews that appeared in New York and in Louisiana were especially favorable.[59] Charles J. Finger praised Saxon in the *Herald Tribune* for not trying to capture readers with "picturesque lies" and for not playing on a "harp of high-pitched heroics." The *New York Times* reviewer went so far as to say that the re-creation of a character in a biography is rarely done so well. *The Booklist* called the book a "true record," and *The Bookman* praised the "charm and distinction" that characterize Saxon's *Lafitte*. The author's friend Stark Young wrote a favorable review for *The New Republic*, calling the book "enchanting and beautiful." J. Fair Hardin, in *The Louisiana Historical Quarterly*, bestowed a wealth of compliments on the work. He described it as a "virile biography" and noted that the account of Lafitte's early days in New Orleans is "the best that we have ever had, in either fact or fiction . . . ." Reactions to the book by Saxon's friends were, of course, communicated to him privately and were perhaps more meaningful than the published reviews. Julia Peterkin congratulated him for writing a "beautiful" book and told her friend that only the fact that she was a good Christian kept her from committing the deadly sin of envy.[60] Grace King wrote a congratulatory note to Saxon also; in it she told the younger writer that "at last" she felt she knew the truth about Lafitte.[61]

Understandably enough, certain patterns emerge from *Lafitte* and the other "eatin' books." In his accounts of the pirate, of old Louisiana, of New Orleans, and of the river, Saxon shows an affinity for certain subjects. A preoccupation with superstitions, for example, permeates the volumes (see *FM* 25, 309, 312; and *OL* 345-52). Saxon's interest in etymology, moreover, is obvious in each of the books. His concern in *Lafitte* with the origin of the word *Barataria* (36-37) is reminiscent of earlier passages, such as those wherein he speculates on the origins of German names (*OL* 354), and on the background to *Creole* (*FNO* 270) and to *Mississippi* (*FM* 68, 90). Saxon's sidetracks on names and word origins may seem initially to be troublesome interruptions, yet most readers will find them, almost without exception, to be enjoyable detours indeed—much like the reaction readers have to Lewis Thomas's wonderful etymological digressions in his essays.

Especially characteristic of all the Louisiana books, of course, is Saxon's interest in trials and his exploitation of the punishments growing out of these trials. Molly Glass in *Father Mississippi*, the soldiers from Ship Island in *Fabulous New Orleans*, the slave and Pauline in *Old Louisiana*, and the brothers Lafitte in his last book are all given their days in court in Saxon's narratives. The sensational and sometimes grotesque punishments that some of these figures and others suffer in the books is another pervasive element in all four. The stories of Molly, Madame Lalaurie, and Pauline in the first three volumes involve torture, and Saxon even manages to slip in a bizarre tale of murder in the last chapter of *Lafitte the Pirate* (294). To fill in the details in many of these accounts, he resorts to a considerable amount of speculation. Like Cable, he loved the "strange true stories of Louisiana," and it seems quite possible that if both of these adjectives did not apply to a story, Saxon preferred the very strange to the strictly true.

In the years following the period from 1927 to 1930, Saxon enjoyed varying degrees of success with the four Louisiana books. *Father Mississippi* and *Old Louisiana* probably netted the author less money than the other two, but even these less successful ones continued to bring him some recognition as the years passed. Various parts of the "autobiographical" first section of *Father Mississippi*, for example, were anthologized as early as 1928, and again in 1938. Other parts of this book included in anthologies are the accounts of the 1927 flood and the chapter about the Indians' visit to Paris.[62] "The Gay Dangerfields," from *Old Louisiana*, has been twice anthologized: in a volume edited by Addison Hibbard and in another by Robert Penn Warren.[63] Although never excerpted, the other chapters about those Southerners who went to pieces seem to be very worthy of consideration—at least in a regional anthology. Several years ago, Tess Crager of New Orleans, a publisher who once owned the rights to all of Saxon's Century books, told me that *Old Louisiana* sold moderately well for decades after the author's death and that she never reissued *Father Mississippi* because of the large amount of outdated factual material about flood control.

Of all four books, *Lafitte the Pirate* probably opened more doors for Saxon than the other volumes. The biography of the pirate was "milked," by the author himself and by others, for all it and the Lafitte name were worth. During the first few months the volume sold very well, and the following spring Saxon and *The Times-Picayune* agreed to a serialization.[64] The gimmickry surrounding the newspaper publication is amazing. The day the first installment appeared, newsboys all over New Orleans dressed as pirates and carried large signs reading "Lafitte the Pirate Beginning To-Day." At the same time the "Lafitte the Pirate Essay Contest" was begun by *The Times-Picayune*. For a prize of twenty-five dollars, all schoolchildren were invited to compose an essay about Lafitte's life based on the serialized articles. The adult readers were not overlooked, however; for the newspaper offered a prize of two hundred dollars in the "Jean Lafitte Treasure Hunt." Clues were given, of course, along with the daily installments of Saxon's story.[65] Such a stunt during the depression must have made Saxon's chapters, or at least the clues accompanying them, one of the most widely read features in *The Times-Picayune* in many years. The final newspaper installment of *Lafitte*, following the serialization of the last chapter of the book, is the description of the ludicrous hunts for the pirate's buried treasure. This account reveals Saxon's somewhat cynical attitude toward the *Times-Picayune* treasure hunt and toward the hunters. Nevertheless, with the serialization of *Lafitte the Pirate* in the newspaper he had left five years before, Saxon the pirate probably unearthed no small booty himself.

Surely less lucrative were still other ventures connected with Saxon's biography of Lafitte. In 1935 the book was translated into French, and the pirate passed "*dans la trouble légende*" to another nation of readers.[66] Ten years later a brief excerpt from *Lafitte* was incorporated into an anthology.[67] The Lafitte story probably reached the widest audience, however, in 1938 and in 1958 when it was adapted, almost completely beyond recognition, for the screenplays of two motion pictures. These films, which I will discuss later, both bore the name *The Buccaneer* and gave on-screen credit to *Lafitte the Pirate* by Lyle Saxon.

Despite these various offshoots and derivations of his Lafitte story, Saxon probably realized more money from *Fabulous New Orleans* than from any of the other Century books. He once remarked that he did not expect the success that came to this volume and jokingly observed that he did not know whether Orleanians would approve his book or burn him in front of the St. Louis Cathedral upon reading it.[68] Orleanians and other readers as well quite heartily approved *Fabulous New Orleans*. By the time *Lafitte the Pirate* was published, the New Orleans book had sold twenty thousand copies and had gone through six editions; by 1934 it had sold fifty thousand copies.[69] In the 1930s *Fabulous New Orleans*, along with *Old Louisiana*, was recommended for supplementary reading in the Louisiana public schools.[70] Throughout the 1930s and '40s, tourists would arrive in New Orleans, according to one account, with Saxon's book about the city "clutched in their hands."[71] Edward Dreyer comments that signed copies of *Fabulous New Orleans* were so prevalent among Saxon's friends and all Orleanians that the author was teased about there being "an unsigned copy of this book . . . under a bell glass in the *Cabildo* . . . . It was the only known *unautographed* copy."[72]

Fabulous New Orleans has proved to be the most enduring of the "eatin' books." Selections were included in two anthologies in 1955, one edited by Willard Thorp and the other by B. A. Botkin.[73] Two years after Saxon's death and twenty years after the original publication of the New Orleans book, Bennett Cerf wrote in his "Trade Winds" column in *The Saturday Review* that of the "countless histories and guides to the Crescent City," Saxon's volume "stands out a mile above all others . . . ."[74] Cerf's remark was on the occasion of the first posthumous edition of the book, issued by the Crager Company in 1948. Tess Crager informed me several years ago that *Fabulous New Orleans* sold consistently well for decades all over Louisiana. The Crager Company's decision not to reissue *Father Mississippi* because it was outdated is interesting since aspects of *Old Louisiana* and *Fabulous New Orleans* are outdated as well, yet I suspect these two books will continue to go in and out of print over the years because of the market created by tourism.[75] That these two books sell steadily in the bookstores around the Vieux Carré is no surprise; that the books sell especially well during certain Super Bowls and at Mardi Gras is no coincidence. Tourists, of course, continue to flood into the "fabulous" city, and many still buy books to clutch in their hands.

Saxon's "eatin' books" are certainly not his greatest achievement or his greatest legacy. As Robert Cantwell points out, they were "considerably in advance" of many similar regional histories that became popular later.[76] Saxon's "histories," however, are scrapbooks, not textbooks. He evidently had no desire that they be taken as anything more than scrapbooks, as the introductory passages to the books indicate; and he should not then be criticized for failing at what he did not attempt. Saxon should be held accountable, though, for other reasons. In at least the first three books, he does seem occasionally to turn over the fictitious sides of his jigsaw pieces while leaving the impression he is dealing only in facts. In the case of his subject matter, the legends were often far more pleasing to write about than were the facts. As histories, moreover, none of the four really adds much new or surprising information. Jay B. Hubbell first noted that one of Saxon's books added "little to what we already know" from King, Cable, and others.[77] Perhaps the most telling indictment of all is another critic's comment that while Saxon's books seem to start well, the final one-third or one-fourth "invariably goes into a decline . . . ."[78] This same writer goes on to surmise that Saxon was a victim of deadlines and of his own procrastination. Both of these observations are quite accurate, and such a combination was as deadly for Saxon as it would be for almost anyone else.

One final aspect of the "eatin' books," which is of particular significance in light of the following chapter, is the author's reasons for turning away from his scrapbook histories and from his lucrative arrangement with Century. One reason was that he undoubtedly still preferred to write fiction; these books were all "just stepping stones" to that end. Saxon shows numerous times in the Century volumes a desire to explore more fully certain historical events he must treat there without elaboration. This desire is seen in chapters like "Perhaps It Was Like This" (*FNO* 156-59), in stories such as that in "Gallatin Street" (*FNO* 291-300), and in comments such as the one wherein Saxon points out that all Louisianans have an inveterate inability to separate history from fiction (*OL* 97). The author once expressed a preference for *Old Louisiana* over the other three volumes;[79] perhaps his reason lay in the fact that this book, especially in the first section, is far more story than history.

That Saxon could ever have achieved a reputation as a scholarly historian of Louisiana is doubtful. What seems certain, however, is that he had no desire for such a reputation. His presentation of the "true" Lafitte notwithstanding, an acquiescence to a Jean Lafitte treasure hunt at Lake Pontchartrain would do little to enhance anyone's reputation as a serious biographer. Earlier, in *Fabulous New Orleans*, Saxon was straining to write even his scrapbook chronicles. He wrote to Olive Lyons as early as May of 1928 that he was incredibly weary of reconstructing New Orleans history.[80] When reviewer Cleveland B. Chase described the author of *Father Mississippi* as being "less happy" in the historical section of the book than in the other parts, he surely did not realize how apt was his choice of words.

In 1930 Lyle Saxon really had only one course to follow and one elusive project to pursue seriously now that he would have some "eatin' " money: he would return to Yucca House to work on his novel. Professor Arlin Turner, in an article on Louisiana authors written for *The Saturday Review*, once catalogued the available subjects open to a Louisiana writer. His list includes New Orleans history, Mardi Gras, yellow fever epidemics, opera houses, quadroon balls, Creole aristocracy, and Jean Lafitte.[81] After his first four books, Saxon very probably had said all he could about these subjects, and he had said some things two or three times. As a historian he had traveled well over a thousand miles and scanned the records of centuries for his materials. As a novelist he would write about a forgotten people from an obscure island community near Natchitoches. Saxon surely could not have guessed in 1923 when he had first visited Melrose that seven years and four books later his dream project, a novel, would still be unwritten. He could not have imagined in 1930, however, that seven agonizing years more would pass before *Children of Strangers* became a reality. By 1937 he must have felt like Jacob, waiting and working all those years for the wife well loved.

5

STRUGGLE AND CLIMAX:
WRITING THE NOVEL, 1923-1937

IN THE SPRING OF 1923 Lyle Saxon wrote to Cammie Henry that he was "tremendously keen" to go to Melrose and write a novel and that the longer he thought about the idea, the more enthusiastic he became. Two years later, when he was finally able to spend an extended period at the plantation, he evidently began to contemplate seriously what first entered his mind in 1923. In his 1925 diary Saxon remarks that on April 10 he was able to write again for the first time in several months.[1] Significantly, this diary entry is the last for the year, and presumably he abandoned his personal record as he began to compose. Surely these writings, Saxon's earliest at Melrose, included various parts of what would become his only novel, *Children of Strangers* (1937). Saxon's "The Long Furrow" and "Lizzie Balize," incorporated as two chapters of the novel, appeared in *The Century Magazine* and *The Dial* and very probably were written in 1925, two years before *Father Mississippi*. One review of Saxon's novel alluded to his already being at work on *Children of Strangers* when the flood of 1927 occasioned his account of the river, and Saxon made the same claim himself at various times.[2]

The years following these initial efforts toward a novel, however, took Saxon far away from what he was "tremendously keen" to do. As I have indicated in the previous chapters, he was busy with *Times-Picayune* work until 1926 and was occupied from 1927 until 1930 with his Century books. Yet even during the hectic writing of these volumes, Saxon was concerned with the composition of *Children of Strangers*.[3] In 1929, in an article about *Old Louisiana*, he again stated his preference for fiction over nonfiction and claimed to be at work on a novel. Earlier in that same year he had told an interviewer that his plans for long fiction were never

completely out of his mind. In January of 1930 he was described in a
Baton Rouge newspaper as having recently arrived from New York with an
unfinished manuscript of a novel "under one arm." In an April interview
that year, moreover, Saxon reaffirmed his "primary interest" in fiction and
claimed to be "halfway through" with a novel. Another article dealing with
Saxon's plans today seems most ironic; it appeared in the December 30,
1930 Baton Rouge *State-Times*. Saxon is quoted here as saying that since
his Melrose cabin gets cold in December, he is on his way to New Orleans
to finish his novel. He outlines his plans quite casually as though finishing
the book would present no difficulties whatsoever. This article is actually
understandable coming from an author who had just completed his fourth
book in three years; it would seem entirely possible, actually quite likely,
that 1931 would bring the fifth volume.

During this year, though, and in those following, Saxon encountered one obstacle after another that prevented his completing the novel. His
grandfather, Michael Chambers, was near death at this time, and Saxon was
called to Baton Rouge where, according to one account, his story "simply
wouldn't perk" under these circumstances.[4] In a letter from Baton Rouge,
written to Caroline Dormon in late 1930, Saxon expresses frustration at not
working on his novel. He then writes bitterly:

> You know . . . I'm gradually becoming convinced . . . that this isn't
> the world after all; it is hell; that we've already lived somewhere else,
> and now we're dead and paying the penalty. Suppose the theory is
> true—what a joke on the Christian religions! How irritated our good
> brothers and sisters will be when they die and find out that they've al-
> ready been in hell and that they haven't got to be afraid of it any more.[5]

At this time, too, the author himself was chronically ill. His letters
and diary entries reflect his nagging problems with neuritis and indicate that
he suffered from a venereal disease as a result of his "criminal stupidity" in
indiscriminate homosexual contacts. Saxon found no relief for the pain of
neuritis, and the treatments he took for the venereal disease were extremely
painful and debilitating.[6] Thus from perhaps as early as mid-1931 until two
or three years later, Saxon was not at all in good health. One of his friends
wrote to Cammie Henry in March 1932, that Saxon's serious illness had
prevented his finishing his book.[7] By the next year, however, he had
progressed on his novel to the extent that it was described in an article as

"soon" to be published; in fact, Saxon himself then referred to *Children of Strangers* by name—still four and a half years before it would appear.[8] Curiously, however, in a letter written six months later, Saxon used the word "soon" to describe when he would complete the book; in mid-1933, he called it "nearly finished again"; and, in a letter of May 10, 1934, Saxon remarked, "Soon I'll turn [the novel] loose on a suspicious public."[9]

His use of "suspicious" rather than "unsuspecting" was especially apt because by 1935 his publishers had already advertised the novel. Exactly why it did not appear then is somewhat of a mystery. Saxon once told a Baton Rouge *Morning Advocate* reporter that *Children of Strangers* was actually completed in 1935 and that the two-year delay was because American readers were not ready to accept the subject matter of the novel.[10] He often alluded also to the delays resulting from his beginning the time-consuming work with the W.P.A. in 1935, and Joseph Henry recalled that there was a widespread rumor that Melrose servants had inadvertently destroyed part of Saxon's manuscript. All of these explanations for the last few years of deferment seem unsatisfactory. It appears unlikely that the American reading public would have viewed Saxon's story of miscegenation as more acceptable reading material in 1937 than in 1935 or that the publisher would have advertised the forthcoming novel without knowing it dealt with such subjects. Likewise unlikely is that the W.P.A. work could have prevented the publication of a "completed" novel for two years. Joseph Henry himself, moreover, admitted no knowledge of a servant's being reprimanded for the destruction of Saxon's chapters and expressed an opinion that this could have been a case of Saxon's "covering up."

Certain publishers became "suspicious" about Saxon's novel long before the reading public did. The author's relationship with various editors and executives at the publishing houses were strained because of his long and erratic work on *Children of Strangers*. According to Joseph Blotner, Faulkner's publisher Hal Smith advanced Saxon one thousand dollars to work on the book.[11] Saxon took Smith's offer over at least two others he received. In 1929, when word of the novel evidently leaked to the New York publishers, William Rose Benét asked Saxon to submit his manuscript to Payson and Clarke, and Cleveland B. Chase solicited his work for Longmans, Green, and Company.[12] Ben Wasson pleaded the case for Jonathan Cape and Harrison Smith, and by 1930 Saxon was contracted with this company.[13] Although the relationship was initially cordial, problems seem to have arisen the next year, probably because the book was publicized and, of course, did not appear. Hal Smith wrote Saxon at this time, telling the author "let me know how you are getting on"; yet the publisher added, "I don't intend to hurry you . . . ."[14] Smith did not intend to wait forever either, though; for by 1932 Saxon had left his first publishers and was contracted with the H. C. Kinsey Company. This arrangement did not last either, and Houghton Mifflin, Saxon's third publishers, eventually issued *Children of Strangers*.

All the problems and delays regarding Saxon's novel seem especially curious in light of the seemingly ideal circumstances under which he returned to his dream project in 1930, after *Lafitte the Pirate*. Financially secure, he could at last turn his full attention to fiction and could compose in his private cabin at the plantation home of his benevolent patroness. Here was the good life in the happy valley. Even under such conditions, however, many problems other than Saxon's health soon arose; and the faults lay both in Melrose and in Saxon.

During the 1920s, '30s, and '40s, the Henry family plantation at Melrose, near Natchitoches, became, as one account points out, "a treasure trove for authors, artists, and historians."[15] Cammie Henry offered the incredible collection of Louisiana lore in her library to all who came to Melrose to work. She wrote no books herself and never indexed her collection. As Harnett Kane points out in *Plantation Parade*, Henry was the index herself, and she "mothered books."[16] Her son Joseph told me that newspapers all over America would carry items about someone's visit to the plantation, and thus more artists and writers would come. Joseph Henry lived at home during many of these years of activity. He described Melrose as "a big hotel." "I've known the time," he told me, "when they would cook thirteen chickens for lunch"; twenty-five or more guests were easily accommodated in the main house and the five cabins.

In addition to those who were engaged with specific projects at the plantation, many paid brief visits or passed through heading north from New Orleans. Several of the guests were friends of Saxon's and very probably came to see him. This group included Edward Suydam, illustrator of three of the Century books, Edward Dreyer and Robert Tallant, Saxon's co-workers on the W.P.A. project, Roark Bradford, Sherwood Anderson, Olive Lyons, *Times-Picayune* reporter and novelist Gwen Bristow, and short story writer Ada Jack Carver. Other authors who were Henry's guests included Rachel Field, Harnett Kane, Alexander Woollcott, Henry Chambers, Josiah Titzell, Frances Parkinson Keyes, Julia Peterkin, William

Spratling, and, according to Joseph Henry, William Faulkner.[17] Prominent figures from various fields who were guests at the plantation included the painter Alberta Kinsey, photographer Doris Ulmann (who collaborated with Julia Peterkin on *Roll Jordan Roll*), botanist Caroline Dormon, the most famous surgeon of his day Dr. Rudolf Matas, and motion picture star Margaret Sullavan.

Francois Mignon, himself a Melrose resident for about thirty years, claims that of all these people who were at the plantation for various lengths of time, Lyle Saxon was Cammie Henry's favorite; for she liked his writings, his personality, and his interest in preserving historical Louisiana.[18] Joseph Henry pointed out that Saxon came to be as much of an attraction to writers as the Melrose library—especially when his Century volumes became widely known. Saxon wrote Olive Lyons in the summer of 1933, telling her of receiving a request from a distant relative in New York:

> . . . I got a good laugh when I received a letter—the first in about thirty years—from an aged cousin in Gloversville, New York, saying that she greatly admired her Louisiana kinsman's work, and would I please write a paper for her on New Orleans, and only about 8000 words, that she could read in 50 minutes, so she could make a nice showing at her local "study club." I refrained from wiring her, collect, this succinct message: "No, you bitch," and just threw the letter away instead . . . It certainly is nice to be rich and famous, like me.[19]

Like it or not, Saxon had attained a degree of fame; and the author who had been drawn to the plantation became a drawing card himself. Although Saxon could ignore his fan mail or withdraw to the seclusion of his cabin regardless of how many guests came to Melrose, at times surely he was more concerned with the social life at the plantation and countless other distractions than with the manuscript of his novel.

Saxon describes Yucca House, his cabin at Melrose in *The Friends of Joe Gilmore*:

> It is very simple—four rooms, all in a row, opening north and south, with a twelve-foot brick-paved gallery on each side . . . . Inside it is all white-painted paneling with open fire-places of brick, painted white. In the sitting-room the walls are lined from floor to ceiling with book shelves, and it is here that I keep my most prized volumes . . . . The

> other large room is a bedroom, in which there is a four-post bed with a
> tester . . . . It is all primitive, but I like it. (19-20)[20]

While composing here, Saxon sat at a desk he kept facing one of the blank
walls, Mignon explains, so that passersby would not disturb him; he wrote
with his back to the windows. Mignon also mentions Saxon's elaborate
garden around Yucca House.[21] Two of the author's friends recalled an
unusual aspect of this garden. Tess Crager and Joseph Henry both remembered that instead of encircling some of his flower beds with oyster shells,
as was the custom, Saxon was fond of ringing his flowers another way: he
alternated whiskey bottles and milk-of-magnesia containers around the
blossoms.

    Under these conditions at his cabin, then, Saxon was at work in
earnest at Melrose by 1933. The diary he kept that year and the next reveals
far more agony than ecstasy as he worked with his manuscript.[22] On
October 20, 1933, Saxon records that Kinsey (his second publisher) liked
the first one hundred pages of the manuscript of his novel, and he confesses
that he is "tremendously pleased" at Kinsey's reaction—especially since he
has kept the publisher waiting almost a year. "I shall write with renewed
interest on Monday," he concludes. Ten days later, however, Saxon has
"nothing to report" concerning further progress; he has been "thinking out"
two scenes of the novel, but has not put them down on paper—"Will do that
tomorrow." More than a month later, the author was evidently becoming
despondent over his failure to progress further with the book:

> Thoroughly discouraged with myself, I got drunk entirely alone tonight.
> I seemed to be possessed by a devil who will not let me write; I waste
> time, do nothing, feed chickens . . . what folly! . . . teach them to
> do tricks, such as flying up on my arm as I call them, one after the
> other . . . and do no work at all, ever. The days pass somehow, I don't
> quite know how.[23]

Obviously, Saxon felt possessed by quite a different devil from those
driving artists' demons Faulkner spoke of in the *Paris Review* interview.

    By the beginning of 1934 Saxon was having no more success with
his manuscript, but was declaring grimly that he would conquer whatever
devils kept him from telling his story. His New Years Day entry laments
receiving a letter from Kinsey in which the publisher "hardly knew what to

say," reminding the author pointedly that his manuscript was long overdue. "My new year's resolution," Saxon continues in his diary, "is that I'll write 2000 words every day in 1934" and that "I'll give Tom Kinsey this book in a month or perish in the attempt." Ironically, Saxon notes in this same entry that he will not have time for his two thousand words that day; and, of course, the other resolution was broken as well, for he neither finished the book nor perished in the attempt in 1934.

Although Saxon had evidently procrastinated in the writing of all the Louisiana books for Century, he met these deadlines nevertheless—even if the latter parts of the books were inferior. He once remarked, however, that he could never seem to get *Children of Strangers* "just right."[24] Obviously, he was not concerned enough with getting his "eatin' books" just right to prevent his sending the manuscripts on for the fall publications. His Melrose diary of 1933-34 is filled with expressions such as "soon," "tomorrow," and "I shall write on Monday." His procrastination is undeniable again, but he was not willing to let this book go before it was "just right," for it seems certain that fiction was always much more important to him than nonfiction.

Whether he drank in despair at his procrastination or put off his work in order to drink, liquor became a problem as well. In later years, working with the W.P.A. in New Orleans, Saxon seemed to drink heavily because he often suffered pain and was in very poor health. The effects of his illnesses, or the treatments, that had plagued him in the early 1930s may have been one of the reasons he drank a good deal at Melrose. He wrote in despair at the beginning of 1934: "For three years I have lain fallow, fattening, getting drunk, deteriorating . . . . Another year like this will finish me."[25] The pressures of Saxon's *Times-Picayune* work and the lean years trying to sell his stories in New York were far in the past. The author had come at last to the peaceful plantation to write his novel, but life in the happy valley was killing him.

Some of Saxon's troubles during this time, of course, were with the story itself. Even when he could make himself take up the manuscript, he struggled with it. In a letter written four months after *Children of Strangers* was finally published, he identifies his major difficulty with the narrative. He points out here that since he had first written a few scenes and several unrelated fragments about life on Cane River, he could not mold these episodes into an organic whole.[26] This task was "the purely technical difficulty" he encountered at Melrose, he explains; and, Saxon continues, "the thing defeated me; I couldn't do it." The author apparently found almost any other writing—including his Melrose diary and the great number of letters he wrote in the early 1930s—easier than working on his novel.

Indeed, Saxon's problems seem to have come in batallions at the time.[27] In 1931 he wrote to Olive Lyons that he was sending regular monthly allowances to his aunts and that they "continue hysterical." Late in 1932, while Saxon was in New Orleans, thieves broke into his Royal Street home and robbed him at gunpoint; "I was cracked over the head and robbed," Saxon wrote Caroline Dormon. Over the next few weeks, he goes on to explain, he was the victim of "every type of intimidation [from the criminals' lawyer] to keep me from testifying." Moreover, Saxon may have still felt a great deal of pain from his unrequited love affair with Muriel Moore. Cathy Harvey points out that Saxon's 1933 Melrose diary entries reveal that his emotions have been "extinct" since he experienced a heartbreak in 1928. Harvey, in fact, feels that Saxon's 1928 New York romance with Muriel Moore "may have permanently impaired his creative drive."

While beset with all these difficulties, Saxon saw his financial security begin steadily to erode. For about three years after the appearance of *Lafitte*, he had evidently earned no money beyond what royalties came from the Century volumes. Although these books remained in print, times were hard and Saxon's income, especially from *Fabulous New Orleans*, was steady but meager. The author was notoriously generous, constantly lending money to friends and even casual acquaintances whom he perceived to be in need. In November of 1933, he recorded in his diary that Roark and Mary Rose Bradford, who had visited him at Melrose, had asked if he needed a loan. Saxon refused their help, but admitted: "I have eighteen dollars left in the world—and I owe . . . God, how much *do* I owe."[28]

About three months later he received another offer that could help him out of his financial bind. *The Times-Picayune* asked him to write a series of articles for the Sunday magazine. Saxon admitted soon after he received the offer that he did not like the idea, but, he confessed, "if I am broke enough I may do it . . . ."[29] He was broke enough. On the day after he made this statement, he signed an agreement with the newspaper for ten stories to run ten consecutive weeks at one hundred dollars per story.[30]

Actually, from February through April of 1934, nine articles by Saxon appeared in the Sunday *Times-Picayune*.[31] They are at best mediocre, reminiscent of the quality of much of the "eatin' books," and probably deserve the term "hack work." The first is a three-part sketch of the life of Adah Isaacs Menken, actress and acquaintance of a wide variety of literary figures. Saxon wrote to a friend that he thought Menken was "a strange and fascinating gal."[32] Another such "gal" was the subject of the next *Times-Picayune* piece: Lola Montez, "companion" to Liszt, Alexandre Dumas, and Louis I of Bavaria. Saxon traces a famous trial in which she was involved in New Orleans, familiar territory for readers of his Century volumes. Three other *Times-Picayune* articles deal with sensational, unusual, or gory aspects of Louisiana history: again, Saxon's recurrent themes in his four Louisiana books. In one he describes (drawing heavily on contemporary news accounts) the gory details of an explosion on a steamboat in 1849, in another he describes an encounter under the notorious dueling oaks, and in a third he rehashes the business between Jackson and Lafitte in 1815. In the midst of writing these, he confided to Olive that his "dull stories of steamboat explosions and duels . . . bore me, and will doubtless bore *Times-Picayune* readers as well."[33] Saxon's other newspaper piece had originally appeared in *The New York Herald Tribune*; this is his account of the blacks' Easter church service at Melrose. The articles indeed aided, perhaps rescued, Saxon financially, but, of course, they also kept him from work on the novel.[34]

Three other ventures surely delayed work on *Children of Strangers* but were also lucrative. In November of 1934 Saxon published "Vanished Paradise," a very pedestrian piece about the decaying old homes of Louisiana. Readers will find nothing here that they could not find in *Fabulous New Orleans* and/or *Old Louisiana*, and Saxon himself called the essay "a very dull thing . . . ."[35] A second article, dealing with yet another "amazing" woman, appeared the same month. Again he was busy with an old theme: the "life and litigation" of a "fascinating gal."[36] Still another money-making venture that took Saxon far away from his manuscript in the cabin was a lecture tour he embarked on in late 1934. This job he found as personally distasteful as it was financially necessary. Saxon's contract was with the Dixie Bureau, "a sort of Lyceum business," and he confided to a friend his feelings about the arrangement:

> As you know, I dislike this sort of thing a great deal; but I had to do something to add to my income—and until my book is out, I must do what I can in order to make the amount necessary to keep my aunts going in Baton Rouge . . . . I'm sick of the whole business. And this

tour of Texas seems to me to be the last degredation . . . but say
nothing of this, for I might as well do it as gracefully as I can.[37]

Saxon was about his "sort of Lyceum business" late in 1934 and in the
spring of 1935, traveling throughout Louisiana and Texas.

As he wrote to friends at the end of the tour, however, the experience did not turn out to be as grim as he feared it would be.[38] He describes
in a letter to Caroline Dormon his delight in witnessing a fellow writer's
upper false teeth fall down in her mouth—while she was speaking. Her
syrupy manner had disgusted Saxon, and "God punished her" with this
embarrassing moment. Saxon wrote to Olive about traveling with his black
driver, one of the Melrose servants, who seemed to meet up with several
relatives wherever they went throughout Texas. Saxon's audiences and
hosts, he says, "thought I was traveling with a group of slaves from the old
plantation." At the conclusion of his tour, Saxon participated in a literary
symposium at L.S.U. Present at this conference also were Robert Penn
Warren, John Peale Bishop, Allen Tate, and Ford Madox Ford. Perhaps
inspired by this distinguished symposium on the present state of Southern
letters, he returned to Yucca House to write again.

"Rather than let my book go before I considered it finished," Saxon
had written on the eve of his lecture tour, "I've had to do all sorts of
things . . . ."[39] By the middle of 1935, he had indeed done many things to
replenish his bank account, but he was evidently beginning to wonder
when—or if—he would ever consider his book finished. He later revealed
that when he worked on his novel, he would get out his fragments and,
failing to integrate them, keep adding more until his manuscript became
extremely long; as he really became immersed in his job with the W.P.A.
Federal Writers' Project, however, he "got back into harness" and decided
to finish his novel and "get rid of it."[40] The enormity of his task with the
project and his acquaintance with other people's very serious problems, he
explained, caused him to put his book in perspective, to integrate and trim
the manuscript, and to send it to the irritated publishers. Saxon must have
cut drastically, for by 1934 he had already written over five hundred
pages;[41] yet what is evidently the final typescript is about half that length.
Saxon was thus probably not exaggerating at all when he claimed that at one
point the book was twice as long as the finished product.[42]

Saxon's wrestling with his novel, especially from 1931 until 1937,
surely taught him certain things about writing—and about himself—that he

did not know before. As he became aware that the novel would not come as easily as the Louisiana books or a feature story for the Sunday supplement, he made several statements about the writer's art that reveal the kind of "anguish and travail" that Faulkner was to speak of later. In one interview Saxon said he felt that writing was "the lonesomest trade in the world . . . . It is impossible to have your friends around you."[43] He added that the idea of teaching a person to write is "bunk"; "no man can teach another man how to create. Technique may be taught, but not creation." By 1934 he had learned from his struggle with the novel that composing a book could be "heartbreaking and backbreaking."[44] In 1935, at the L.S.U. symposium, he expressed a view again reminiscent of Faulkner's statements in the 1956 *Paris Review* interview. Saxon was quoted in a Baton Rouge newspaper as having pointed out "that writers wrote because they had to and what they had to, knowing that they would be both criticized and praised . . . ."[45] After the ordeal with his novel, he stated summarily: "And the writer cannot help writing. I don't know why."[46] During the midst of his work at Melrose, Lyle Saxon—in quite the opposite sense from Faulkner—had felt possessed by a devil who would *not* let him write; and he wondered in his diary if anyone would save him from the frustration and anguish he was going through. He answered his own question, however: "No. If there is any saving done, I must do it myself . . . and I will, by God, I will."[47] Saxon saved himself and somehow endured the lonely, heartbreaking, backbreaking time; the novel was published on July 6, 1937.

   Children of Strangers is the story of Euphémie (Famie) Vidal, a mulatto woman from the Cane River country.[48] When the book begins, in 1905, Famie is a sixteen-year-old girl living with her grandparents in a cabin only eleven steps from the river. The girl and her grandmother do ironing and needlework for Adelaide Randolph, the mistress of nearby Yucca Plantation.[49] Early in the novel, the author presents members of all four groups who dwell in this country, for he has the two mulatto women visit the whites at Yucca and, soon after, shows them encountering a low-class, "hill country" white clerk and several black women in the plantation commissary.

   Famie's life up to the time the novel begins has been somewhat uneventful. She has studied in the mulatto Catholic school across the river, performed her daily chores in the cabin, and, recently, been courted by one of her second cousins. This boy, Numa Lacour, is so much like a brother to Famie, however, that she feels no passion for him. The new white clerk

at the commissary offers an indecent proposal to the girl, and she is somewhat perplexed as to how she feels about him. When Famie confides in her
cousin Nita, whom Saxon calls "the bad one" as he had the wild Susie in
"Cane River," the cousin takes the clerk up on the invitation he had extended to Famie.[50] Soon afterward, at a dance, Famie is mildly stimulated
by Christophe, a mulatto boy who has recently returned from New Orleans;
but, when she goes to bed that night in her cabin, she dreams of "a man in a
pink shirt with a bare chest. The man in her dream was not Christophe.
His skin was white" (51).

Two days later something happens to Famie that changes her life
forever. On her way back from school, crossing the river in her skiff, the
girl decides to try to see what stranger has been camping on a secluded part
of the bank of Cane River. What Famie discovers is, to her, quite
extraordinary: ". . . the man was standing in the sunlight on the path beside
the fire. He was naked and his hair flamed red in the sun. His body was
startlingly white against the green leaves" (56). The mulatto girl, of course,
has never seen anything like this apparition, but, Saxon writes, the whole
incident had "the quality of a familiar dream; it seemed to her that she had
waited for this, had known it would happen." The red-haired man soon
discovers Famie spying on him and, first brutally then gently, has sexual
relations with the girl. Famie, the narrator points out, "lay as if in a dream,
hardly conscious, without thought or reason" (59).

During the next several nights, Famie goes in secret to the white
man's camp. The girl realizes that the red-haired man, who has told her to
call him "Joe," thinks that she too is white, and this realization makes her
"proud and afraid" (69). Numa, her mulatto cousin, soon guesses Famie's
secret, follows her to the inlet, and discovers the relationship with Joe.
Soon afterward Numa learns from the sheriff that a criminal has fled from
Texas and is thought to be in the Cane River country; the man's hair is
"fiery red" (80). Numa tells what he knows of Joe, and Famie's lover is
killed by the sheriff's men. The mulatto boy later swears on a crucifix to
his beloved Famie that he has not turned Joe in. He is afraid to accept three
hundred dollars as reward money for his act for fear that Famie may someday find out that he, in essence, killed her white lover. Numa does eventually take the money, however, hides it in the base of an old clock, and
leaves the Cane River country.

Saxon's narrative skips several months at this point, and the reader
next encounters a very pregnant Famie Vidal. Numa returns at about this

same time, Christmas of 1905. Lizzie Balize, a black "nurse," is summoned to the Vidal cabin to deliver Famie's child. The girl has a terrible time in labor, however, and is saved by the white doctor, whom Numa has hired form Cloutierville with part of his reward money. Famie gives birth to "a strong, healthy boy with blue eyes," and there is "no mistaking" the color of his hair: a fiery red (131). Famie realizes that neither she nor her baby would have survived without the medical aid acquired by Numa. Now more than ever, the girl comes to depend on her cousin, and, the next spring, she agrees to marry him. Long-suffering Numa realizes on the wedding day, however, "that, in Famie's affections, the white man's child would always come first" (135).

Saxon begins to widen his scope beyond just the story of Famie Vidal after the girl's marriage to Numa. He introduces additional upper-class white characters about midway in the novel. Two are Flossie and Harry Smith, Orleanians who come to visit Guy and Adelaide Randolph at Yucca. Flossie is stunned to see the nearly white mulattoes at the plantation and tells Famie that she could pass for white almost anywhere (151). The next new white character is Guy Randolph's brother Paul, an artist who returns to Yucca dying of tuberculosis. The relationship between Paul and Henry Tyler, a black sharecropper at the plantation, is the subject of Saxon's chapter that was originally published in *The Century Magazine* as "The Long Furrow." Henry longs for a life beyond and above his demeaning and deadening plowing of the furrows. He does not believe, as his wife and other blacks do, that "Nigger is nigger" (161). Paul senses Henry's despair and frustration and promises to take him far away from Yucca, from the long furrows; but Paul never leaves the plantation again himself. He dies one night in a cabin near Henry's own, and all the dogs begin to howl "as faint and final as death cries heard in a dream" (172).

Henry Tyler, trapped then at Yucca, becomes a very important character in Saxon's novel. As Numa, also a consumptive, becomes weaker with each passing day, Henry begins to do various chores for Famie and her son Joel, who "grew to look more and more like the red-haired man . . ." (187). Numa dies before his thirtieth birthday. Famie "was only twenty-six . . . , but she looked forty. Youth was gone, and already there were streaks of gray in her dark hair" (213). With her companion of almost ten years gone, Famie turns her full attention to Joel. She loves his whiteness, the narrator reveals, and she gains a curious "ecstasy" from bathing him and caressing him (215-16). Joel, however, soon grows annoyed with his smothering mother and, at age thirteen, begs to live with a Vidal relative in Chicago and to go to school there. Famie begins to sell her valuable antiques and to earn money, as would one of the "niggers," by working at menial tasks in the big-house. During all this time, she loses caste with the mulattoes, and black Henry Tyler, now a widower, is her only friend. "She felt," Saxon writes, "that she was no longer a mulatto, nor was she a negro; she was nothing" (250).

The final picture of Famie involves the resolutions of the relation-ships between Famie and her son and between her and Henry Tyler. Joel goes to Chicago and stays away from Yucca for seven years. He has lived well on the money Famie has sent him, and when he returns his design is to secure a large sum from the sale of his mother's only remaining possession of value, her land. This acreage is the only thing that distinguishes Famie, or any other mulatto in the Cane River country, from the blacks. Against the desires of her own people, Famie sells her land to Guy Randolph and gives the money to the boy. She thinks he will now take her to Chicago, but he explains that he has "crossed the line" and could not have his mulatto mother live with him (281). The other mulattoes, upon learning that Famie has sold her land to the white planter, formally disown her. The matriarch of the group even tells her: "If yo' meet me in the road, don't speak to me" (273). Saxon's final chapter is the account of Henry Tyler's calling on Famie to take her to the Baptist Easter service. "Their appearance would serve," the narrator explains, "as an announcement that their future lives would be spent together . . . that she had left her own people and had gone to his" (283).

The last scene in the novel is quite well done. It involves Henry and Famie, who is wearing a large sunbonnet, riding home from the blacks' church on a mule. First they encounter a group of mulattoes on their way to Mass; among them is the old woman who had driven Famie from their fellowship. None of the mulattoes acknowledges her. The couple on the mule next encounter Flossie and Harry, driving toward Yucca for another visit to the Randolphs. Although Flossie knows Famie, she does not recog-nize her on Henry's mule with her face turned downward, weeping beneath the sunbonnet. The white woman from New Orleans assumes, of course, that she has encountered "some niggers on their way home from church" (294). The scene strikes Flossie as so quaint as to deserve a picture, and, as she tells Harry to give the black husband a dime, she snaps the photo-graph. Flossie is overjoyed at the result: "Harry, I'll bet I've got the *grandest* picture. They were so *typical.* You know, Harry, I always say that niggers are the *happiest* people. Not a care in the world."

The historical background of Saxon's characters of "mixed blood" in *Children of Strangers* indicates clearly that he drew on the facts and legends regarding the people of French-African descent who lived on Isle Brevelle, an area in Natchitoches Parish about twelve miles from Natchitoches and just across the Cane River from Melrose.[51] The French soldiers at Fort Natchitoches, early in the eighteenth century, had several offspring by the female slaves in the area. To many of these "children of strangers" went substantial land grants.[52] According to a tradition that one local history states "has a sound basis," the mulattoes established and owned what is now known as Melrose plantation.[53] These people married among themselves, accumulated great wealth as planters, and owned many black slaves. Augustin Metoyer was the real-life patriarch of the clan, and in the novel Saxon alludes to *"Grandpère"* Augustin's establishment of the Catholic church Famie and the other mulattoes attend (32). Saxon also has Guy Randolph give the history of Augustin Metoyer in the novel and comments, through Randolph, that the old man became a "sort of king" to the mulattoes (227).

Because of economic depressions, "untimely family deaths," and oftentimes because of unfortunate prodigality, the "free people of color," by the second half of the nineteenth century, began to lose the great wealth of their ancestors.[54] The vast Metoyer landholdings were so subdivided among his heirs, moreover, that no one had a great acreage, and some, like Famie, sold their birthrights to the whites. By the time Saxon's novel begins, in 1905, the mulattoes had surely fallen far, and a few had become, as does Famie, no different from the black servants at the big-house.

Whether the great patriarch Augustin, the mulatto "king," had actually established and operated Melrose plantation before the whites purchased it is questionable. Even Francois Mignon, who has written many times of this legendary background to the plantation, admitted to me that the story did not always check and was probably family legend with some basis in fact. Joseph Henry, whose family owned Melrose for many years, accumulated an impressive amount of information from parish records indicating that the story of the mulattoes' having once controlled the entire plantation is probably exaggerated. What seems important in light of the novel, however, is that the story was given wide credence in Saxon's day and that he probably believed it. In terms of the novel, if Famie's ancestors once enjoyed the position of the Randolphs themselves, the irony of her becoming a house servant is considerably heightened.

Evidently Saxon drew on more than the general legends and facts of the people of Isle Brevelle for *Children of Strangers*. Although the novelist's prefatory statement claims that his characters are "entirely fictional" with no intentional similarity to "any living person," several residents of the area are present in the novel. Madame Aubert Rocque, whom Saxon and the Bradfords visited at her cabin, appears throughout the book, and there was an actual Henry Tyler, an uneducated, very strong black man who headed the Black Masonic Order in the parish. This man's personal life, however, was unlike that of Henry in the novel, and he did not marry a mulatto woman.[55] The two black house servants of the Randolphs, Mug and Henry-Jack in *Children of Strangers*, bear the same names as two servants employed by the Henrys at Melrose. Certainly the Randolphs themselves are drawn from John H. and Cammie Henry. Close parallels between Mrs. Henry and Mrs. Randolph are obvious in comparable passages from the novel and from some random notes Saxon made during one of his stays at Melrose.[56] Joseph Henry, in fact, felt that the Randolphs were essentially fictional portraits of his parents.

Real-life models for other characters in the novel are not nearly so easily identifiable, however. Famie Vidal, many feel, is a fictional counterpart of a woman named Josephine Monette Metoyer. Saxon outlines the story of this woman's life in some of his early notes from Melrose. One parallel does exist: Josephine, a mulatto, became a servant at the plantation big-house and eventually ate with the blacks who worked there. Almost all other facts of this woman's life, however, are far different from anything regarding Famie Vidal.[57] Joseph Henry discovered another real-life resident of the Cane River country of long ago—one whose life story much more closely resembles that of Famie. Henry, who verified most of his findings by Natchitoches Parish records, points out that a mulatto woman named Amelia Llorens, while married to a kinsman, Joseph Llorens, Sr., had an illegitimate child by a white man in 1897. The white father was probably the priest at St. Augustine Church on Isle Brevelle.[58] The child, whom Saxon met at Melrose, was named Joseph Llorens, Jr., and was, Henry told me, the "Joel" of the novel. If the novelist was drawing on this Llorens family history, it is interesting that he made Famie's white lover a criminal rather than a priest. The latter might have seemed too close a real-life parallel; or Saxon possibly felt such an affair between a girl (especially one who does fine needlework) and a clergyman might have reminded too many readers of *The Scarlet Letter*. At any rate, the novelist's disclaimer about the people in *Children of Strangers* being purely fictional seems little more than a stock formality, and he even admitted in an interview shortly after publication that "a good deal" of what he had written was factual.[59]

As indicated by the above, then, Saxon's primary sources were what he had heard as a resident of the Cane River country and what he had observed from his Melrose cabin over a period of fourteen years. Although his main inspiration was surely from life and not from literary sources, certain parallels between *Children of Strangers* and other works do indicate the possibility of additional influences. In a general sense Saxon was very probably influenced by George Washington Cable, once called "the first writer to question the validity of aristocratic tradition in Southern fiction" and identified as the "spiritual godfather" of Southern realists.[60] The influence of the Louisiana writer on Saxon, however, seems to have been scant, for, as Saxon's friend Catherine Dillon once noted, he never read Cable's best works.[61]

What he read by Kate Chopin is unknown, but it seems very likely that he was familiar with the stories of this writer from Cloutierville, a town about twenty miles from Natchitoches. Chopin had dealt with the theme of mixed blood, in stories such as "Désirée's Baby," and had also written about Natchitoches.[62] In *The Awakening*, moreover, Chopin's Edna tells a sultry story of a woman and her lover in a pirogue, depicting a scene reminiscent of Saxon's picture of Famie and the red-haired man. By far Saxon's most likely inspiration, if any exists, from the works of Kate Chopin would be "La Belle Zoraïde." This story deals with a mulatto who has an illegitimate child by a black man. At one point, when she realizes she will never be able to marry her lover, Zoraïde "took comfort and hope in the thought of her baby . . . ." A loyal mulatto friend desires to marry the girl, as Numa does Famie, but before this union can take place, Zoraïde's child is taken from her. Chopin's character is called "*Malheureuse*"—a term that would describe Famie as well.

Two works of the 1920s might also have had some small influence on *Children of Strangers*. The first book Saxon was definitely familiar with: his friend La Farge's *Laughing Boy*. As Famie is neither black nor white culturally, neither is La Farge's Slim Girl Indian or American. Slim Girl also has a white man as a lover (although her feelings for him are far different from those of Famie for Joe) and is, like Saxon's mulatto, discovered in her lover's arms. One more possible influence on *Children of Strangers* is Jean Toomer's novel of 1923, *Cane*. The possibility of influence here is not quite as remote as might appear from the fact that the first edition of *Cane* sold less than five hundred copies; for two of Saxon's New York acquaintances, Paul Rosenfeld and Alfred Kreymborg, reviewed Toomer's works during the time Saxon lived in Greenwich Village. As I have suggested, too, certain passages in *Cane* seem echoed in Saxon's 1926 story "Cane River." Like Famie Vidal, Toomer's Becky, in the section of *Cane* so named, lives alone in a cabin and is an outcast to both blacks and whites. Becky, a white woman, bore two sons by a black man. Although the parallels among Slim Girl and Becky and Famie are only general and these influences, if present at all, may be somewhat minor, Saxon's reading of these two earlier novels possibly contributed to his overall plan and may have played their parts in the shaping of Famie Vidal.

Structurally *Children of Strangers* is an orderly book, and the story is nicely framed. Saxon divides the novel into four sections: "Easter 1905," "Numa," "The Big-House and the Cabin," and "Black and White." The first and last sections of the novel, like Faulkner's *The Sound and the Fury*, are set at Easter time, and, like the earlier novel which Saxon so much admired, the final section contains an account of an Easter sermon at a black church. Saxon also frames the book by opening and closing in the early morning hours of two April days twenty-one years apart. Even his descriptions of the Cane River country in the first and last chapters serve to frame the narrative. "Fog covered Cane River" is the opening sentence of the novel (3), and Saxon includes this description a few pages from the end: "Mist hung low over the river, and the foggy fields seemed to end in a white wall of clouds" (284).

The three previously published parts of the book are integrated quite well despite the great difficulty Saxon claimed to have had in doing so. The story of Henry Tyler and Paul, "The Long Furrow," is well anticipated by Saxon's early use of the title of the story (13) and by the reference to Paul's homecoming (151-52). The end of "The Long Furrow," the memorable account of the dogs howling mournfully at the man's death, is reinforced by later references to the dogs (175, 177, 178). Saxon also neatly fits the "Lizzie Balize" story, originally published in *The Dial*, into the structure of the whole. The novelist introduces Lizzie's son Bull, a major character in the *Dial* story, in an earlier scene in the novel (116) and foreshadows black Lizzie's awful vengeance against a mulatto by her scornful pronouncement, seventy pages before "Lizzie Balize," that mulattoes are "uppity" (118). The third previously published chapter of the novel is the last, the one in which Famie and Henry attend the Baptist church service. The adaptation of this chapter, originally a first-person account in which Saxon accompanies Henry, is remarkably well done. Essentially Famie is substituted for the first-person narrator of the earlier version of the story, and the scene with Flossie is added at the end.

Considering the extensive revisions, especially the vast amount of cutting, Saxon could easily have produced a stylistically disastrous book. Sentences written perhaps fourteen years apart, characters who were altered and cut to the bone, and the extensive deletion of syntactical elements all invite disaster.[63] Thus, not surprisingly, *Children of Strangers* is flawed; but the novel is far from poorly written, and some passages are remarkably well done.[64] Especially noteworthy is Saxon's differentiation between black and mulatto dialect, both of which are quite unlike the speech of either the low- or high-class whites. Well done too are the vivid descriptions of the Cane River country, none of which, happily enough, is overly poeticized. Saxon consistently manages to describe the country he found beautiful in a restrained manner—not wasting words telling his readers how quaint or beautiful they ought to feel it to be. Similarly the novelist manages to treat quite emotional scenes with a degree of decorum and restraint, and his pathos does not become bathos. Numa's death, the death of Famie's lover, and the mulattoes' disowning of the girl are scenes of potential bathos, but, as Roark Bradford pointed out in regard to the disowning scene, the novelist's restraint successfully saves the book from mawkishness.[65]

Saxon's narrative involves a somewhat shifting point of view, but the changes in the narrative voice are unobtrusive and natural. His "shifts" involve entering a character's mind during a particularly emotional moment for him or her, such as Saxon's focusing on Numa immediately after he has forsworn himself to Famie (98) or on Famie the night she marries Numa (138).[66] For the most part, however, the speaker in *Children of Strangers* is a detached, omniscient, objective one who makes no didactic point about Famie's or the mulattoes' decline, about the black sharecroppers' entrapment, or about the white characters' patronizing and exploitation of the others. "I tried to keep from preaching," Saxon once explained.[67] How well he succeeds in this effort is obvious and is a distinctive feature of the book. His narrative was judged by various reviewers as reflective of a "highly trained reporter," as one in which "objectivity never really fails," and in which the reader finds "few asides."[68]

As successful as Saxon's handling of point of view in the novel is his employment of symbols to enrich his story. Nicely suggestive beyond the literal level, for example, are Famie's soiling her dress when she meets her lover (61), the fire at Joe's camp burning itself out at the same time the affair is terminated (84), and the terrible thunderstorms raging while Famie suffers the emotional storm of Joe's death (90-91). Later in the novel Saxon skillfully describes the pecans hanging in their green husks, "gathering oily nutriment" as they ripen, immediately before he introduces readers to the fact that Famie is pregnant (107-08). He also employs Famie's headdresses as symbols throughout *Children of Strangers*. She initially wears a sunbonnet like her grandmother's and the other mulattoes'; she is given a white hat by Mrs. Randolph during the time she meets her white lover; and, late in the story, she begins to wear a *tignon* like the blacks with whom she works and with whom, eventually, she lives. Perhaps the most extensive single symbol (and one of the most obvious) in the novel is the fence that separates the field Henry Tyler plows from the cabin where Paul Randolph stays at Yucca. This high wire fence was constructed, Saxon writes, to keep in some valuable game chickens; the birds were gone long ago, "but the barrier remained" (159). The novelist chose "barrier" judiciously, for this is what the symbolic fence is. It prevents Paul and the black man from visiting each other, and, on the night the two transcend the barriers of race and class and communicate with each other, Paul cuts an opening in the fence (165).

Saxon extensively employs color symbols in *Children of Strangers*. The races he is depicting of course lend themselves logically to this device, and the novelist explores, perhaps exploits, all possible significances from things white, black, white-and-black, and yellow. Famie's longings for whiteness, as well as her eventually taking a white lover, are foreshadowed by all sorts of symbols involving whiteness. One of the first pictures of the girl involves her sitting with Numa under the "white" moon, in a "white" dress, holding a "white" rose (8). Famie picks out a white dotted Swiss material for her Easter dress (21) and derives an almost erotic pleasure from fingering the white washbowl in which she bathed Joel (243-44). When she is abandoned by her son, she breaks this white bowl and, soon after, goes to live with black Henry Tyler (282).

Yellow seems to be used in *Children of Strangers* almost as a leitmotif suggesting the mulattoes' mixed blood. Early in the book Saxon employs yellow literally to describe a mulatto's skin (10). He mentions the yellow lamps at a mulatto dance, in Numa's cabin, and in the Vidal house (43, 112, 136). He also has Famie receive an old, "yellowed" prayerbook from the old mulatto matriarch, and he places Famie's cousin Nita at one point "beside a yellow rosebush" (133, 203).

More subtle and more meaningful seems his use of black and white. This color mixture sometimes suggests the obvious—a mixture of Caucasian and African blood—such as when a mulatto woman wears a black-and-white dress or when a black-and-white dog sleeps at Famie's feet (132, 263). Saxon is not consistent with his use of this kind of symbol, however, and he transcends, fortunately, this quaint but really inconsequential identification of color with mulatto by his other uses of black-and-white elements. Famie, like all mulattoes, "black" as far as the laws of Louisiana were concerned, is linked symbolically to this color and Joe to white in the initial love scene on the shores of Cane River. The criminal's dog is "black-and-white spotted" (55). Famie first sees the dog, then is startled by a mockingbird, who "flirted his tail," which would of course reveal his two colors. At this point the girl spies the "startlingly white" Joe. When the two lie together, "the dog lay watching," and the birds "chirped angrily . . ." (59). In this scene, then, black-and-white creatures watch what is—in the eyes of the law and Cane River society—a union of black and white.

Certainly not surprising is Saxon's symbolic use of red in his novel. This color is linked, conventionally enough, to illicit sex and to sin. Joe is of course red-haired, and Famie is obsessed by his hair.[69] Joel is also a redhead and is a cruel, ungrateful son. Nita, "the bad one," appears at the Easter dance in a red silk dress, having skipped Mass and spent the previous night with a white man. The best figurative use of this color seems to be in the subtle touch Saxon employs at Famie and Numa's wedding. For this occasion Famie wears her best white dress, but it has rust stains on it "from the chain of her rowboat . . ." (132). She has stained the dress on her trips to the inlet to meet Joe. Also on her wedding day, Famie removes the red poppies from the hat she has chosen to wear, an appropriate deflowering.

As he had already done in "Cane River," in one of his *Times-Picayune* features, and in *Old Louisiana*, Saxon shows in *Children of*

Strangers a familiarity and an adeptness with local superstitions. As Philip Tapley has pointed out, Saxon's "observation and collection of superstitions are unusually thorough" in the novel.[70] Tapley catalogues the characters' superstitions and demonstrates how geographically widespread several of them are. The superstitions are not only extensive, he concludes, but quite accurate—"not 'fakelore' or the mere contrivance of the author." Indeed Saxon very likely would not have to resort to contrivances, that is construct a superstition to fit a fictional situation; nor would he have needed to consult some classic study like Puckett's *Folk Beliefs of the Southern Negro*. In Saxon's own seven-page compilation in *Old Louisiana* are virtually all those superstitions he had encountered among the Cane River residents over the years. Saxon's introductory comments to the list in *Old Louisiana* provide a nice gloss on the characters' superstitions in *Children of Strangers* and, incidentally, are reminiscent of Richard Wright's comments in *Black Boy* concerning blacks and superstitions:

> He [the black man] lives in a world apart from the white man's world, and in a world infinitely more interesting and terrible; for every breeze brings an omen for good or bad luck and the sunlight itself must be watched for shadows of passing birds. (*OL* 345)

In addition to his skillful handling of symbolic elements and local superstitions, Saxon shows in *Children of Strangers* an ability to create quite vivid characters. The novel is Famie's story, and this characterization is, of course, the fullest and most memorable. This mulatto girl is in some ways reminiscent of certain other literary figures. Her playing with Joel's toys and fingering his washbowl years after he has left home is similar to the behavior of Chopin's Zoraïde, who caresses and carries around a rag doll after her child is gone. Famie's strange "ceremonial" involving the washbowl, moreover, is the kind of behavior readers might expect in someone from Winesburg, Ohio. As I have mentioned already, Famie's talent in doing "delicate" needlework calls to mind Hester Prynne; and the girl's washing herself and her clothes and looking in the mirror after her loss of virginity is reminiscent of Caddy Compson's actions. To cite another, far more recent literary point of comparison, Famie, with her great losses of status and self respect stand in dramatic contrast to Alice Walker's Celie and her great gains in pride and self-awareness.

Despite these and other parallels that could be mentioned, however, Famie is a fully rounded character. She is neither derivative, nor a foil; her individuality is not lost in the symbolism she carries. Her unique personality is vividly drawn. Everything that happens to her in the twenty-one years covered by the novel is skillfully anticipated and poignantly depicted as her story unfolds. Her relationships with Joe and with Joel seem well motivated and are foreshadowed early in the story by the oblique revelations of her longing for whiteness. The pleasure she takes in discovering that her African blood is difficult to detect, her admiration of Mrs. Randolph's white child, and her dream of a white lover all prepare readers for her actions throughout the first parts of the novel (see 16, 17, and 51).

Also aptly foreshadowed is Famie's eventual assumption of blackness, of life with Henry Tyler. Saxon's main character consistently manifests either a favorable attitude toward blacks or a refusal to scorn them as other mulattoes do. Early in the novel, she fails to understand "her grandmother's distaste" for blacks (16), and before attending Mass, she "caught herself" humming some of the blacks' hymns she overhears as they pass by on their way to the Baptist church (38-39). Later in the book, when Famie works at the big-house with the black house servants, she eats with them, enjoys the same jokes they do, adopts their superstitions, and, eventually, she begins frequently to sing (not merely hum) "a negro baptizing hymn . . ." (see 246, 248, 252, and 256). Famie's feelings for Henry Tyler are likewise consistently warm and foreshadow the eventual union. While still married to Numa, she befriends Henry and gets him to cut firewood for the family; after Numa's death her friendship with Henry grows, and she sews for him. By this time Famie "had come to depend on his strength" (257).

Having begun with such an individual as Famie Vidal, Saxon seems to have ended quite nicely with a type. The reviewer in *The New York Times* pointed out that Famie is a representative character, one in whom the fate of all the mulattoes is synthesized. She was also seen as a synthesis of tragic, long-suffering motherhood.[71] Famie's individual "fall" from identification with whiteness to identification with blackness reflects the general social decline of her people at the time *Children of Strangers* was written. Her loss of caste with the mulattoes comes not from bearing the white criminal's child; it comes instead from her association with the blacks and her "selling out," quite literally by her acreage, to the white planter. Famie too, as representative motherhood, is made to suffer pain from the ungrate-

ful child, but Saxon allows her to maintain her dignity—and her sanity—
after the cruelest rejection, after she receives the blow from Joel. Perhaps
the novelist's finest accomplishment in *Children of Strangers* is his ability to
incorporate such social and universal elements in his individual without
Famie's suffering a fatal loss of individuality.

It seems appropriate to mention here too that Famie—that is,
Euphémie Vidal—is very well named. If a pun is intended on *fame*, it is in
regard first to her notoriety—her scandal and shame—then perhaps quite
ironically to the loss of any kind of fame, whether from her youthful beauty
or from her sins; for she will surely end her days in obscurity. The Greek
roots for Euphémie, moreover, denote "fair of speech" or "well reputed,"
suggestive of the "virtuous woman" of Proverbs 31—the kind of hard-
working, long-suffering, devoted wife and mother Famie in many ways
becomes. More significantly, I suspect that Euphémie's name is a subtle
reminder of what a mulatto—a "free person of color," one of "mixed
blood"—really was in the old South. After all, in that milieu and in the eyes
of the law long afterwards, "mulatto" was never more than a euphemism.
Faulkner's Shreve and Quentin finally surmise that miscegenation is
more unbearable to Henry Sutpen than even incest; Bon was really Bond
all along.

Also very successful in *Children of Strangers* is the characterization
of Henry Tyler. One writer has identified Henry as an example of the
frustrated black character who is "intelligent enough to want to ask
questions, but there is no one to ask."[72] Henry does know that "nigger is
nigger" is not true (161), but he also loses his only chance, Paul Randolph,
to escape his "nigger" existence at Yucca. Saxon presents a full-bodied
black character in Henry—one who is neither a devoted servant or a shuf-
fling eye-roller. Henry's lack of awareness and knowledge are not sources
of humor. Rather than having fun with Henry's ignorance, Saxon makes
clear why the sharecropper cannot improve his mind. Saxon does not
ridicule Henry's religion, but demonstrates that it is true, passionate, and
genuine to Henry and his people. Tragic and dignified, a man whose "eyes
asked questions," an example of the black man Cable described as "freed—
not free," Henry Tyler makes a lasting impression: harnessed behind his
mule in the east field of Yucca, plowing the long furrows forever.

These two memorable characters, Famie and Henry, are really the
only fully developed people in the novel. Numa, whose role was probably
reduced considerably as Saxon revised, emerges as somewhat of an

underdeveloped character. His devotion to Famie is admirable, of course, but taxes credibility. Whereas Henry is more man than "nigger" and Famie is more woman than mulatto, Numa's full humanity never quite emerges. One reviewer's comment that Numa is more symbol than real seems accurate.[73] The picture of him as long-suffering, devoted lover and solid, dependable mulatto husband is perhaps too good to be true.

Other characters are one-dimensional and shallow. Nita, who is rarely mentioned without the epithet "the bad one," is simply this: bad. Her sexual activities first with the white clerk and then with black Bull Balize precede, and foreshadow in a sense, the two relationships Famie will enter into with white and black. This foreshadowing and Nita's serving as a foil to Famie seem Saxon's only purposes for the inclusion of Nita, but even a "bad one" deserves a little fuller treatment than this girl receives. Readers may find themselves wishing for some good—or at least for some more good badness—from Nita. Also disappointing is the treatment of Joel. The boy once had a larger role in Saxon's story, but the novelist here seems to have cut the life out of his character along with the lines he cut in manuscript.[74] Perhaps even more of a disappointment is the shadowy figure of Paul Randolph, whose life span is only about twenty pages in the novel. Saxon's blue pencil was evidently as fatal to Paul as was tuberculosis, for "sickly-like and puny," he cannot carry the allegorical weight Saxon has him bear. Paul is the literally and figuratively weak white who wants to cut barriers, like the wire fence, but who is ineffectual despite his noble aims. Saxon's paring down and deletions regarding these minor characters seem unfortunate. I find it quite regrettable that he apparently trimmed them so, and I think most readers will find themselves wishing Nita, Joel, Numa, Paul, and some of the others were more fully drawn and clearly motivated.

Other one-dimensional personalities in *Children of Strangers*, however, seem appropriately shallow. Famie's lover, the aptly anonymous Joe, is important for his whiteness, but not as an individual. A fuller picture of him as a personality would seem to serve no purpose. Even to Famie only his white skin and red hair are exciting. He is a "stranger" to her and should be no more; Technical Sergeant Garp, after all, does not need a first name. George Stevens noted in *The Saturday Review* that the plantation whites in Saxon's novel are also "superficial" characters.[75] This reviewer mildly criticizes what seemed like abortive scenes taking place between the whites and the mulattoes and between the whites and the blacks at Yucca.

What seems to explain and to justify such scenes in *Children of Strangers*, however, is that surely any such relationships in Cane River life were abortive and superficial.

The really masterful stroke among Saxon's minor, "superficial" characterizations is Flossie, Mrs. Randolph's effusively garrulous visitor from New Orleans. In fact, to paraphrase an old paradox, Flossie is very shallow way down deep. Saxon's most richly superficial character, she works well in several ways in the novel. Roark Bradford, in his review of *Children of Strangers*, noted that instead of including the ludicrous black character for comic relief from a serious story about whites, Saxon employs Flossie, a ludicrous white character, as comic relief from the seriousness of the blacks' story.[76] Flossie Smith is also used for purposes beyond the strictly humorous. As an observer of Famie, she makes especially pertinent and timely comments. She functions essentially as the chorus in the tragedy of Famie Vidal. When Flossie first sees the girl, she tells Famie: "Why, you could pass for white . . ." (151). The last time the two meet, Flossie assumes she is photographing an old "nigger" woman on a mule (294). Saxon's ironic thrust is potent as he has Flossie, delighted over the "*typical*" picture Famie and Henry make, proclaim that "niggers are the *happiest* people. Not a care in the world." Readers thus come away from the book with a feeling not unlike that evoked by Hemingway's final scene in *The Old Man and the Sea*, wherein the woman discusses the tail of the "shark." Saxon's and Hemingway's tourists are indeed floss compared to the people of substance whose painful struggles readers have seen endured.

Undoubtedly Saxon wanted to reveal to readers from all parts of the country the carefully structured, regional caste system of the Cane River section of Louisiana. As several reviewers pointed out, however, he merely presents this stratified society and does not explicitly condemn it. The four classes—mulatto, black, low white, and the white planters—fascinated Saxon, and he wanted to depict them in all their interrelationships. This aim is admirably fulfilled, among many other ways, in Famie's various associations with her cousin Numa, Henry Tyler, the low-class white clerk, and Flossie. The novelist manages throughout to capture the blacks' resentment of the "uppity" mulattoes and the mulattoes' contempt for the lowly blacks. He aptly has the low whites, like the commissary clerk, refer to both groups as "damned niggers" and the high whites, like Mr. Guy, carefully and respectfully preserve class distinctions between blacks and mulattoes (see 123 and 119-22).

Saxon, trying "to keep from preaching," succeeded well enough in avoiding propagandizing and in depicting this caste society objectively that his feelings about the four peoples of the Cane River country are not easily inferred. Certain elements in *Children of Strangers* suggest a few ideas worth noting briefly, however. It is perhaps significant, for example, that Famie's three men represent, in the eyes of her people, a decline from a white, to a mulatto, to a black mate. The white man with whom she shares her life, however, is a criminal, the mulatto is her own rather ordinary cousin, and the black is strong, dignified, noble Henry Tyler. This is clearly an upward progression, thus belying the whole idea that any character's transition from white to black would be an inherent, and unfortunate, fall. In fact, Famie's changed life suggests not even a *felix culpa*, but definite amelioration. Her turning to a life with the blacks, though, is far from an affirmation that she and Henry have found the good life on Cane River, that the world is all before them; for Famie is left weeping, an outcast, and Henry Tyler has that very day heard an owl call—a bad omen that causes him to shiver.[77] Though as individuals, both have triumphed in spirit, in point of fact Famie and Henry are now forever fixed on the lowest level of Cane River life.

Twice in his novel, Saxon alludes to the problems of the Cane River society. He has Guy Randolph summarize a conversation he has had with his brother on the possibility that the whites exploit the blacks. Paul makes some good points, Guy admits, but "he couldn't find a solution any more than I can" (232). Saxon evidently had no solution for either brother to present. The other scene in which the novelist seems to be pondering the problems with no answers occurs very early. As Famie and her grandmother look out from their cabin near Yucca, Saxon writes:

> As they stood in their doorway they could see the big-house rising above its trees not more than half a mile away. But the big-house at Yucca was remote, for all that. There are barriers far greater than distance: race and timidity and old, threadbare pride. (12)

This passage, in essence, seems to be the crux of Saxon's Cane River story. Above all, *Children of Strangers* suggests poignantly, from beginning to end, that there are barriers far greater than distance. In the final scene he juxtaposes the two classes furthest apart, the black sharecroppers and the white Orleanians; and nowhere in the book are the barriers greater or the distances more remote than when Henry Tyler and Flossie Smith are side by side in the road.

Reviews of Saxon's novel spawned all sorts of comments about how a reader ought to react to the book. The author wrote once to a friend that "the difference between the Northern and the Southern reviews would make God laugh."[78] This vast difference is surely apparent: Carl Van Doren's view that "any decent white person" should feel "a sense of shame" when reading the book stands in stark contrast to the caution in *The Times-Picayune* that a large portion of *Children of Strangers* is "not good reading for Southerners."[79]   Aside from such comments regarding the readers of the book, the vast majority of the reviews do deal with the novel itself and are quite favorable.

The New York reviews must have been very gratifying to the novelist.[80] Comments such as "absorbing" and "eminently readable" appeared in the *Herald Tribune*. The *New York Times* reviewer hailed the book as "a sincerely felt and poignantly written story," and Harry Hansen, in the *World-Telegram*, praised Saxon's "sensitive" achievement. In *The New Republic* Hamilton Basso, understandably enough, recommended the novel and especially lauded the portrait of the mother's sacrifice for the "adored and unadoring son." The most prominent review of *Children of Strangers*, or of any book Saxon ever wrote or edited, came on July 10, 1937. The novelist's picture appeared on the cover of *The Saturday Review of Literature*, and George Stevens wrote a very favorable critique of the book. Stevens told the vast *Saturday Review* audience that the Louisiana novelist had created a beautiful book, "genuine and moving as it is unpretentious," memorable for "its poignancy and its considerable distinction."

British reviews were equally favorable.[81] *Children of Strangers* was lavishly praised in *The Spectator,* called "fine and unusual" by the *Scotsman*, and described as a "very human story" in *The Birmingham Post*. *The Times Literary Supplement* contained the fullest and most laudatory British review. Saxon, the *Times* reviewer noted, tells his story with pity but not with sentimentality and skillfully keeps his individual, Famie, representative of her people throughout. The novel's "abiding effect," this reviewer concluded, "is one of unusual poise, of authentic tragic beauty, of material fined and refined until every episode, every word, has its place in an artistic whole."

Ironically, in light of such comments in New York and London, Saxon's book received a largely negative review in New Orleans. George

W. Healy, Jr., editor of *The Times-Picayune*, wrote what Saxon's friend Tess Crager remembered as "a blast of a review." Although Healy's article does contain several favorable comments about the novel, Saxon remembered the adverse criticism long afterward.[82] In assessing *Children of Strangers* Healy wondered "just how long" Saxon would remain many Louisianans' favorite author after they read the novel.[83] He especially disapproved of the first section of the book—not for its slowness, a fault George Stevens and even Saxon himself had recognized, but for its subject matter. The story of Famie and Joe the *Times-Picayune* reviewer saw as a tale of "concubinage"—"not fit . . . for anyone." The fact that such comments appeared in *The Times-Picayune* must have been embarrassing as well as disappointing for Saxon.

In the long run, *Children of Strangers* made the author neither rich nor famous. The four printings of 1937 totaled 12,500 copies, not a sensational sales rate but a good one (despite the warning in *The Times-Picayune*). Saxon confessed shortly after the book was published that he had been advanced so much money that unless the book sold at a "phenomenal" pace, he would do well to break even.[84] Surely he fared better than this, but probably not much better. *Children of Strangers* did not make any of the major "Best Seller" lists, dominated at the time by *Northwest Passage, Of Mice and Men,* and *To Have and Have Not.* Saxon's novel was published in England by John Lane, but he was told jokingly by a friend that "English publication . . . is an honor only, you make in cash about $45."[85]

The novelist was, without question, proud of *Children of Strangers.* Many of Saxon's friends stressed to me how the author thought the book to be his best accomplishment, and, yet again, Saxon's assessment of his own work seems quite sound. He even foresaw the relative obscurity into which the book would fall. Only a month after the publication, Saxon told a Baton Rouge reporter that he felt *Children of Strangers* would sell well for several weeks "then drift off into desultory buys by the reading public." He went on to explain that his subject matter was "quaky ground" and, in another interview published the same day, remarked that readers would soon spend their money on "more pleasant things."[86] Such statements seem admirably philosophical in light of the way he felt about the book, for he even confessed once that everything he had written before *Children of Strangers* seemed only "preparation" for the novel.[87]

Long out of print, Saxon's novel was revived in 1974. John R. Egle, then a publisher with Ballantine Books, included *Children of Strangers* in a series of Southern novels. Egle explains that Saxon's book was chosen "because it is excellent fiction, long out of print . . . ."[88] The paperback *Children of Strangers* was not widely reviewed, but a few praised the story as lavishly as many had the first edition thirty-seven years before.[89] The only unfavorable review appeared in the *Roanoke World-News.* The reviewer was evidently under the impression that the novel had just been written and that Saxon was still alive; ironically, his major complaint is that Saxon writes about a time and place "that never actually existed."

That *Children of Strangers* has not disappeared completely is fortunate and, to me, entirely appropriate; for this book about the Cane River country does not seem deserving of the relative obscurity it has shared with scores of other Southern regional novels. In an essay in Louis D. Rubin's 1985 *History of Southern Literature,* Anne Goodwyn Jones comments quite favorably on *Children of Strangers.*[90] In contrasting Saxon's characters with Roark Bradford's fictional blacks, Jones says Saxon avoids the "obvious white stereotyping" of Bradford and "does a better job of imagining black life with some sensitivity to the fullness of the black experience." She concludes that while Bradford "seems to want to monumentalize the old view of blacks, Saxon seems to want to deconstruct it."

Considering the milieu in which it was written, *Children of Strangers* is noteworthy in many senses for what it is not; it does not suffer from either picturesque quaintness or heavy-handed propagandizing—the two dangers of writing about the Cane River country that Saxon has Guy Randolph identify (230-231). In addition, the novel does not depict nonwhites in a dehumanizing or degrading manner. With the exception of only a few very minor characters, the nonwhites in Saxon's novel, whether of pure or of mixed African ancestry, are not the grateful servants, the carefree buffoons, or the blissful, lazy children who populate countless fictional plantations from Swallow Barn to Tara. They are not "typical," but individual; and they are not the happiest people in the world—regardless of what Flossie Smith will see in her glossy photograph.

6

ANTICLIMAX:
THE RETURN TO NEW ORLEANS, 1935-1946

L YLE SAXON CHRONICALLY COMPLAINED of being bound by "facts" in writing such books as the four Century volumes. The facts of his histories do seem almost to shackle him in the Louisiana books. In *Children of Strangers* he was at last free from the facts and could create, experiment, and exercise poetic license in his tale of the Cane River country. By the time his novel was finally published, however, Saxon had already been involved for two years with the W.P.A. Federal Writers' Project, a monumental work concerned largely with the collection of facts—far more facts than Saxon had ever felt shackled by before. He would be occupied with this project until 1943, and he published no new fiction the last nine years of his life.

The Federal Writers' Project was established in July of 1935. One historian of the project calls it "an extraordinary governmental enterprise" to aid needy writers.[1] Harry Hopkins, then director of the Works Progress Administration, curtly told critics of the Writers' Project that artists had to eat like anybody else.[2] Essentially, the program yielded three kinds of books: folklore studies, biographies, and the volumes that made up the bulk of the work, regional guidebooks. Well-known writers were the exception rather than the rule in the project. Many who were to become widely known, such as Eudora Welty and Richard Wright, were just beginning their careers when the project started. Lyle Saxon, named state director for Louisiana, was among the most widely published of the administrators and has been identified as one who played a major role in the project.[3]

When Saxon began his W.P.A. duties in New Orleans in the summer of 1935, he was assuming his first regular job in nine years. Not since his days at *The Times-Picayune* had he been regularly employed, and, as indicated in the previous chapter, his bank account had suffered recently. As state director he was well salaried and occupied a large office in the Canal Bank building.[4] Under the national director of the Writers' Project, Henry G. Alsberg, Saxon supervised the Louisiana program, assisted by Edward Dreyer and, later, Robert Tallant. The work in Louisiana officially began on October 15, 1935, and the New Orleans workers, as well as those in the several district offices, began gathering information for the New Orleans and Louisiana guidebooks.

Saxon's duties included, of course, the editing of the material gathered for these guidebooks. The fieldworkers, numbering nearly a hundred, sent Saxon a steady stream of data: interviews, descriptions, anecdotes, and a hodgepodge of information about the subject at hand. His task was to assimilate, revise, and improve what reached his desk. The whole process, as William F. McDonald writes, "was a problem in directing multiple efforts toward a single end."[5] All the old jokes about committees come immediately to mind.

As difficult as this editing task seems, however, Saxon's really hard job, at first anyway, was the hiring of personnel. Although the official policy was to employ those on the W.P.A. roles who had previously earned their livings as writers, this criterion was not always followed; and the state directors actually could hire whom they chose. This was a terrible onus for Saxon, or anyone in such a position, in the midst of the depression; for he had money to give, and he could hire anyone who claimed to be a writer.

In a sense Saxon was like the wedding guest buttonholed by scores of ragged mariners and in a position to give them more than just an ear. He was overwhelmed. He wrote Cammie Henry three days after the New Orleans office opened: "I'm talking to a great many people who need work badly—and to a lot of others who are anxious to grab any government money they can—and not work for it."[6] Even when he could identify those who genuinely needed the work, however, he could not always help them. After three months at his job, he wrote: "I still have daily visitors asking for jobs—and no funds for new workers. Nice. And it always tears me up to refuse people who need work so badly."[7] Caroline Durieux, Baton Rouge artist who worked with Saxon on the project, recalled that several fellow employees and hundreds of people interviewed "were practically starving" in New Orleans in those days.[8] Virtually all of Saxon's co-workers and friends with whom I talked took note of his compassion, his genuine feeling for those whose sad stories he heard daily.

During his early years as state director of the writers' program, Saxon's personal literary production was slowed but not stymied completely.[9] He wrote a brief tourists' pamphlet for the Dinkler hotel chain in 1935 and in August of the next year published a piece in the *Southern Architectural Review* about a haunted house. Late in 1936 and throughout 1937, Saxon somehow found the time to write seven reviews for *The New York Herald Tribune*. He favorably reviewed Herbert Asbury's *The French Quarter*, which was concerned with many of the same topics as *Fabulous New Orleans*. Actually Saxon helped Asbury in the writing of the book and was acknowledged for his assistance by Asbury himself. Ward Greene's *Death in the Deep South* was also recommended heartily by Saxon, possibly because it contains a lengthy and sensational trial. Saxon called Hamilton Basso's *Courthouse Square* his "best novel to date," made a very similar statement about Robert Rylee's latest book, and enthusiastically recommended Roark Bradford's *The Three-Headed Angel*. Like Saxon's critiques in the *Herald Tribune* a few years before, these reviews and the two written late in 1937 are genteel. "If any criticism is to be made," Saxon writes in one, "it is perhaps . . . "; the "if" and the "perhaps" are typical qualifiers in the few passages that adversely comment on the book at hand.

Saxon's seven reviews of 1936 and '37 steadily decrease in length and in prominence in the *Herald Tribune* book review section. The first five are among the "featured" reviews and are essentially sound analyses—even if they are somewhat reticent about the faults of the books. The last two, however, are relegated to the back pages of the book review section and are included among general fiction headings. They are also relatively worthless in analyzing the books or in providing readers with any information to determine whether or not to purchase the volume. "I like the book," Saxon says in one review, and he says little else.

It seems very likely that the W.P.A. work, surely becoming quite heavy by late 1937, was already detracting from the time and the effort Saxon was able to put on other projects, such as these reviews. He did not publish another in the *Herald Tribune* after the rather shabby and superficial one in late September. From the inception of the W.P.A. work until 1938, Saxon's only new productions, other than these inconsequential reviews, were a guest editorial in a relatively obscure New Orleans magazine and one article in *The Times-Picayune*.[10] By far the major part of Saxon's day was spent at this time readying the *New Orleans City Guide* for publication.

In the midst of his undoubtedly difficult work on the city guide, a diversion came to Saxon in early 1938: the motion picture *The Buccaneer*, based quite loosely on the author's *Lafitte the Pirate*. Cecil B. De Mille, producer-director of the film, first came to New Orleans in November of 1936 with the idea of making the movie. De Mille and his crew returned to shoot the location scenes early the next year. Although he interviewed many Orleanians and authorities on Lafitte, De Mille specifically acknowledged Saxon and his biography in the movie credits, and the screenplay was "based on [an] adaptation by Jeanie Macpherson of Lyle Saxon's book, 'Lafitte the Pirate' . . . ."[11] De Mille's screenplay no more resembles Saxon's book than could be expected of something "based on [an] adaptation." Especially ironic are two elements: the introduction of major female characters and the thoroughly romanticized picture of the pirate—a picture that Saxon not only strives to avoid, but that he ridicules in *Lafitte the Pirate*. As he sails out into the murky sea, De Mille's Lafitte proclaims to a fair damsel at the end of the screenplay: "This deck under our feet—(He glances quietly along the deck)—is our only country."[12] "Well—it's a good deck," the pirate girl answers, and the pair sail away with their love to sustain them until they reach their eventual "home port . . . the bottom of the sea."

The Buccaneer premiered in New Orleans on January 7, 1938. The *Times-Picayune* reviewer noted that Frederic March, as Jean Lafitte, would "capture a million new hearts," but that Akim Tamiroff (Dominique You) "steals the show."[13] Neither Tamiroff nor the show was as warmly received outside New Orleans, however. The *New York Times* reviewer called the film "a run of De Mille picture" by the "professor demeritus of history . . . ."[14] The film was not, to be sure, one of De Mille's finest efforts, and Saxon, whom *The Times-Picayune* noted "gets credit" for the picture, was possibly the recipient of the proverbial dubious honor in 1938.[15]

Although Saxon complimented the film publicly, he criticized and ridiculed it privately and did not make a great deal of money from the movie.[16] What the author received beyond the "credit" for *The Buccaneer* evidently amounted to about three thousand dollars, a sum mentioned by several of Saxon's friends with whom I spoke. Although this was certainly a substantial sum, the movie was budgeted at "more than 1,000,000" and, according to one film historian, made "a handsome profit."[17] Muriel Saxon Lambert recalled that her cousin felt that he did not receive a fair financial deal from Paramount. Francois Mignon got this impression from the author also but added that Saxon would never have given a negative public reaction to the film, since he was not in the least vindictive.

At any rate, when *The Buccaneer* appeared, Saxon was surely far too busy with the W.P.A. work to try to resolve any unsatisfactory arrangements with Paramount—even if he wished to do so. Less than two months after Frederic March and Akim Tamiroff saved New Orleans on the screen at the old Saenger theater, the *New Orleans City Guide* was at the bookstores.[18] This guidebook consists of three sections: one dealing with the historical background of New Orleans, one with the economic and social development of the city, and, the longest, with the various tours by which the city can be viewed.

Certain subjects in the book were quite probably included or emphasized because of Saxon's influence. A brief "Plantation Tour" of old Louisiana homes (371-78), a chapter on the street names in New Orleans (403-04), and an extended treatment of the Lalaurie mansion (249-50) all reflect favorite topics with which the editor had concerned himself in his own books. None of these topics, however, is as fully or as interestingly treated as in the Century volumes. Although much of the same territory is covered in the historical section of this book as is found in *Fabulous New Orleans*, Saxon's style and the personality of the earlier book, understandably enough, are not present. The *New Orleans City Guide* is indeed a production of a group, and little about the book is individualized. Much of the original W.P.A. volume is by now quite an anachronism as well. Once-practical references to where the visitor might see the New Orleans Pelicans play baseball or to the fact that a tourist's meal at Antoine's restaurant might cost as much as $3.50 are now quaint but hardly useful.

During the first few years after its original publication, however, the Saxon-edited *New Orleans City Guide* was indeed useful to many and was quite well received critically. Like all the W.P.A. guidebooks, it was a tourist's delight. Edna Ferber borrowed Saxon's copy of the book and used it to provide much of the New Orleans background for *Saratoga Trunk*.[19] Judging by the glowing comments in some of the reviews, Ferber would have needed little else to create the genuine atmosphere of the old city.[20] The *New Orleans City Guide*, Edward Tinker wrote in *The New York Times*, "is a colorful jambalaya of fact, folklore, tradition . . . ." The volume was also described as "a faithful guide for the stranger in New Orleans." Many of the local guidebooks were reviewed together, and Jerre Mangione, historian of the Federal Writers' Project, recalls that the New Orleans volume was praised highly in a Washington newspaper, which panned the Philadelphia guidebook on the same review page. Mangione calls the *New Orleans City Guide* "one of the literary gems in the American Guide Series . . . ."

During the year in which this first volume from the Louisiana W.P.A. project was published, Saxon's individual writing efforts continued to decline.[21] Early in 1938 he wrote various articles about Mardi Gras for *The Times-Picayune.* A prefatory verse by Saxon appeared in his friend Olive Leonhardt's thin volume of drawings, *New Orleans Drawn and Quartered,* and a brief pamphlet sketching the life of novelist Gwen Bristow was published at this time also. Only one featured *Times-Picayune* article by Saxon appeared in 1938, a rebuttal of J. B. Priestley's adverse comments about New Orleans. The author's only other published work unrelated to the project that year was a very brief piece about one of the quaint streets in the Vieux Carré.

Despite the steady decline of his own literary activity and the ever-increasing workload with the project, Saxon maintained many friendships with the literati of New Orleans in the 1930s. He reestablished his relationships with old friends from the 1920s and made many new contacts—often through the W.P.A. work. He aided Stark Young, an acquaintance of many years, in his plans for a book set in East Feliciana parish and was the dedicatee of Young's volume.[22] In addition to the above-mentioned encounters with Edna Ferber and with J. B. Priestley, Saxon became acquainted, essentially because of his work on the project, with two Tennessee writers at this time. T. S. Stribling, who wrote Saxon expressing admiration for *Children of Strangers,* came to New Orleans and addressed the staff of the Writers' Project in 1937; Harry Harrison Kroll visited Saxon during the 1930s also. Kroll's purpose, according to one who witnessed the encounter between Saxon and Kroll, was to pump his host for information about New Orleans voodoo in preparation for a book he was planning dealing with the subject. Saxon did not like Kroll's manner, however, and would change the subject; he provided little information about voodoo for the Tennessee novelist.[23] Thomas Wolfe visited New Orleans in January 1937, and on this trip encountered Saxon in the Vieux Carré.[24] Katy and John Dos Passos also visited the French Quarter at this time and evidently spent a great deal of time with Saxon. In 1938 Katy Dos Passos wrote Saxon acknowledging that he was largely responsible for the good times she and "Dos" had on a recent trip to New Orleans.[25]

Throughout the 1930s and early '40s, Saxon's friendship with Roark and Mary Rose Bradford deepened. Richard Bradford recalls several boyhood memories of this friendship. He writes that his parents used to feed Saxon dinner almost nightly and that he would look forward to these visits from his "Uncle Sack."[26] He reveals further regarding his parents' and his own good friend:

> Thinking back on it, I would guess that he was six feet one or two and somewhere between 240 and 260 pounds. He had the most perfect New Orleans accent I ever heard—soft, Southern, crisp, and comprehensible and easy on the ears. Not a mushmouthed Delta accent, but the best kind of Southern way of speaking.
>
> Lyle had also the most exquisite manners of any person I have ever known. No matter how young, or stupid, or boring, or banal you might be, he listened with a sort of gracious intensity and made you feel smart and witty.

Each Christmas Roark Bradford and Saxon composed a sacrilegious musical comedy, and "Uncle Sack," Richard Bradford further recalls, painted "primitive oils," also sacrilegious, of ludicrous madonna-and-child scenes. The Bradfords usually gave Saxon a birthday party. For his fiftieth birthday, they threw an elaborate party in their French Quarter home and gave Saxon one-half of a century plant. Tess Crager recalled to me the very active social life at the Bradfords' home and noted that Lyle was almost invariably present for the fun.

When he first returned to New Orleans, Saxon had not lived in the heart of the Vieux Carré as he had during his *Times-Picayune* days. He soon began to make plans, however, to acquire another home in the Quarter. With the money he received from *The Buccaneer*, he purchased a large house at 534 Madison Street in 1937. His plans were to restore the home, as he had the two on Royal Street in the 1920s, and retire there. The house, with its elaborate courtyard, was, according to Saxon "so peaceful and quiet . . . [that] I wanted to stay on, with Joe [Gilmore] to take care of me, and dream the rest of my life away, while I listened to the chiming of the Cathedral clock" (*FJG* 16). The house that he had bought, as Dreyer writes "to keep him in his old age," however, did nothing but "ruin his middle years."[27] Not only did Saxon pour enormous amounts of money into the restoration project, but his health failed in the late 1930s; and the W.P.A. duties became increasingly demanding of his time. Instead of moving permanently to the Madison Street home, he continued to reside in his suite at the St. Charles Hotel, near his office, and eventually sold this French Quarter property in 1945.

The beginning of the steady decline in Saxon's health came in 1938, just when he was first planning to move all his furniture from the hotel to Madison Street. While writing some articles related to Mardi Gras for *The Times-Picayune*, his appendix ruptured, and he was hospitalized. Complications arose after the surgery, however; for Saxon's appendix, according to Edward Dreyer, "was larger than any appendix previously uncovered in all of south Louisiana and it got into places in his anatomy where no Louisiana appendix had ever ventured before."[28] Richard Bradford, then aged seven, had an appendectomy at this same time. He recalled his own two-inch scar looking quite unimpressive compared to Saxon's "eighteen-inch exploratory masterpiece."[29] Uncle Sack's appendix, Bradford writes, was "wrapped around his spleen or his inner ear, or some place."

Saxon's medical problems at the time actually became quite serious, however. Pneumonia set in after the lengthy surgery to remove the appendix, and his doctor indicated that his recovery would be slow and tedious. Saxon continued to have problems for months afterwards. Several of his friends became understandably worried. Sherwood Anderson wrote a note expressing his concern, as did Hamilton Basso, who had heard in Washington of Saxon's serious illnesses.[30] Saxon himself wrote Cammie Henry after he had been in the hospital for over three weeks: "All of this has been like a long nightmare—now nearly over. It's been too painful and bad to talk about . . . . I'm still not quite sure that I haven't made a mistake in trying to recover."[31] His remark to Henry may seem lighthearted in this letter, but after many months of complications and relapses, this passage in his 1939 diary seems less than comic: "Left hospital after pneumonia, etc. Back at St. Charles. 'It would have been better and cheaper to have died,' Dreyer said laughing. It is quite true nevertheless."[32]

Evidently Saxon either never fully recovered from this series of maladies, or the effects of the malignancy that would eventually kill him had begun by 1939 or '40. One of his friends recalled at Saxon's death that he was "never well" after the extended hospitalization in March of 1939.[33]

This was also about the time he began to drink quite heavily. By the time Saxon died, Richard Bradford recalls his mother saying, the author was "a fifth-a-day man."[34] In 1939 Saxon's literary production declined to almost nothing, to less than he had written probably since his first newspaper job in about 1912. Except for the publication of his short story "Cane River" in a regional anthology, Saxon's literary output during almost a three-year period consisted of two articles in the *Jefferson Parish Yearly Review*.[35] There in 1939 he wrote a piece dealing with the historical background of the parish, and the next year he wrote an article on the elderly residents of Barataria.

After the decline in Saxon's health, he surely knew fewer and fewer happy times in the "fabulous" city. One incident from mid-1939 serves as a poignant footnote here and as an indication of the emptiness and loneliness that probably characterized Saxon's late years. Apparently in the summer of 1939, Hugh Saxon had visited New Orleans from California. Well aware of his famous son's rejection and denial, he made no attempt at reconciliation or even contact; yet he saw his son one day in the city. Hugh Saxon wrote his son afterwards: "I stood beside you upstairs in Holmes Dry Goods Store right after luncheon. I gave you the up-and-down and moved on."[36]

Lyle Saxon's failing health, depression, or increasing dependence on alcohol are surely reasons enough for a hiatus in his literary life, but during this same period his work at the W.P.A. office was building to a peak. Saxon's staff, like those in almost every other state, was behind schedule on the next guidebook. In fact, only five of the forty-eight states met the first Congressional deadline. In 1938 the W.P.A. administrators in Washington had begun appointing regional directors in an effort to accelerate the work on these lagging state guides, and Saxon became supervisor of the work in Arkansas, Mississippi, Oklahoma, and Texas, as well as in Louisiana. With these added responsibilities, it is not surprising that the Louisiana guidebook was one of the last ones published in the series.

The W.P.A. volumes, such as the one Saxon and his co-workers labored over from about 1938 to 1941, are quite interesting even now. The several state guidebooks still in print make for stimulating reading a half century or so after their completions. Although the origin of the guidebooks has been linked to Baedeker, the W.P.A. state guides, as Alfred Kazin aptly notes, "became something more than a super-Baedeker . . . ."[37] The books have had their champions over the years, and Kazin feels that they are surveys that are "anything but mechanical," constituting "an extraordinary contemporary epic."

Louisiana: A Guide to the State appeared in March, 1941. The Saxon-edited volume consists of three major sections: "Louisiana: Past and Present," "Cities and Towns," and "Tours," the most lengthy section. This was the general format followed in the other books of the series. As in the case of the *New Orleans City Guide*, much of the volume is humorously outdated now. The wealth of historical data, nevertheless, is quite valuable, and the wider scope of this statewide survey yields more still-useful material than the local guidebook. The tone of *Louisiana* is informal, the voice friendly, despite the continually informative nature of the book. "If you will look at a map," the volume begins, "you will see that Louisiana resembles a boot . . . ."[38] The book is packed with Louisiana facts and legends, from this amicable beginning to the invaluable glossary of Louisiana terms at the end (685-92). There readers find fascinating explanations of words curious tourists might hear throughout the state: from *allée* to *zombie*.

Louisiana is one of the longest of the W.P.A. guidebooks, numbering 746 pages, and was immediately hailed as one of the finest in the series.[39] "I am not a guidebook man," one reviewer admitted, but added that the Louisiana guide "deserves all kinds of praise." The *Herald Tribune* reviewer, Gilbert Govan, cited errors in the Georgia, Alabama, and South Carolina state guides, but, when he turned his attention to *Louisiana*, confessed: ". . . not every state was fortunate enough to have a Lyle Saxon, whose editorial work has made the Louisiana guide the best I have seen in the whole series." Actually reviews, such as this one, that mention Saxon specifically, upset him considerably. After Carl Carmer was quoted in the *New Orleans Item*, identifying *Louisiana* as "Lyle's . . . book," Saxon promptly replied. After properly thanking Carmer for his praise, he told the *Item* readers that the volume was not at all his book, but that credit was due to the project workers, "who labored long and hard . . . ."[40] Saxon's concern that his staff be appreciated seems quite genuine, and he was surely not being overly magnanimous.

At the same time the work progressed in the W.P.A. office on Canal Street, a related project among black writers was under way at Dillard University. Saxon had organized the Negro History Unit of the Louisiana project in 1935. The purpose of this program was "the collection and utilization of material on the history of the Negro in Louisiana."[41] Understandably in Louisiana in the 1930s, this program was completely separate from the Saxon-directed work on the two guidebooks; but, former W.P.A. worker Caroline Durieux told me that Saxon aided the Dillard group in any way he could. He seems to have been especially proud of this project; he specifically mentioned it in an interview dealing with his W.P.A. accomplishments.[42] One worker on the Dillard project commented at Saxon's death: "He was not only a tolerant and painstaking director, but also an understanding friend to those who worked under him."[43]

Beyond the scope of the W.P.A. work, Saxon encouraged black artists in New Orleans in a variety of ways. He helped found the all-black Les Cenelles Society of Arts and Letters and encouraged the work of a black sculptor. Saxon also aided a group of black poets from New Orleans and was the dedicatee of their initial volume of poetry.[44] He collected, over a long period of years, rare miniatures painted by black slave artists. Saxon very possibly had responded in 1933, moreover, to the appeal of Langston Hughes on behalf of the "Scottsboro nine." In asking for financial help and for a statement of support for a new trial for the nine, Hughes wrote to Saxon: "I know the great sympathy which you have shown for the Negro peoples and the beauty you have given them in your writing. I feel that you would not want these nine Negro boys to die."[45] Octave Lilly, who worked on the Dillard project, told me that Saxon's "whole attitude toward black people" was unquestionably "rather advanced" for the place and time in which he lived.[46]

Lilly's qualifiers are quite proper, of course; for although others among Saxon's friends assessed his feelings toward blacks as "liberal," they too added that this was not at all an attitude that would today be viewed thusly. Richard Bradford aptly summarizes the feelings that Saxon, as well as his father Roark, held about blacks: "He was probably a paternal sort of man when it came to black people. Like my father, he was a man of gentle and loving arrogance."[47] Notwithstanding the arrogance and the patronizing in Saxon, an unusual sensitivity and affection were characteristic of his feelings for blacks as well; his failure to show affection or support more fully than he did was probably because of the times, not Saxon. Almost forty years since the W.P.A. project, Octave Lilly remembered how embarrassed and saddened Saxon was one day when he was not allowed to have some of the black workers visit him at the St. Charles Hotel.

As the W.P.A. projects at Dillard and on Canal Street continued following the publication of *Louisiana*, Saxon's life in New Orleans gradually became a kind of unquiet desperation. The parties and the social life continued from the partly restored Madison Street house or from the St. Charles suite, with Saxon's valet Joe Gilmore pouring drinks and welcoming guests. Saxon surely knew, however, that the days of the project were numbered after the advent of World War II. Work on the third volume, a folklore book, was by then in full swing, and Saxon's own literary output in the early 1940s was amazingly scant. He published two more articles in the *Jefferson Parish Yearly Review* at this time.[48] The first is a rehash of some tours readers might take in the parish, and the other is a piece about the moss that covers Louisiana's trees. Another long period, two years, thus passed with the director of dozens of writers turning out nothing of note himself.

In December of 1942 the New Orleans office of the Federal Writers' Project closed. Most of the others around America shut down at about the same time. Catherine B. Dillon worked with Saxon on the Louisiana project, and, shortly after his death, she described the scene in the Canal Street office the day the project closed. Dillon writes of lingering to talk with Saxon and of leaving the office when Joe Gilmore came to pick up his employer:

> . . . I left now that he had something [Joe] to divert his mind from the solemnity of the last of a seven year period in his life. As I glanced back from the doorway at Lyle's great figure and the small black man beside him, there was a tenseness about the scene, and there came a feeling of fear and futility that printed a picture on my mind—Lyle Saxon, alone except for Joe Gilmore.[49]

When the national project was officially discontinued in Washington early in 1943, Saxon, one of only four state directors who had been with the program since the beginning, was summoned to "preside over the funeral arrangements."[50] Specifically, he supervised the skeleton staff that composed the official report of the accomplishments of the project. Saxon's task in Washington was not so much a distinguished honor, however, as it was a distasteful job. That he was not exactly looking forward to it and was really rather desperate is obvious since Saxon, even with his distaste for the military, had attempted to enlist in both the army and the navy beforehand. "He despised statistics," Dillon writes, and Saxon himself later confessed that the W.P.A. Washington assignment made him "miserable."[51] The group writing the obituary for the lame-duck project nicknamed themselves "The Remainders." In what one historian depicts as a grim atmosphere, they went about their business: answering letters that begged the W.P.A. not to close the project, and composing the statistical story of the past seven years.[52] Surely there was little cheerful about what Saxon and the other "Remainders" did in 1943. When their jobs were done, they held a cocktail party in the office, and someone suggested that they always remember that "once upon a time the United States Government had actually hired writers to be writers."[53]

When Saxon left Washington in the spring of 1943, he did so gladly; "I'll say goodbye to this fine place with no regrets," he wrote to Cammie Henry.[54] The future, however, was not bright. Now evidently never quite well anymore, drinking very heavily, and financially strained because of the Madison Street restoration and medical bills, Lyle Saxon was unemployed again. Glad as he was to finish the "funeral arrangements" in Washington, he wrote in the same letter to Henry: "I'll have no worries now except where Maude and Lizzie's next meal is coming from." The well-being of his Baton Rouge aunts was now his responsibility, and he was suddenly without an income or without any good prospects for new work. He had given eight years of his life to the Federal Writers' Project, had written no new fiction himself in this period, and had even ended up as financially insecure as he had been in 1935. In the midst of the war, with none of his Century volumes "in stock" because of the paper shortages, Saxon was forced to begin job hunting at the age of fifty-one.

The paradox of Saxon's involvement with the W.P.A. project is that while it was his salvation, it was as much his ruination. Although he always seemed to spend and give away about as much as he made, he did obtain some financial security in his job as state director. He also managed to harness himself and, not long after the W.P.A. work began, finish his novel. As the W.P.A. workload increased, however, his own literary aspirations went unfulfilled, and his own writing activity all but ceased. Cammie Henry and many other friends had advised him not to take the W.P.A. position in 1935 for fear that his personal literary career would be curtailed. Francois Mignon records Henry's argument that someone less talented as a writer could assume the essentially administrative and editorial position in New Orleans while Saxon could remain at Melrose and write more fiction.[55] Saxon had felt, however, that he had a duty to his state to accept this job he thought he could fill well. In all likelihood he would have written some additional fiction at Melrose during all those years. Within the context of the Writers' Project, by contrast, "the individual was subordinated to the group, and the creative concept to that of the socially useful."[56]

It seems fitting to note here that Saxon's patroness was not merely flattering him when she argued that his writing career was just beginning on the incline, for the author missed out on numerous literary opportunities in the early days of the project. Soon after the appearance of *Children of Strangers*, for example, Saxon received a bona fide offer to have the book dramatized, but he was never able to pursue this possibility.[57] Mignon writes that De Mille even talked with Saxon about filming the novel.[58] Saxon wrote T. S. Stribling a month after *Children of Strangers* was published saying that he had been so overwhelmed with the work of the project that he had not even been able "to enjoy the good things that people have done" regarding the novel.[59] Obviously he was likewise unable to take advantage of the good things that could have grown out of the publication of his book.

Many other opportunities were lost very probably because of the W.P.A. work. Malcolm Cowley solicited a long article for *The New Republic* about Louisiana local color and flattered Saxon with the statement that "there is nobody in the whole United States who is better qualified to undertake this job."[60] In the same letter Cowley says he is waiting for Saxon's review of a book by Caroline Gordon. Neither article nor review ever appeared. Other offers included an invitation to write about Molly Glass in a journal published by Thurber, Benchley, and Heywood Broun and to do an article on Louisiana writers for *The Saturday Review*.[61] Saxon accepted the former offer, but the editors who wanted the Molly Glass story were "still waiting" a month after Saxon promised the manuscript.[62] This article would surely have been a natural for Saxon, the raconteur capable of burlesque and rollicking good humor like that of the early sections of *Old Louisiana*. The *Saturday Review* article on Louisiana writers was never written by Saxon either and was evidently later given to Arlin Turner.[63] F. Meredith Dietz wrote Saxon explaining the revival of the *Southern Literary Messenger* and asking for stories or articles, and Saxon missed out on an opportunity himself to revive "The Centaur Plays Croquet."[64]

Although most of the author's lost opportunities came during and shortly after the publication of *Children of Strangers*, many possibilities to further his career came much later during the W.P.A. work. In 1940

Coronet solicited fiction from him and explained that although "our top price always has been \$100," the editors would pay Saxon more.[65] A representative with Doubleday was "more than anxious" in inviting Saxon to contribute a Christmas story set in New Orleans for a 1942 anthology.[66] Tess Crager recalled, moreover, that during the days when the state guidebook was in progress, Saxon used to think of plots for new fiction, novels, and short stories, but that he would suggest them to other writers who had the time and the strength to write them. The greatest disappointment for Saxon during these W.P.A. years must surely have been the gradual realization that his first novel was going to be his last. He had already "mapped out" the plot of a second novel by August of 1937.[67] A few months later, however, he confessed:

> If I have enough energy, I may begin another novel before that time [June 1938], but I doubt it. I have an idea for a novel of present-day New Orleans, and my publishers are urging me to write it, but whether I can write it—and work at my present job at the same time—is problematical.[68]

As the years passed, Saxon continued to mention his proposed novel, even calling it "Uneasy Blood" in one interview;[69] but, of course, the book was never done, and no fragments survive.

In his early days with the project, while working on the *New Orleans City Guide*, Saxon wrote to a friend: "You don't know how I miss Melrose. It seems a shame that I got my cabin all fixed up with all my books in place and everything the way I wanted it and then I got this job and had to leave it."[70] Of course Saxon had had his problems composing at Melrose, but when *Children of Strangers* was completed everything indeed was the way he had wanted it. If the Cane River country could have inspired more fiction, "it seems a shame" indeed—in a sense Saxon did not fully realize at the time—that he had to leave his private cabin to begin his work with the Writers' Project. Through the depression and during the war, then, Lyle Saxon, like so many others, served his country at considerable—even irreparable—personal expense.

Saxon's almost frantic attempts to find work after his final W.P.A. Washington assignment thus emerge as terribly ironic in light of the numerous missed opportunities of the previous years. Whereas in the late 1930s and early '40s, he had to ignore and refuse offers, by 1943 the offers had ceased and he simply could not find a job for several months. He applied for work with *Fortune* magazine in New York, and, although he felt confident he would get a position there, he was finally told nothing was available for him.[71] He also wrote to the Office of War Information seeking work. His letter shows all too clearly his desperation:

> May I have a reply as soon as possible? My ticket is bought for a return to New Orleans on June 24th, but how gladly I would turn it back if there is a chance of doing a useful job. I am unmarried and am willing to go anywhere. I know something of personnel work and executive work as well as writing and editing. I will be glad to come up for an interview if you hold out any hope.[72]

Although Saxon had confided to Cammie Henry, in a letter of only three days earlier, that he was eager to leave Washington "with no regrets," "how gladly" he would have remained there or gone anywhere else for "any hope" of work.

One letter Saxon wrote in the desperate days of mid-1943 paid off, however. Before the year's end he acquired work with the Louisiana state government. He had written the wife of Governor Sam Jones, offering his services as a state historian. Saxon explains in this letter that he could somehow employ the unused Louisiana material gathered by his W.P.A. workers to write new volumes on the history and folklore of the state.[73] Saxon confides to Mrs. Jones that he has failed a physical examination to try to get into the armed services, that although he could get a job in New York he would much rather "come home" and continue writing about Louisiana, and that his request of her is "not a request for a soft State job . . . ." Whether through the influence of the governor's wife or not, Saxon was given a position with the Louisiana State Library Commission, was able to reemploy many of his W.P.A. workers, and was given free reign to make a book of the remaining data gathered during the project.

The connection with the library commission was probably formalized late in 1943. *Gumbo Ya-Ya*, the volume which would eventually grow out of this work, did not appear, however, until December of 1945—largely because of printing delays due to the paper shortages. As before with the W.P.A., Saxon's individual literary production was practically stymied during the preparation of the folklore book. In 1943 he wrote one article, the next year he published nothing, and in 1945 "Fame" was reprinted in a new magazine.[74] Saxon's failure to write this time, though, was probably due less to his workload than to his poor health. One of his friends recalls in an article that his health was so bad during the work on *Gumbo Ya-Ya* that "he was usually too ill to do even the little that was required of him . . . ."[75]

The idea for a book on Louisiana folklore had come in 1936 from Henry G. Alsberg, then national director of the Federal Writers' Project. Houghton Mifflin, the publishers, had expressed an interest in the volume as early as 1937. The material relating to Louisiana folklore, gathered "at every possible opportunity" from 1936 until 1943, was assembled, rewritten, and edited by a staff headed by Saxon, Edward Dreyer, and Robert Tallant, and sponsored by the Louisiana Library Commission. Thus while *Gumbo Ya-Ya* is not really a Federal Writers' Project volume, the fieldworkers and the personnel editing the book were all former W.P.A. employees, and the genesis of the book was within the context of the project itself. Saxon once called *Gumbo Ya-Ya* a "final W.P.A. fling . . . ."[76]

Exactly how much of *Gumbo Ya-Ya* Saxon wrote is impossible to determine. Most of the raw material from which the book was compiled is now at Northwestern State University of Louisiana. Many individual file folders originally bore individuals' names, indicating the fieldworker and/or editor of the material therein. Saxon's name is seldom present, and, judging by this criterion alone, Robert Tallant seems to have done the bulk of the writing.[77] The material at Northwestern State University related to *Gumbo Ya-Ya* is voluminous, and what Saxon, Dreyer, and Tallant received from the field workers must have literally inundated them. Saxon had colorfully described their struggles with the sheer bulk of the materials in a letter written during the work on the state guidebook: "Dreyer and I are knee deep in folklore at the moment; editing like beavers building a dam, working with claw and tooth."[78]

I doubt that Saxon joked very often about the arduous job of editing the *Gumbo Ya-Ya* material. At times his failing health prevented his doing any work at all on the project. In a letter of February 1944 to Houghton Mifflin, signed by all three *Gumbo Ya-Ya* editors, reference is made to the fact that Saxon had been ill "for six months."[79] In this same letter Saxon, surely recalling the reviews of the guidebooks that lauded him as an individual, insists that when this book is published all three editors be given equal credit.

Suffice it to say that the subject matter in *Gumbo Ya-Ya* is in keeping with the things Saxon had written about in his Century volumes and that, whoever the writer of a particular chapter happened to be, the volume is "typical" of Saxon. "Gumbo Ya-Ya" is a "Cajun" term for "everybody talks at once" and, in essence, everybody does just this throughout the book. This hodgepodge of Louisiana folklore, replete with the superstitions Saxon found fascinating (525-58), is in large part made up of quotations and summaries of the words of the colorful characters encountered by the fieldworkers. The editors were neither very reticent nor very selective; readers meet all sorts of Louisiana characters—from a woman on Perdido Street who will "do it for twenty cents" to Mother Catherine, who "healed an' blessed," presumably for free (1, 210). The book skips all over the state in its effort to record and preserve the folk beliefs of the people. It often seems unorganized, but hardly ever uninteresting.

Reviews of the Saxon-Dreyer-Tallant volume were basically laudatory.[80] Arna Bontemps said the book makes "the liveliest kind of reading" and that Lyle Saxon has never been associated with a dull book. *Gumbo Ya-Ya* was described in *The Saturday Review* as "big, rich, juicy . . . amiable and good natured . . . ." Eudora Welty, who reviewed the volume in *The New York Times*, was aware of where the editors got their material and called the book "a dish made of left-overs . . . ." Welty admitted, however, that like many leftover dishes, *Gumbo Ya-Ya* "has the luck to be seasoned highly enough to get by." The volume got by quite well actually and was a success for Houghton Mifflin; four printings soon sold nineteen thousand copies. It was reissued in 1988 by Pelican Publishing Company.

While Saxon worked with the Louisiana Library Commission, his social life in New Orleans continued to be quite active—albeit not by the standard of his earlier French Quarter days. As he had presided over a kind of salon from his Royal Street house twenty years earlier, Saxon became the social director for New Orleans literati from his suite on the fifth floor of the St. Charles Hotel. He called this suite "a labyrinth with fourteen doors."[81] The apartment was furnished lavishly with antique pieces and decorated with Mexican sculpture, given by William Spratling, and several paintings. One of the paintings was of a group of centaurs, and another was an unusual portrait of Cupid. When John Dos Passos saw this latter painting, he is reported to have said: "My God! Is that a portrait of Lyle's appendix?"[82] In *The New York Herald Tribune* in 1944, Lucius Beebe called Saxon, whom he had recently visited at the St. Charles, the "official patriarch" of New Orleans.[83]

During the last few years at the hotel, the New Orleans "patriarch" established a friendship with John Steinbeck and Gwyndolen Conger, who was to become Steinbeck's second wife. Upon leaving New Orleans after one visit, Steinbeck wrote Saxon a farewell note in which he said that "we," evidently he and Conger, "more than like you" and that "you are bigger than your myth and that is a rare thing."[84] A little over a year later, when Steinbeck was divorced from his first wife, he and Gwyn Conger married in the courtyard of Saxon's Madison Street home. Gwyn wrote a note to Saxon on the first anniversary of her marriage. In it she tells her friend of the pleasant memories brought to her mind as she looks at her "wedding 'document' and the collection of nervous and drunken signatures . . . your's amongst them."[85] John Steinbeck called his New Orleans wedding a "good and noisy" affair where the guests "cried and laughed and shouted and got drunk. Oh! It was a fine wedding."[86]

Visitors to Saxon at the St. Charles Hotel at this time were indeed numerous. Dorothy Parker came, and her reputation had so preceded her that when she left, Joe Gilmore expressed disappointment to his employer that she had not said anything unpleasant to Saxon.[87] The honorable Judith Hyams Douglas, the first woman admitted to the Louisiana bar, was a neighbor down the hall in the hotel and a frequent visitor. Saxon also probably first met Sinclair Lewis at the St. Charles, for Lewis stayed there in October of 1939. Elizabeth Kell, Saxon's longtime friend and employee of *The Times-Picayune*, told me that Saxon once called her to come to his suite; he had arranged for her to interview Lewis, quite a scoop for a young reporter. Actually almost anyone could turn up at Saxon's apartment during these years. Robert Tallant writes in his "Salute to Saxon":

> A typical gathering might include an internationally known author, a complete stranger who knew Lyle Saxon only by name but had come to borrow five dollars, perhaps a cowboy movie star and a colored former hotel waiter. All met in Lyle Saxon's rooms on a perfectly equal plane.[88]

Tallant goes on to point out an undeniable fact about Saxon's ostensibly hilarious party life of the 1940s; despite the crowds who surrounded him and in the midst of all the hilarity, he was essentially a lonely man. By 1945 he was also a desperately ill man. The last time Elizabeth Kell saw

Saxon at the St. Charles, shortly before his death, she remembered him as extremely ill and in great pain. Saxon was surely aware that he was in a serious condition and that there would be no blissful retirement on Madison Street. Writing shortly after his last piece of Vieux Carré property was sold, he implied that those who live in the St. Charles have no place else to go; "We stay until we die. It is a sort of joke" (*FJG* 76).

It was in this kind of mood and yet in the party atmosphere of the final St. Charles days that Saxon dictated what became *The Friends of Joe Gilmore*. As early as 1943 Saxon's publishers had asked him about writing his memoirs. He apparently began this project the next year, after the work on *Gumbo Ya-Ya* was completed. The idea he hit upon was to write autobiography indirectly, by recording Joe Gilmore's impressions of the "friends" who had wandered in and out of the St. Charles suite and in and out of Saxon's life. The book is only as much about Joe as Gertrude Stein's is about Alice B. Toklas. Robert Tallant recalled in 1948 that Saxon would dictate his reminiscences and "Joe's" impressions to a secretary, often during a party, with Saxon "prone upon his magnificent bed."[89] This last book was unfinished at Saxon's death, and it was largely through the efforts of Edward Dreyer that the slim amount completed was published in 1948.[90]

Despite the abortive nature of *The Friends of Joe Gilmore*, Joe Gilmore himself emerges as a memorable personality. Gilmore was hired in 1935, the same day Saxon reported to his New Orleans W.P.A. office for the first time. His "first act" as Saxon's employee was to give the author a massage for his neuritis (*FJG* 3). Gilmore's "pretty, pleasant, black, and fat" wife was soon hired as Saxon's cook, and Joe became "major-domo, valet, butler, and yardman" (*FJG* 6). Richard Bradford remarks that Gilmore "kept the apartment and Lyle together."[91] Joe also became barman for the St. Charles parties, ordering the workers under him with such gusto that they called him "Black Saxon" (*FJG* 6).

Although essentially autobiographical, *The Friends of Joe Gilmore* is of little value in reconstructing the facts of Saxon's life; too much important information is lacking. The incidents that are related, moreover, are not very well documented. The book is permeated by rambling "tales" of Gilmore and Saxon's friends and contains very few specific dates and places. Most of *The Friends of Joe Gilmore* is set during the years in which Gilmore and Saxon were together, with flashbacks to earlier days—usually triggered by an account of one of the friends.

At times Saxon's last book is reminiscent of the whimsical parts of
Old Louisiana. The author recounts, for example, the enjoyable story of
Bessie, who "died dry." This tale, told several years before to Gilmore and
Saxon by an elderly woman, involves "a proud family" and the problems
that grow out of the leaking roof on their plantation home. Bessie's son,
Culpepper, orders shingles to fix the leak, which drops the rain on his
mother's bed. An impertinent neighbor, however, sees the pile of shingles
and implies that the family has fallen on hard times. This is a blow to
Culpepper's pride, and he never has the leak repaired. The months pass,
the rains fall on Bessie in bed, pneumonia sets in, and Bessie becomes
critically ill. Although too late, a nurse procures a fruit peddler's umbrella
and places it over the lady right before the end, so the "one comfort" is that
"Bessie died dry" (109). In a similar tone Saxon relates the story of when
the Vieux Carré painter Alberta Kinsey visited the Cane River country and,
"waving her diminishing glass," saw compositions everywhere (57).
Saxon writes that on one visit Kinsey, with palate, smock, and diminishing
glass, was busily preparing to paint a picture of a Cane River church. The
artist was almost taken to the nearby mental asylum as an escaped patient,
however; for all she had told the passersby, Saxon explains, was that she
intended to "paint the church" (63). They saw no ladders, brushes, or
buckets and knew that the asylum paid ten dollars for returning runaway
patients, one of whom she surely seemed to be. Kinsey was rescued by
Saxon and Gilmore.

Other parts of *The Friends of Joe Gilmore* seem well done for the
sentiments they evoke. The passages, for example, in which the author
somewhat wistfully recalls "nearly perfect" evenings at the various homes
he and Edward Suydam visited during the work on *Old Louisiana* make for
pleasant reading. Saxon may be merely remembering the way he wishes it
was, but his nostalgic treatment of so many lost days that were "pleasant
and easy" is often winsome. The final chapter of the book, the account of
the time when Joe Gilmore left Saxon's employment for a brief stint as a
Pullman porter, is moving. Notwithstanding the obviously patronizing
attitude of Saxon toward Gilmore, the scene of the reunion of the two is
well done and admirably restrained. Saxon recalls lying on his bed at the
St. Charles, "miserably sick," hearing a knock on his door, and, upon
opening it, encountering "Joe Gilmore—my friend . . ." (112). Gilmore
explains that he has returned because of the abuses he suffered and the
names he had been called by the white passengers on the trains; " ' . . . you

never called me names like that, Mr. Saxon' " (112). At this point readers infer who is foremost among the friends of Joe Gilmore.

Saxon's posthumous volume received limited attention from critics.[92] In a brief review *The New Yorker* called the book "a sympathetic and lively memoir," but added, quite accurately, that most of the stories are of "local reference." Hodding Carter called the book "a rarity and a delight" and pointed out that readers could imagine Saxon telling the tales therein with "a glass in his hand and his head thrown back laughing." This appraisal assumes, however, that readers had previously seen such a picture in life; very few, of course, had actually heard Saxon spin such tales, and the book did not sell well.[93] The reviewer in the Baton Rouge *State-Times* remarked that reading the book is like having Saxon back "vibrantly with us anew" and wrongly predicted that the "rollicking wit" of *The Friends of Joe Gilmore* will cause it to be widely read.

The description of the book as "rollicking" does not seem accurate. Catherine Dillon recalls that Saxon wrestled with his manuscript and that, although the volume was intended to be whimsical, the critically ill author was usually in no mood to be whimsical.[94] Many of the jokes in *The Friends of Joe Gilmore* do indeed fall flat; the punch lines lack punch, and readers are often left not laughing, but wondering if they have just missed something funny. Tess Crager told me that Saxon realized the book was inferior to what he would like to have written, but that he simply could do no better under the circumstances. *The Friends of Joe Gilmore* suffers too from a lack of continuity. Although Gilmore turns up from time to time and place to place, he is far from a unifying element; and at times readers may feel that the title character, remembered after a time, is dragged against his will back onto the stage. The book is a hodgepodge of reminiscences— humorous but not uproarious, light but not lighthearted. Occasionally readers of *The Friends of Joe Gilmore* sense that they are in the midst of a wonderful party, like one of the summer's best at the mansion on West Egg. Far more often, though, readers will get the same sobering sensation as when Gatsby's last guest has gone; for this party is almost over, too, and it has been a last desperately hilarious gathering of the friends of Lyle Saxon.

By the end of 1944 Saxon had become very seriously ill from cancer. During the final year-and-a-half of his life, he was constantly in and out of the Baptist Hospital in New Orleans. One friend writes that he lost a great deal of weight, becoming painfully thin and leaning heavily on a cane.[95] All this time he evidently grew increasingly aware that death was imminent, and, although he was not told until quite late that he suffered from cancer of the bladder, he held at no time any real hope for full recovery.[96] Actually, during one period in October of 1944, Saxon's doctors gave him only a slim chance to live; he recovered this time, but fell gravely ill again the next spring.[97] He had improved somewhat by late 1945 and wrote to Cammie Henry then that he no longer had to sleep with a cane beside his bed.[98] At this time Henry had been quite ill also, and Saxon jokingly told his old friend that they must both get well "so that you and I can make a comeback that will bring confusion to our enemies." He remarked a week later, "I guess that we've both got to keep on living; what a nuisance, but I don't seem to die easy."[99]

Nineteen forty-six began with Saxon evidently in better health than the previous few months. He had even written a little recently. Robert Tallant's *Voodoo in New Orleans* appeared with a brief foreword by Saxon, and, as usual, Mardi Gras occasioned a few words from Saxon in *The Times-Picayune*.[100] He was well enough during the carnival to sit on a balcony and broadcast the Rex parade nationally over the Mutual radio network.

As he often had done in years past, Saxon decided to go to Melrose for a rest after Mardi Gras. On February 24, 1946, he wrote Cammie Henry to tell her of his plans to visit. A few days later Saxon, Robert Tallant, and Joe Gilmore set out for Melrose. When they reached Baton Rouge, however, Saxon began hemorrhaging, and they quickly returned to the Baptist Hospital in New Orleans. Francois Mignon told me of the two telephone calls he received at Melrose that day; both were from Joe Gilmore—one to announce the departure for the plantation, and the other to tell what had happened to Saxon. Robert Tallant later told Cammie Henry that in a very real sense Saxon was on the way home in March 1946; this is what Melrose had come to mean to him.[101]

His final hospitalization in New Orleans lasted a little over a month. Following a desperate operation in early April, Saxon's condition worsened, and pneumonia developed. Tess Crager told me that about this time, she and her husband had almost convinced Century to reissue the "eatin' books," which were out of print. The Cragers went to the hospital one night to show Saxon a bundle of letters from booksellers asking for *Fabulous New Orleans* to be reprinted, but he was in a coma. He did not regain consciousness, and at 9:16 P.M. on Tuesday, April 9, 1946, Saxon died.

Outside the room were the Cragers, his cousin Muriel Saxon Lambert, Robert Tallant, and Joe Gilmore. Tallant wrote Cammie Henry a few days later, telling her that although Saxon's breathing was harsh and difficult during the early part of the final day, "the last few hours his breathing became softer. At the end it simply stopped. That was all there was to it."[102]

Funeral arrangements were supervised in New Orleans by Muriel Saxon Lambert, who worked with the two aunts when they arrived from Baton Rouge. Hugh Saxon was not notified of his son's death, Lambert recalled, because her cousin had requested that he not be contacted. Memorial services were held in New Orleans on April 10, and in Baton Rouge the next day. After the Episcopal services at St. James, Saxon was buried in Baton Rouge, in the Magnolia Cemetery.

Understandably enough, numerous eulogies appeared at Saxon's death.[103] In the Baton Rouge newspaper he was remembered as "always considerate and courteous, and professionally generous." *The Times-Picayune* called him "the dean of New Orleans writers" and noted that he was a man whose character was "as clear-cut and unforgettable as his writings." Brief obituary notes about Saxon appeared also in *Time*, *Newsweek*, *The Publishers' Weekly*, and *The Wilson Library Bulletin*.

In another national magazine, what was ostensibly an article on New Orleans in "The Cities of America" series turned out to be more of a memorial to Saxon. George Sessions Perry wrote this *Saturday Evening Post* article, which appeared two months after Saxon's death. In it Perry not only quotes *Fabulous New Orleans* several times, but implicitly identifies the city with Saxon himself. After quoting Saxon's 1919 *Times-Picayune* story about the burning of the French Opera House, with the final line that the "heart of the old French Quarter has stopped beating," Perry says that this statement actually came true only recently—when Saxon died.[104] Ironically, in his one-liner about the loss of the opera house, the climax of his first big *Times-Picayune* story, Lyle Saxon had written his own—and perhaps his best—epitaph.

The comments of Saxon's close friends with whom I have been able to speak reveal a more vivid picture of the writer than even the most sensitive of the published obituaries. Tess Crager told me that she remembered Saxon as an extremely gentle and very generous person. Caroline Durieux, his co-worker on the W.P.A. projects, recalled how agonizingly hard Saxon always tried to help others during those very difficult times.

Francois Mignon described his longtime friend as a delightful raconteur and as a man without arrogance about his achievements, a selfless person; but Mignon remembered too that Saxon's life was one of much personal disappointment and sadness. Several people with whom I talked mentioned that despite Saxon's countless friendships and sexual affairs with many men and women, he never had a really intimate relationship with another person. Muriel Saxon Lambert recalled that he could appear very witty and quite happy, but that he was an essentially lonely man. This whimsical facade seems to be behind the statement that Tallant says Saxon often repeated in his last years: "Don't grieve for me when I die. I've had a wonderful time."[105] This attitude and the rime he once made that there is "no answer to cancer" are surely less genuine than Lambert's memories of one of the last times she saw her cousin alive. Saxon began to weep, she explained, and was grieved deeply that he was going to die before he could meet more people and write more books.

During the final years, while living at the St. Charles, Saxon had become a tourist attraction. At times, guides would actually take groups into the hotel to "show" the author.[106] When tourists first began to seek him out and to gawk at him, Saxon had remarked: "I began as a writer, and I end as a souvenir."[107] Ironically, his words were a prophetic description of the last nine years of his life—a period of sustained literary anticlimax following the appearance of *Children of Strangers*.

Now more than four decades after his death, the city of New Orleans has "officially" forgotten, or failed to remember, Lyle Saxon. As Tess Crager once pointed out to me, whereas streets and parks have been named "after everything and everybody," there is no city memorial to Saxon. His New Orleans years at *The Times-Picayune* and with the Writers' Project, along with his central position among the literati of two different generations who enjoyed his hospitality on Royal Street or at the St. Charles, mark Saxon's best years in the city. By 1946 "Mr. New Orleans" had ended up as a "souvenir" for strangers. Now, in the city where he began as a writer, he is not even that.

CHOICES AND LIMITATIONS

PROFESSOR LEWIS SIMPSON of Louisiana State University has pointed out that Lyle Saxon "had his vogue and then more or less disappeared."[1] At present, the author's work is not at all well known—even in Louisiana. One of his friends I talked with in New Orleans many years ago commented on how depressing the fading of Saxon's reputation has been to those who knew him.[2] This friend, along with almost all whom I have met, admitted that awareness and appreciation of the author had been limited to the older Louisianans, that Saxon's work was known best by Saxon's contemporaries. Academic concern with his works has been very slight—again, even in Louisiana. As Professor Walter L. Mosley of Northwestern State University once said, "It's strange that Saxon has been so ignored by those in his backyard, but he has."[3] As I have mentioned in the earlier chapters, Saxon's attitude toward black characters in *Children of Strangers* and his role in Faulkner's early New Orleans and New York experiences have occasioned discussion in a few recent scholarly studies such as those by Rubin, Grimwood, Blotner, Minter, and Karl.

Saxon has received little attention in the pages of Louisiana newspapers in the years since his death. Occasionally his name will turn up in connection with one of the guidebooks or *Gumbo Ya-Ya*. When I wrote *The Times-Picayune* several years ago asking for information on Saxon, I received only the 1946 obituary and a letter stating that "this is the most complete [information] we have."[4] Saxon's name appeared prominently in the Baton Rouge newspapers early in 1974, however, on the occasion of a memorial service in his honor.[5] The Foundation for Historical Louisiana, headed at the time by Joan Samuel of Baton Rouge, dedicated a new stone at Saxon's grave and invited friends and readers of Saxon to attend. This "tribute of respect" took place on January 27, 1974, and was well attended. Pat Baldridge, *State-Times* reporter who helped plan the service, told me that although the weather was very bad, several people came, some from great distances, to honor the writer.[6] Joan Samuel estimated the crowd to be about seventy persons, but remarked too that almost all were elderly, some quite infirm, a few in wheelchairs.[7] Needless to say, very few who knew Saxon personally are left today.

Despite the fact that Saxon's works are now little known to students of American literature, four of the author's books are still in print. Tess Crager, who acquired the rights to the Century volumes and to *Children of Strangers* before Saxon's death, for several years issued *Fabulous New Orleans*, *Old Louisiana*, *Lafitte the Pirate*, and the novel. All but *Lafitte* have since been issued as paperbacks, along with, most recently, *Gumbo Ya-Ya*. The *New Orleans City Guide* and *Louisiana* have been reprinted by Somerset Publishers, the latter volume having been revised in 1971 by Harry Hansen. In my opinion, however, the volumes still in print, with the exception of the novel and parts of *Old Louisiana*, do not represent Saxon at his best. A miscellany—containing, for example, excerpts of the liveliest parts of all the Century books, some of the best *Times-Picayune* fiction, and the two prizewinning stories "Cane River" and "The Centaur Plays Croquet"—would represent Saxon well and make a creditable volume.

At any rate, whichever of Saxon's works may, or may not, be known to readers in the years to come will surely be from his previously published material; he apparently left no significant unpublished works. A few fragments of stories are in the Saxon Collection at Tulane, and, as I have mentioned, some W.P.A. papers by the author are in the Northwestern State University archives; nothing in either collection, however, would enhance Saxon's stature as a writer of fiction or nonfiction. One reason for his scant unpublished literary remains is surely that he wrote so little during the W.P.A. years. Any unused parts of his novel and of his Century books, moreover, were evidently destroyed; and any significant work he may have done on his second novel is now lost as well. Even an illustrated edition of "The Centaur Plays Croquet," returned several years ago by Hastings House to Saxon's aunts, has now disappeared.[8]

Since much of Saxon's best work, then, has not been resurrected and since nothing significant is still unpublished, he may indeed remain as obscure as he is, known to fewer with each passing year. I am convinced from the facts of his personal and literary life which I have tried to focus on in the previous chapters that this obscurity is unmerited, that Saxon's life and achievements have been unduly neglected. His literary accomplishments were far from insignificant. In the end he surely knew his failures and accomplishments, for he was consistently an astute judge of his own work and was, one friend recalled, a man of unusually good literary taste.[9] He knew when he had done "outrageous" or "florid" work in *The Times-Picayune*, he knew that in many ways *Old Louisiana* was the best of the "eatin' books," he knew that Ada Calander was a lively creation, and he knew finally that *Children of Strangers* was his finest work. He seemed as sure in all such extraordinarily objective views of his own work as he was in his unqualified early praise of *The Sound and the Fury*.

The friends of Lyle Saxon were numerous. Many who knew him and worked with him delighted years later in talking about the author. The number of literary personalities he knew or met is impressive indeed. Over about a quarter of a century, Saxon met scores of well-known writers who visited or lived in New York and New Orleans. Accounts by or about authors more widely known than Saxon—such as books dealing with Wolfe, Steinbeck, or Faulkner—continue to reveal facts about Saxon or his friendships with these writers.

Evidently Saxon was unusually well liked. He was eulogized as a writer "without an enemy."[10] He was considered an ally by the black artists of New Orleans. He was a friend and a source of encouragement to greater and to lesser literary figures. He may well have encouraged Faulkner, but he surely inspired now obscure writers such as Evans Wall as well. Robert Tallant wrote to Cammie Henry in 1946:

> As a writer, I owe him everything. He gave me encouragement, faith and actual help. No matter how badly he felt he would force himself to read what I had done. When I needed it he bawled me out very thoroughly. He would go to any extreme to help me. As a friend he gave himself completely. I am more than grateful that I knew him.[11]

It seems not at all unrealistic to suppose that dozens of writers could have echoed Tallant's sentiments.

At Saxon's death the Baton Rouge *Morning Advocate* obituary pointed out: "New Orleans loved Saxon as much as Saxon loved New Orleans."[12] Exactly how much he loved New Orleans, especially the Vieux Carré, is difficult to overestimate. Likewise hard to exaggerate is the important role Saxon played in the restoration of the structures in the old section of the city. He was also, it should be remembered, among the earliest writers to live in the French Quarter—even before Sherwood Anderson moved to his Pontalba apartment. To contend that the artists' colony in the Vieux Carré in the 1920s would not have evolved if Lyle Saxon had not restored his Royal Street home seems a rash claim indeed. To ignore or underestimate the significance of the young *Times-Picayune* reporter's determination to make the Quarter livable for himself and his friends, however, seems an equally rash omission. Robert Tallant writes of an incident illustrative of his friend's love for the French Quarter. In the 1940s, Tallant explains, Saxon was fond of walking down Royal Street and pointing out a certain vine that, by 1946, covered five houses; Saxon had planted the vine more than twenty-five years before in the courtyard of his first Royal Street home.[13] It would be pointless to attempt a more appropriate symbol of Lyle Saxon's influence on the Vieux Carré.

In light of the relative obscurity of Saxon and of the mammoth reputations of some of his friends from the French Quarter and New York, it is tempting to speculate on what happened to Lyle Saxon. That he admired and/or envied the successes that came to many of these other authors seems a fair assumption. Repeatedly he stated a desire to write fiction himself. After the long-delayed appearance of *Children of Strangers*, however, he wrote no more short stories or novels. Despite the W.P.A. work, Saxon's nine-year drought seems curious—especially since he had once remarked that a person who really wants to write can do so "in spite of the odds, and nothing except a physical calamity can crush him."[14] Of course his life after 1937 was something of a physical calamity, and the W.P.A. work was not all that burdened the critically ill author.

It is entirely conceivable, however, that Lyle Saxon simply lost the desire, the drive, the vitality necessary to attain a higher level of literary excellence. He may have become no longer possessed by that demon Faulkner eloquently associated with creativity, or Saxon may have been overcome by another demon, one he identified once in his diary as "a devil who will not let me write." Saxon once said: "Creation and vitality usually go together."[15] Apparently well before his W.P.A. work and the onset on his many serious illnesses, he had lost the vitality he felt necessary for creativity. Thus while the portrait of this artist sapped of his strength and thus his potential for new creations because of his editing work and his illnesses is an appealing one, it is surely an oversimplified one too. After all, Saxon had terrible problems in composition at Melrose and was, it seems, an essentially lazy person. Many of his friends recalled this aspect of his personality, and the author even described himself once as "lazy."[16] As early as 1930 one writer characterized Saxon as a procrastinator and "a lotus-eater," a seemingly apt indictment.[17] That anyone who had written countless newspaper articles and five books in a decade could be called "lazy" may seem strange indeed; actually "weary" may be a more appropriate word for Saxon in the 1930s. Yet by his own admission in numerous letters, speeches, and diary entries, the Century books and the newspaper work came easy for him, indeed too easy to be really good. It was fiction he found to be "heartbreaking and backbreaking."

So, then, as talented as Saxon was and as wrongfully neglected as he has become, he did not achieve greatness as a creative writer. He wrote adequate "eatin' books," a few excellent short stories, and one very impressive novel. He befriended, aided, entertained, and, in some cases, inspired countless other writers. He once showed tremendous promise himself as a writer of fiction. Perhaps if he had enjoyed better health, or could have freed himself from the many mundane writing and editing tasks he had to perform, or left his newspaper work earlier, he would have become a first-rate literary artist. Perhaps not even then, though. After all, like several of his illustrious friends, he was a lotus-eater, and he was not possessed by Faulkner's demon.

Late in 1925 Saxon wrote a long and extraordinary letter to his friend Noel Straus.[18] Like many of his letters, this one shows a facility of expression, a keen wit, pathos, and a great deal of originality and creativity. In one part of the letter, Saxon relates in considerable detail his meeting a dwarf named Julia, a young woman who cared for the sick in a rural community a few miles from Baton Rouge. He had driven his Aunt Maude, a registered nurse, to Greenwell Springs where she was to aid those stricken in a local diphtheria epidemic. Saxon sets the scene:

> It was a lovely, balmy, sunlit afternoon, with just enough crispness to make the old brown overcoat feel very comfortable . . . . We started about two o'clock, and got to the village just in time to meet a funeral. One of the poor children had died, just strangled to death, before the doctor arrived—and the mother and father were carrying the body to the cemetery in a rough box in order to satisfy the restrictions for speedy burial. There was something supremely tragic in that funeral. Just the

mother and father, poverty-stricken and pinched looking; crying, both of
them, and driving a thin brown horse with its tail full of cockle-burrs.

Saxon and his aunt followed the couple back to their house so that
Maude could examine the other children in the family to try to determine if
any needed to be taken away for treatment. Leaving the burial site, Saxon
describes the countryside:

> We drove for miles, far off of the graveled highway and into a beautiful
> country road, all curves and depressions, and little hills, with tall trees
> beside it, and with great clumps of yupon trees full of crimson berries;
> at intervals there were typical cabins of poor whites, behind old snake
> fences.

When they arrived at the house, Saxon says, "I—coward that I
am—remained outside . . . ." As he waited for Aunt Maude, he writes, he
gazed down the "beautiful curving road," observing "its deep shadows and
streaks of sunshine which turned the berries to a remarkable metallic red and
made them glisten and gleam like some poisonous fruits in a fairy tale."
This was a moment, Saxon writes, when "I had just reached that strange
mental state where nothing seems natural, and everything seems like
something in a dream . . . ." He then heard "a woman's deep voice," and
looking around—then down—for the source of the voice, he saw "a
fantastic little woman, just about a yard high." Julia was standing near
Saxon with her arms raised "in a gesture that I can never describe, but it had
in it all the mockery of all the clowns of all the ages . . . ."
Julia had asked Saxon for a ride back to her house; he tells Straus of
his odd feelings upon first seeing her:

> . . . I knew that here was a life-long friend, a sort of witch and fairy
> combined that had been waiting for me all these years, and was ready to
> step into my life. I knew that this dwarf—whoever she was—was
> destined to become my friend. Odd that I never felt just exactly this
> thing before; but so it was. I knew all this even before I got my
> breath to answer her. . . . I felt as though sky-rockets were exploding in
> my mind. Fairy tales were true after all. Something had happened
> to me . . . .

As Saxon talked with Julia, he learned that she lived far back in the woods. She pointed in the direction with "another gesture of those inadequate arms that embraced all the horizon before us." Saxon then elaborates further on Julia's background:

> She had been nursing the child that died—"That's my ambition, to become a trained nurse!"—but the child had died, and so she had stayed and cooked supper for the other children while the father and mother went to the funeral. . . . There was a great deal of sickness in the community, she said, and she helped nurse the sick and bury the dead. She even helped dig a grave once.

Saxon continues in his letter to Straus, detailing Julia's girlhood, the cruelties she suffered in school, and her dream "that someday she would get a chance to . . . study to be a trained nurse . . . ." On the way back to Baton Rouge, Saxon discovered that his aunt had known Julia for years, although "she couldn't see why I thought the dwarf was remarkable" and wondered if her nephew could make some money by writing about Julia in *The Times-Picayune*. At this point Saxon tells Straus that such a story would probably turn out to be outrageously sentimental "blah."

The account of his encounter with Julia—along with what grew out of this chance meeting—seems quite typical, even symbolic, of Lyle Saxon's life and literary career. This relatively minor incident one day when he was turning from newspaper work to writing fiction not only provides an extraordinary insight into Saxon, but what followed his meeting Julia Allen is actually quite predictable. He did write about Julia later for a *Times-Picayune* assignment—if not outrageously at least quite prosaically compared to the account he gives his friend in the letter. Saxon also established a fund at L.S.U., contributing money himself and raising a nice sum from others so that Julia could attend nursing school and fulfill her dream. The one thing he did not do was write a short story based on that day in the country, though he certainly could have formed a fine work of fiction from the Julia story. Many other writers surely would have; yet they may not have written such a marvelous letter to an old friend, or enabled Julia to become a nurse. While Lyle Saxon had his limitations, he also made his choices.

NOTES

Chapter 1

[1] Lyle Saxon, *Old Louisiana* (New York: The Century Co., 1929), vii. Subsequent references are to this edition and will appear parenthetically in the text.

[2] Lyle Saxon, *The Friends of Joe Gilmore* (New York: Hastings House, 1948), 95. Subsequent references are to this edition and will appear parenthetically in the text.

[3] Harris Downey, personal interview, 25 Aug. 1974. Subsequent references to Downey are to this interview unless otherwise noted.

[4] Muriel Saxon Lambert, personal interview, 24 Aug. 1974. Subsequent references to Lambert are to this interview unless otherwise noted.

[5] Pat Baldridge, "Memorial Service Will Honor Writer Lyle Saxon," *BRST*, 25 Jan. 1974: 14.

[6] Virginius Dabney, *Liberalism in the South* (Chapel Hill: U of NC P, 1932), 375.

[7] Elizabeth Lyle Saxon, *A Southern Woman's War Time Reminiscences* (Memphis: Pilcher Printing Co., 1905), 11.

[8] Elizabeth Lyle Saxon, 14.

[9] Elizabeth Lyle Saxon, 16-17.

[10] "Lyddell A. Saxon," [*NOTP* ?] [1901], LSL.

[11] "Lyle Saxon Dies at Home After Stroke," *Dallas Morning News* [Apr. 1939], NSU.

[12] I am indebted to Betty Chambers Campbell's investigation of Baton Rouge cemetery records (and other East Baton Rouge Parish records) for most of the life dates of the Chambers relatives. Campbell includes a great deal of information regarding the Chamberses in a letter to the author, 8 Nov. 1974. This Baton Rouge Chambers family, incidentally, was not the same branch of the family as that of the Louisiana historian Henry Chambers.

[13] Cathy Harvey located the record of the marriage (Marriage License Index, Health Department, Orleans Parish, Vol. 15, Part 2, p. 74; Vol. 27, Part 4, p. 405) in her research for her 1980 dissertation. See Cathy Chance Harvey, "Lyle Saxon: A Portrait in Letters, 1917-1945," diss., Tulane U, 1980, 6.

[14]Thomas C. Atkinson, personal interview, 28 Aug. 1974. Subsequent references to Thomas Atkinson are to this interview unless otherwise noted.

[15]Charles Elder, personal interview, 13 Apr. 1974.

[16]Edith Atkinson, letter to the author, 5 May 1974.

[17]As evidence of Saxon's birth in Washington, Harvey cites the facts that (1) in a notebook Katherine Chambers alludes to a visit to British Columbia in the spring of 1891, (2) in one of Katherine's books from the period is a Los Angeles obstetrician's business card, and, perhaps most convincingly, (3) Calvin Fixx (once Lyle Saxon's secretary) says in a letter to Saxon, "No, I'm sure you never mentioned you were born in Bellingham." All these materials are at the Tulane University library. See Harvey, "Portrait," 8-9.

[18]"Lyle Saxon," *BRST*, 11 Apr. 1946: 4.

[19]"Saxon Known Everywhere—Best Here," *BRST*, 24 Mar. 1938: 7.

[20]Katherine Chambers Saxon, Notebook: 1892-95, ms., TU.

[21]See, for example, Stanley J. Kunitz and Howard Haycraft, eds., *Twentieth Century Authors* (New York: H. W. Wilson, 1942), 1236-37; "Lyle Saxon Dead at 54," *NOSI*, 10 Apr. 1946, LSL; and Viva Begbie, "A Writer Without an Enemy," *Shreveport Times*, 23 Mar. 1969: 14.

[22]Caroline Dormon, "Southern Personalities—Lyle Saxon," *Holland's Magazine*, Jan. 1931: 26.

[23]See Joseph Blotner, *Faulkner: A Biography*, 2 vols. (New York: Random House, 1974) 1: 394; and Frederick R. Karl, *William Faulkner: American Writer* (New York: Weidenfeld and Nicolson, 1989), 344.

[24]Lyle Saxon, *Father Mississippi* (New York: The Century Co., 1927), [v]. Subsequent references are to this edition and will appear parenthetically in the text. Incidentally, the family members Saxon focuses on, the main characters in this opening section of *Father Mississippi*, have names that do not correspond to any Saxon or Chambers relatives.

[25]Jo Thompson, "Lyle Saxon, Seasoned Reporter, Likes Reporting Far More than Writing Books—But Writes Books," *BRST*, 5 Aug. 1937: 3.

[26]"Saxon Known Everywhere—Best Here," 7.

[27]"Lyle Saxon," *BRST*, 4.

[28]Catherine B. Dillon, "Flickers through the Cypress Boughs: An Intimate Sketch of Lyle Saxon," *Inn Dixie*, Sept. 1946: 5.

[29]Robert Cantwell, letter to the author, 22 Aug. 1974.

[30]"Saxon Known Everywhere—Best Here," 7.

[31]Edward Dreyer, "Some Friends of Lyle Saxon," *The Friends of Joe Gilmore*, by Lyle Saxon (New York: Hastings House, 1948), 118.

[32]"Lyle Saxon, Famous Louisiana Author, Gives Opinions on Southern Literature," *Fair Park* [High School, Shreveport] *Pow Wow*, 21 Mar. 1934: 1.

[33]Dreyer, 116-17, 139.

[34]Francois Mignon, personal interview, 3 Sep. 1974. Subsequent references to Mignon are to this interview unless otherwise noted.

[35]Precisely when he died is difficult to determine. He was still alive at the end of 1930, for in a newspaper article late that year Saxon reveals plans to visit his grandfather; the next year he refers to his grandfather's critical illness. Dr. Sherburne Anderson of Baton Rouge examined old city directories (issued biennially) and found Michael listed in 1929 but not in 1931 (Sherburne Anderson, letter to the author, 26 Dec. 1974.) Since Saxon's grandfather was born in 1838, he was at least ninety when he died.

[36]Lyle Saxon, letter to Noel Straus, 21 Dec. 1925, TU.

[37]Betty Chambers Campbell, letter to the author, 3 Oct. 1974.

[38]Lyle Saxon, Story of Mary Nelson, ms., TU.

[39]Sherburne Anderson, letter to the author, 26 Dec. 1974.

[40]Dreyer, 123.

[41]Richard Bradford, letter to the author, 12 Nov. 1974.

[42]"Lyle Saxon, Famous Louisiana Author," 1.

[43]Lyle Saxon, *Fabulous New Orleans* (New York: The Century Co., 1928), 6. Subsequent references are to this edition and will appear parenthetically in the text.

[44]Josiah Titzell, "Chronicler of the Fabulous," *St. Nicholas* 56 (1929): 467.

[45]The photograph "Summer" is in *St. Nicholas* 35 (1908): 370; "The Dusty Road," *St. Nicholas* 35 (1908): 850; and "Rowing," *St. Nicholas* 35 (1908): 1142.

[46]Sherburne Anderson, letter to the author, 26 Dec. 1974.

[47]Dreyer, 122.

[48]Lyle Saxon, Story of Mary Nelson, ms., TU.

[49]Henry O. Cazentre, letter to the author, 19 Feb. 1975. Cazentre, then Assistant Registrar of L.S.U., provided me with the entrance date, initial course of study, and the fact that Saxon listed "M. Chambers" as his guardian.

[50]Although only signed with the last name, this drawing was surely done by Lyle Chambers Saxon. He is the only Saxon listed in any yearbook during his years at L.S.U.

[51]Sherburne Anderson, letter to the author, 26 Dec. 1974.

[52]This first bookstore, incidentally, was the basis for Claitor's, now a large Baton Rouge bookstore and a part of the chain of stores owned by Anderson News Company. John Albert Anderson, Michael Chambers's successor, became partners with and later sold out to Otto Claitor. In an article about the Claitor business, the founders refer to Chambers's store and acknowledge that "our store is descended from the pioneer bookshop here" (Mr. and Mrs. Otto Claitor, "We Progress from Sidelines to Books," *The Publishers' Weekly* 132 (1937): 1413.

[53]Dreyer, 125.

[54]"Lyle Saxon's New Book Dedicated to Miss Mercedes Garig, First Woman Ever on L.S.U. Faculty," *BRST*, 5 Nov. 1930, LSL.

[55]Lyle Saxon, letter to Cammie Henry, 24 Feb. 1946, NSU.

[56]"Body of Saxon Due Here Today," *BRST*, 10 Apr. 1946: 1.

57"Lyle Saxon, Famous Louisiana Author," 3.

58Dreyer, 126.

59This is the assertion of Helen Gilkison in her unfinished master's thesis, "Lyle Saxon: Louisiana Writer" at L.S.U. See Harvey, "Portrait," 23. Harvey's examination of L.S.U. records "confirms Miss Gilkison's statement that he did not graduate."

60Gilkison in Harvey, "Portrait," 29.

61Saxon seems less than thrilled with this Pensacola experience as he describes it in his "Who Would Go Hunt for Spanish Doubloons and Pieces of Eight?" *NOTP* magazine, 9 Apr. 1922: 3.

62Dreyer, 127.

63Joseph M. Henry, personal interview, 3 Sep. 1974. Subsequent references to Henry are to this interview unless otherwise noted.

64There is a good deal of guesswork involving these early years in Saxon's journalistic career. Drawing on Gilkison's narrative, several Saxon obituaries, and *Item* and *Picayune* records, Harvey provides a useful discussion. See Harvey, "Portrait," 28-32.

65Thompson, 3.

66"Good Loser," [ca. Oct. 1917], LSL. This clipping bears no date, page number, newspaper title, or even city. I assume it relates to the Chicago days because on the reverse side of the article about Saxon is an address of a church located at Oakwood Boulevard and Langley Avenue. In the church treasurer's report there is a current balance-on-hand figure dated October 1, 1917. The item appeared in some Chicago paper other than the *Daily News* since there is also a reference in it to Saxon's work in one of the other "local dailies."

67A. P. Mc Graw, "Saxon, First Fiction Work Through, Has Guidebooks to Edit; Plans for Future Include Only 'More Writing,' " *BRMA*, 5 Aug. 1937: 2.

68Thompson, 3.

69Dillon, 6.

70Edward J. O'Brien, ed., *The Best Short Stories of 1927* (New York: Dodd, Mead, 1928), 330.

71Lyle Saxon, 1918 Diary, ms., 2 Mar. 1918, NSU; Harvey, "Portrait," 33.

72Dreyer, 130-31.

73Lyle Saxon, Résumé, ts., TU. Saxon himself composed this list of chief jobs and literary works apparently for use by the various persons who introduced him at speaking engagements (there are several carbon copies).

Chapter 2

1See Alberta Lawrence, ed., *Who's Who Among North American Authors, VI: 1933-35* (Los Angeles: Golden Syndicate, 1935), 880; Robert Penn Warren, ed., *A Southern Harvest* (Boston: Houghton Mifflin, 1937), 358; Stanley J. Kunitz and Howard

Haycraft, eds., *Twentieth Century Authors* (New York: H. W. Wilson, 1942), 1237; and "Noted Historian Lyle Saxon Dies," *NOTP,* 10 Apr. 1947: 3.

[2]Robert Tallant, *The Romantic New Orleanians* (New York: E. P. Dutton, 1950), 311.

[3]Lyle Saxon, letter to Maude Chambers, 13 Dec. 1919, LSL.

[4]Thomas E. Dabney, *One Hundred Great Years: The Story of the* Times-Picayune *From Its Founding to 1940* (Baton Rouge: LSU P, 1944), 402.

[5]This comment occurs in *Fabulous New Orleans* after the reprinted story about the fire and reflects the author's view nine years after the original *Times-Picayune* article. Saxon's original account is "Fire Leaves Famous Home of Lyric Drama Heap of Ruins," *NOTP,* 5 Dec. 1919: 1+.

[6]Lyle Saxon, letter to Maude Chambers, 13 Dec. 1919, LSL.

[7]Dillon, 6 and Dreyer, 142.

[8]The *Times-Picayune* "Literature and Less" book review continued under that same title until January, 1988.

[9]Lyle Saxon, "Make This a Book Christmas," *The Publishers' Weekly* 112 (1927): 2022.

[10]Lyle Saxon, "Make This a Book Christmas," 2022.

[11]Lyle Saxon, "At the Gates of Empire," *NOTP,* 24 Apr. 1921: 2.

[12]Lyle Saxon, "At the Gates of Empire," ms., LSL, 10. Subsequent references to the story are to the manuscript rather than the installments in *The Times-Picayune* and will appear parenthetically in the text.

[13]Charles East, letter to the author, 5 Apr. 1974.

[14]Dillon, 33.

[15]Lyle Saxon, *My Love: From Lyle Saxon's 1924 Scrapbook and By the Fire: From Lyle Saxon's 1925-26 Scrapbook* (Baton Rouge: n.p., 1950), 3.

[16]Lillian Hellman, *Pentimento: A Book of Portraits* (Boston: Little, Brown, 1973), 78.

[17]"Saxon Known Everywhere—Best Here," 7.

[18]Karl, 344.

[19]Ray M. Thompson, "The Three Decades of Lyle Saxon," *Down South,* May-Jun. 1960: 5.

[20]Dormon, 26.

[21]Tess Crager, personal interview, 24 Aug. 1974.

[22]Tallant, *The Romantic New Orleanians,* 311.

[23]Robert Tallant, introduction, *Fabulous New Orleans,* by Lyle Saxon (1928; New Orleans: Crager, 1950), xiv.

[24]In two letters, Saxon mentions that Lea used his house for a description of a character's French Quarter dwelling in her story "Yellow Roses," *Harper's Bazaar,* Apr. 1920: 88+. See Lyle Saxon, letter to Maude Chambers, 13 Dec. 1919, LSL; and Lyle Saxon, letter to Cammie G. Henry, 4 Apr. 1923, NSU.

[25]See Titzell, 467; Robert Tallant, "My Fabulous Friend Lyle Saxon," *NOTP* magazine, 21 Nov. 1948: 8; and Dormon, 65.

[26]William Spratling, *File on Spratling: An Autobiography* (Boston: Little, Brown, 1967), 16.

[27]Lyle Saxon, introduction, *Picturesque New Orleans*, by William Spratling (New Orleans: Tulane U P, 1923), n. pag.

[28]King also knew Sherwood Anderson and, through Saxon, met Edmund Wilson. It is doubtful, however, that she ever met Faulkner. See Robert Bush, *Grace King: A Southern Dynasty* (Baton Rouge: LSU P, 1983), 297-300. Saxon's speech at King's memorial service is quoted in Henry P. Dart, ed., "The Death of Grace King," *Louisiana Historical Quarterly* 15 (1932): 334-35.

[29]Dillon, 33.

[30]Mary Rose Bradford, letter to Cammie Henry, 21 May 1946, NSU.

[31]Mary Rose Bradford, "The Story of Annie Christmas," *A Treasury of Mississippi River Folklore*, ed. B. A. Botkin (New York: Crown, 1955), 36.

[32]Roark Bradford, letter to Lyle Saxon, [1927?], TU.

[33]Meigs O. Frost, "Annie Christmas," *NOTP* magazine, 23 May 1948: 16.

[34]Mary Rose Bradford, "The Story of Annie Christmas," 35.

[35]These accounts are found in *Father Mississippi*, 138; and in Lyle Saxon, Edward Dreyer, and Robert Tallant, eds. *Gumbo Ya-Ya* (Boston: Houghton Mifflin, 1945), 376-77. Subsequent references to *GYY* are to this edition and will appear parenthetically in the text.

[36]Frost, 16.

[37]These remarkable volumes, over 250 of them, contain all sorts of material relative to prominent Louisianans and important historical events. They were used, during Cammie Henry's lifetime, by various students and writers as reference materials. Mary Linn Bandaries, archivist at the NSU Library, told me recently that researchers continue to make frequent use of the scrapbooks and other materials in Natchitoches. Melrose plantation, incidentally, is now a National Historical Landmark and is still visited by many tourists each year (Mary Linn Bandaries, personal interview, 5 May 1989).

[38]Lyle Saxon, letter to Cammie Henry, 4 Apr. 1923, NSU.

[39]Lyle Saxon, "Easter Sunday at Aunt Cammie's," *NOTP* magazine, 22 Apr. 1923: 1.

[40]Lyle Saxon, "The One Thing," *NOTP* magazine, 27 May 1923: 1. The previous week Saxon had published two brief sketches: "An Interlude" and "The Forgotten Cigarette," *NOTP* magazine, 20 May 1923: 4, 7. These are very brief and inconsequential.

[41]F. L. Pattee, "The Age of O. Henry," *Side-Lights on American Literature* (New York: The Century Co., 1922), 36-37.

[42]Lyle Saxon, "The Perfume of Her Presence," *NOTP* magazine, 30 Sept. 1923: 1.

[43]See Jean Toomer, *Cane*, ed. Darwin T. Turner (1923; New York: W. W. Norton, 1988), 44-49. I am not suggesting an influence here, incidentally, although it is entirely possible that Saxon, by September of 1923, would already be familiar with some of Toomer's work. *Cane* appeared in late 1923, but over the previous several months Toomer had published in *The Double Dealer*.

[44]Lyle Saxon, "Blackmail," *NOTP* magazine, 30 Mar. 1924: 1-2.

[45]Lyle Saxon, "The Man Who Hated Women," *NOTP* magazine, 25 May 1924: 7.

[46]Lyle Saxon, "The Return," *NOTP* magazine, 13 Jul. 1924: 1.

[47]Blotner, 1: 457.

[48]Lyle Saxon, "Epitaph: A Play in One Act," *NOTP* magazine, 16 Sept. 1923: 2+.

[49]The newspaper clipping that describes the performance bears no date, page number, or title of newspaper. The article is entitled "Lyle Saxon Play 'Epitaph' Given at Petit Theatre," TU.

[50]See, for example, McGraw 2; and Wendell Tynes, "A Talk With Lyle Saxon," *The Haversack,* 22 Jan. 1933: 4.

[51]Lyle Saxon, "After All These Years," *NOTP* magazine, 24 Jun. 1923: 4.

[52]Lyle Saxon, letter to Noel Straus, 21 Dec. 1925, TU.

[53]See Lyle Saxon, "A Breath from the Vieux Carré," *House and Garden,* Nov. 1923: 72+; "The Mistletoe Trail: Christmas on a Louisiana Plantation," *NOTP* magazine, 23 Dec. 1923: 1+; "Gallatin Street," *NOTP* magazine, 6 Jan. 1924: 1+; and "Jewels of a Century," *NOTP* magazine, 17 Feb. 1924: 5.

[54]Lyle Saxon, "The Toil of Worship," *NOTP* magazine, 27 Apr. 1924: 4.

[55]No letters survive to shed light on this long period of illness, yet Harvey cites as evidence Saxon's failure to make a planned European voyage and an extended sick leave he took from *The Times-Picayune.* See Harvey, "Portrait," 109-11.

[56]Pieter Stuvyesant, "Parnassas Under the Levee," *The New Orleanian,* 25 Oct. 1930: 18.

[57]Karl, 196, 214.

[58]Blotner, 1: 394.

[59]Pat M. Barnes, "Saxon Relates Stories About Noted Writers," *The Houston Post,* 15 Mar. 1935, NSU.

[60]Ben Franklin, personal interview, 28 Aug. 1974.

[61]Spratling, *File on Spratling,* 17.

[62]Ray Thompson, 18.

[63]Cathy Harvey, "Dear Lyle/Sherwood Anderson," *Southern Studies* 18 (1979): 322. Elsewhere Harvey comments on the essentially impersonal nature of the two writers' letters; "they are primarily progress reports from pupil to master." See Harvey, "Portrait," 113.

[64]Lyle Saxon, letter to Noel Straus, 21 Dec. 1925, TU.

[65]T. M. Pearce, *Oliver La Farge* (New York: Twayne, 1972), 40.

[66]Oliver La Farge, letter to Lyle Saxon, 10 Aug. 1929, TU. La Farge, incidentally, inscribed Saxon's copy of *Laughing Boy* with a message of gratitude for Saxon's help and encouragement. See Harvey, "Portrait," 137.

[67]Elizabeth Kell, personal interview, 24 Aug. 1974. Subsequent references to Kell are to this interview unless otherwise noted.

[68]David Minter, *William Faulkner: His Life and Work* (Baltimore: Johns Hopkins U P, 1980), 48.

[69]Blotner, 1: 419.

[70]This is Faulkner's "Mirrors of Chartres Street," rpt. in Carvel Collins, ed., *William Faulkner: New Orleans Sketches* (New York: Random House, 1958), 15-18. The article appeared originally in the *NOTP* on 8 Feb. 1925.

[71]Blotner, 1: 424. See, in Collins, for example Faulkner's "Jealousy," 34-40; "The Kingdom of God," 55-60; "The Rosary," 61-65; and, especially, "Chance," 70-75. These stories appeared originally during March, April, and May, 1925 in the *NOTP* magazine.

[72]Karl, 240. Karl is referring to Faulkner's "The Liar."

[73]Blotner, 1: 394. Blotner's sources for this information are Harold Levy, Flo Field, and James K. Feibleman.

[74]Mary Rose Bradford, "The Story of Annie Christmas," 36.

[75]Former *NOTP* reporter George Tichenor quoted in Collins, xxvi.

[76]George W. Healy, Jr., "No Beck and Call for Bill," *William Faulkner of Oxford*, ed. James W. Webb and Wigfall Green (Baton Rouge: LSU P, 1965), 59-60.

[77]"Frank Recollections of His Pals Told by Saxon," *Shreveport Times*, 8 Mar. 1934, NSU.

[78]Collins, xxvii.

[79]Collins, xxvii.

[80]See Frances Jean Bowen, "*The New Orleans Double Dealer*, 1921-May 1926: A Critical History," diss., Vanderbilt U, 1954.

[81]Harvey, "Portrait," 114. Harvey's informants on these matters are the wife of *Double Dealer* founder Julius Friend, James K. Feibleman, Daniel Wogan, and George Healy, Jr.

[82]Karl, 282. See William Spratling and William Faulkner, *Sherwood Anderson and Other Famous Creoles: A Gallery of Contemporary New Orleans* (1926; Austin: U of Texas P, 1966), n. pag.

[83]"Frank Recollections," NSU.

[84]See Edmund Wilson, letter to John Peale Bishop, 4 Dec. 1934, *Letters on Literature and Politics*, ed. Elena Wilson (New York: Farrar, Straus and Giroux, 1977), 252; and "South: New Orleans' Literary Mentor Weeps for Mulattoes," *Newsweek*, 10 Jul. 1937: 20.

[85]McGraw, 2.

[86]Elizabeth Kell, personal interview, 24 Aug. 1974.

[87]Various clippings from the architecture series (dating from 9 Apr. to 19 Apr. 1922) and from the "Ways of Making a Living" series (dating from 26 Jul. to 17 Aug. 1922) are found at NSU. See also Lyle Saxon,"Fingers in the Dark," *NOTP*, 27 May 1923, NSU; Lyle Saxon and Wilbur Wright, "Two Writers Do Time For Story 'Behind Bars,' " *NOTP*, 15 Jul. 1923, NSU; and Lyle Saxon, "Brilliant Throng Meets Movie Fold at Opening of Loew's State Theater," *NOTP*, 4 Apr. 1926, TU. Saxon's final *Times-Picayune* feature before he moved to New York, incidentally, was "Baroness Pontalba Goes Home," *NOTP* magazine, 10 Oct. 1926: 7.

[88]Lyle Saxon, letter to Mercedes Garig, 24 Sep. 1918, Harvey, "Portrait," 86-92.

[89]Lyle Saxon, letter to Mercedes Garig, 28 Dec. 1918, Harvey, "Portrait," 96-98.

[90]Lyle Saxon, letter to Maude Chambers, 13 Dec. 1919, LSL.

[91]Lyle Saxon, letter to Sherwood and Elizabeth Anderson, 12 Sep. 1926, Harvey, "Dear Lyle," 328-31.

[92]Lyle Saxon, letter to Noel Straus, 21 Dec. 1925, TU.

[93]Tynes, 4

[94]Pattee, 5

[95]Pattee, 37, 40.

[96]Harold L. Leisure, "Presenting Lyle Saxon," *Southern Literary Messenger* 2 (1940): 509.

Chapter 3

[1]Edmund Wilson, letter to Hamilton Basso, 25 Jan. 1927, *Letters*, 133.

[2]Karl, 344.

[3]Blotner, 1: 394, 583.

[4]Harvey, "Portrait," 118-19. Harvey's informants regarding Saxon's appearance are Elizabeth Kell, James K. Feibleman, and Daniel Wogan.

[5]Bernard De Voto, letter to Lyle Saxon, 13 Apr. [1930?], TU.

[6]Lyle Saxon, "A Breath from the Vieux Carré," *House and Garden*, Nov. 1923: 72+.

[7]Lyle Saxon, 1925 Diary, 7 Feb. entry, ms., NSU.

[8]Harvey, "Portrait," 127-31. Harvey's informants regarding Olive Lyons include Marc Antony and Barbara Miller, Olive Lyons's godchild.

[9]Muriel Saxon Lambert, personal interview, 24 Aug. 1974.

[10]Adaline Samuel, personal interview, 24 Aug. 1974. Subsequent references to Samuel are to this interview unless otherwise noted.

[11]Elizabeth Kell, personal interview, 24 Aug. 1974.

[12]Dreyer, 150.

¹³In a letter written after his move to New York, Saxon tells Olive that since a visitor has seen her photograph by his bed, "we may hear new scandals about ourselves in the early spring." Evidently the author and Lyons had grown accustomed previously to hearing gossip in New Orleans about their relationship. See Lyle Saxon, letter to Olive Lyons, 18 Feb. 1927, TU.

¹⁴This view was expressed, for example, in my interview with Tess Crager and in Richard Bradford, letter to the author, 12 Nov. 1974.

¹⁵Harvey cites letters from Josiah Titzell and another man, known only as Arthur, which indicate sexual relationships with Saxon; she also cites passages from a Saxon diary referring to homosexual relations with a "J. C." or "C. J." (Harvey, "Portrait," 234, 340-41). On the other hand, Harvey infers from Saxon's letters that he had some kind of love relationship with Olive Lyons and with a relative of Olive's sister, Muriel Moore (Harvey, "Portrait," 129-31, 239-43). Harvey concludes, "Like the relationship with Olive, this love affair [with Muriel Moore] attests to the duality of Saxon's sexual nature," 234.

¹⁶Lyle Saxon, 1925 Diary, 8 and 9 Apr. entries, ms., NSU.

¹⁷Lyle Saxon, "Cane River," *The Dial* 80 (1926): 207. Subsequent references to this story are to this printing and will appear parenthetically in the text.

¹⁸Saxon had written a piece for *The Times-Picayune* during the fall of 1925 on various superstitions among the blacks of Cane River. See Lyle Saxon, "Cane River Superstitions," *NOTP*, 20 Sep. 1925: 3. I will discuss Cane River superstitions further in my treatment of *Children of Strangers* in Chapter 5.

¹⁹Frances E. Jones, "Background of the Louisiana Short Story," thesis, LSU, 1936, 66.

²⁰As I have already suggested—and as I will discuss further in my analysis of *Children of Strangers*—Saxon very well could have been familiar with *Cane*, published three years before "Cane River."

²¹Robert Wilson Neal, introduction, *O. Henry Memorial Award Prize Stories of 1926*, ed. Blanche Colton Williams, et. al. (Garden City: Doubleday Page, 1927), xiii.

²²Lyle Saxon, letter to Caroline Dormon, 7 Aug. 1925, Harvey, "Portrait," 158-62.

²³Lyle Saxon, letter to Olive Lyons, [Sep. 1925], Harvey, "Portrait," 164-67.

²⁴Lyle Saxon, letter to Sherwood Anderson, 3 Mar. 1926, Harvey, "Dear Lyle," 328.

²⁵Dorothy Dix, letter to Lyle Saxon, 18 Mar. 1926, personal library of Joseph M. Henry.

²⁶Roark Bradford, letter to Lyle Saxon, [1927?], TU.

²⁷Grace King, letter to Lyle Saxon, [Mar. 1926?], NSU. Saxon published two stories in *The Dial*, and King's undated note does not reveal whether she means "Cane River" or the later story. Because of its proximity to early materials in the Melrose scrapbook in which it is located—as well as because of the allusion to Saxon's

arriving—the note seems surely intended to congratulate the author regarding the earlier story.

[28]Pattee, 38.

[29]Lyle Saxon, letter to Noel Straus, 21 Dec. 1925, TU.

[30]Sherwood Anderson, letter to Lyle Saxon, [Nov. 1925], TU. Anderson refers in this letter to the New York reaction to his *Dark Laughter* (1925) and mentions that he will be in New York until November 10.

[31]Lyle Saxon, 1925 Diary, 16 Mar. entry, ms., NSU.

[32]The sum Saxon received on this sale was perhaps two or three thousand dollars. The former figure is given in McGraw, 2; the latter in Alvin C. Hamer, Transcript of WXYZ Radio Broadcast, 8 Jul. 1937, NSU.

[33]McGraw, 2.

[34]Lyle Saxon, letter to Elizabeth Chambers, 18 Oct. 1926, LSL.

[35]Lyle Saxon, letter to Olive Lyons, 18 Feb. 1927, TU.

[36]Lyle Saxon, letter to Olive Lyons, 7 Jan. 1927, TU. The next several references are to this early letter to Olive. Later letters will be identified and noted.

[37]Wilson, *Letters,* 132.

[38]Harvey suggests March of 1925 as the date for this first "Abe Buzzard" letter. See Harvey, "Portrait," 154.

[39]In fact, O'Connor occasionally appropriated characters from people described in newspaper ads and articles. See Harvey Klevar, "Image and Imagination: Flannery O'Connor's Front Page Fiction," *Journal of Modern Literature* 4 (1974): 121-32.

[40]Elizabeth Chambers, letter to Lyle Saxon, [Oct. 1926], LSL.

[41]Michael Grimwood, "Lyle Saxon's *Father Mississippi* as a Source for Faulkner's 'Old Man' and 'Mississippi,' " *Notes on Mississippi Writers* 17 (1985): 56.

[42]Harvey, "Dear Lyle," 321-22.

[43]Lyle Saxon, letter to Olive Lyons, 18 Feb. 1927, TU.

[44]Lyle Saxon, "Voodoo," *The New Republic* 50 (1927): 135-39.

[45]Lyle Saxon, letter to Olive Lyons, 18 Feb. 1927, TU.

[46]Roark Bradford, letter to Lyle Saxon, [Mar. 1927], TU.

[47]Neal in Williams, xiv; Robert L. Ramsey in Williams, xiv.

[48]Lyle Saxon, "Fame," *New Orleans Life,* May 1927: 9-11.

[49]See, for example, Kunitz and Haycraft, 1237; and "Lyle Saxon: Author of *Old Louisiana,*" *The Wilson Bulletin* 4 (1929): 148.

[50]Lyle Saxon, letter to Olive Lyons, 4 May 1927, TU; and Lyle Saxon, letter to Olive Lyons, 7 May 1927, TU.

[51]These articles were published in the July, August, and September numbers of the magazine. See Lyle Saxon, "Down on the Levee: A True Story of the Mississippi Tragedy," *The Century Magazine* 114 (1927): 292-98; "Acadians in the Flood: Waiting for Safety and Sunrise and Dry Land," *The Century Magazine* 114 (1927): 462-68; and

"And the Waters Receded: But What about Bigger and Better Floods Next Year," *The Century Magazine,* 114 (1927): 583-89.

[52]Francois Mignon, *Plantation Memo* (Baton Rouge: Claitor's, 1972), 42.

[53]Lyle Saxon, letter to Olive Lyons, [1928], TU.

[54]Lyle Saxon, letter to Olive Lyons, 15 Jun. 1929, TU.

[55]Lyle Saxon, Melrose Diary, 20 Oct. and 6 Nov. 1933 entries, ms., TU.

[56]Sherwood Anderson, letter to Lyle Saxon, [1927], TU.

[57]Lyle Saxon, letter to Olive Lyons, 31 Aug. 1927, TU.

[58]Lyle Saxon, letter to Olive Lyons, 7 Jan. 1927, TU.

[59]Henry Longan Stuart, "The First 'American Caravan' Comes to the Bazaars," *NYTBR,* 18 Sep. 1927: 24.

[60]Gilbert Seldes, "An Enquiry into the Present State of Letters," *The Dial* 83 (1927): 435.

[61]Saxon worked on the story during the summer and alludes to the finished product in a letter at year's end. See Lyle Saxon, letter to Noel Straus, 21 Dec. 1925, TU; and Lyle Saxon, letter to Olive Lyons, 7 Jan. 1927, TU.

[62]Lyle Saxon, letter to Olive Lyons, 18 Feb. 1927, TU.

[63]Lyle Saxon, letter to Caroline Dormon, 7 Aug. 1925, Harvey, "Portrait," 158-62.

[64]Crager and Downey interviews; "Lyle Saxon Dead at 54," LSL.

[65]Lyle Saxon, "The Centaur Plays Croquet," *The American Caravan,* ed. Van Wyck Brooks, Alfred Kreymborg, Lewis Mumford, and Paul Rosenfeld (New York: Literary Guild, 1927), 344. Subsequent references are to this printing and will appear parenthetically in the text.

[66]Saxon evidently gave careful thought to the selection of names in the story. Several of them, discussed in the paragraphs and notes that follow, add to the understanding of the characters in the context of the story. "Ada," on the other hand, is surely named for Saxon's close friend and fellow author Ada Jack Carver. She, Caroline Dormon, and Saxon, in fact, all agreed to write about centaurs and, according to Carver's biographer, Ada Jack Carver was not pleased with Saxon's story (Harvey, "Portrait," 161-62). Saxon had earlier used friends' names in stories as well: for example, "Olive" in "The One Thing" and "George" in "The Return." "Marie," incidentally, was a favorite fictional name, appearing in "At the Gates of Empire" and in two *Times-Picayune* stories. I know of no Maries among Saxon's relatives or circle of friends, however.

[67]Saxon's choice of the surname, along with the switching of the last two vowels of *calendar,* is somewhat puzzling. Neither of the two *calenders* listed in the *OED* seems to have anything whatsoever to do with the story. (One is traced to the Greek for *cylinder,* and the other is from a Persian word for a wandering dervish.) Thus the origins of *calendar* would seem the source of the suggestiveness or wordplay here—if any is intended. The Latin *calendarium* means an account book or register; *calare* (root for *calendae*) means to announce solemnly. Neither has obvious application to Ada or John

David, beyond the fact that they both make solemn announcements from time to time. Perhaps Saxon simply had the idea of a court calendar in mind, these being the six sworn testimonies in this current strange case on the calendar.

[68]Stuart, 24.

[69]Although no such poems as the ones mentioned in the story appear in these issues of *Harper's* for 1883 and 1884, some do appear occasionally, as Saxon surely knew, on topics similar to those with which Ada was concerned. See, for example, William Allen Butler, "The Garden of the Gods," *Harper's Magazine* 64 (1881-82): 96; and Mary A. Barr, "Lethe," *Harper's Magazine* 66 (1882-83): 605.

[70]The only indexed reference to centaurs in Burton's work, incidentally, is to a passage that lists humans who have had sexual relationships with beasts. These people have given in to lust, Burton says, "either out of their own weakness, a depraved nature, or love's tyranny . . . ." See Robert Burton, *The Anatomy of Melancholy*, ed. and trans. Floyd Dell and Paul Jordan-Smith (New York: Tudor, 1927), 651-53. It is significant in light of Ada's situation that Burton's reference to centaurs is to the sexual relationship of the beasts with women rather than to the Chiron story or to some more noble aspect of the creatures. Very likely, Saxon had checked Burton's work before he made this a favorite book in Ada's library.

[71]Elsewhere Saxon, in listing the figures encountered at Mardi Gras, notes that "occasionally one meets a centaur." See Lyle Saxon, "The South Parades," *Theatre Arts Monthly* 14 (1930): 685.

[72]The author may have been thinking of James Branch Cabell when he named this character. Saxon, who had read Cabell during his boyhood, may have more recently encountered *Jurgen*. One of the characters therein in Nessus—a centaur. Tenuous as such a connection may be, it does seem possibly intended—especially in light of the allusion to Burton and of subtle touches such as Ada's map of Sagittarius (360).

[73]Once again Saxon enjoys a private joke with names, for a Boudousquie of the late nineteenth century was instrumental in the construction of the French Opera House. See *Fabulous New Orleans*, 280ff.

[74]This character's name could have been chosen because of the similarity in sound to "make-bride," a function of a preacher who performs wedding ceremonies. In McBryde's first sentence, he refers to the fact that he married Ada and John David (367).

[75]The wordplay involved with the stonecutter's German name and its English translation is understandable coming form Saxon, a former member of the German Club at L.S.U.

[76]"Lyle Saxon: Author of *Old Louisiana*," 148.

[77]Again, Saxon seems to want to bring to mind only the sensual, lustful, and wine-guzzling associations with centaurs—not the richer aspects of the centaur myths, such as those involving Chiron.

[78]Lyle Saxon, letter to Noel Straus, 21 Dec. 1925, TU.

[79]The story never appeared again in Saxon's lifetime and was anthologized once in 1948 in a regional collection edited by Hamilton Basso's wife. See Lyle Saxon, "The Centaur Plays Croquet," *The World From Jackson Square*, ed. Etolia S. Basso (New York: Farrar, Straus, 1948), 277-300.

[80]Brooks et al., ix.

[81]Seldes, 435, 437.

[82]Lyle Saxon, "The Long Furrow," *The Century Magazine* 114 (1927), 688-96.

[83]Hewitt H. Howland, letter to Lyle Saxon, 4 May 1927, TU.

[84]Lyle Saxon, letter to Olive Lyons, 4 May 1927, TU.

[85]Lyle Saxon, letter to Caroline Dormon, 29 Aug. 1927, Harvey, "Portrait," 291-92.

[86]Lyle Saxon, letter to Olive Lyons, 31 Aug. 1927, TU.

[87]Lyle Saxon, letter to Elizabeth Chambers, 26 Oct. 1927, LSL.

[88]Lyle Saxon, "Cane River," *The Best Short Stories of 1927*, ed. Edward J. O'Brien (New York: Dodd, Mead, 1927), 240-54; the review is "Three Collections of the 'Best Short Stories' of 1927," *NYTBR*, 11 Dec. 1927: 2.

[89]Lyle Saxon, "Make This a Book Christmas," 2021.

[90]See Lyle Saxon, letter to Olive Lyons, 7 Jan. 1927, TU; and letter to Olive Lyons, 18 Feb. 1927, TU.

[91]Sherwood Anderson, letter to Lyle Saxon, [Aug. 1927], TU. Harvey has aptly noted the similarity between Anderson's comparison here (involving the writer bearing tales and women bearing children) and similar comments in "The Book of the Grotesque" in *Winesburg, Ohio* and in Anderson's dedication of his *Memoirs*. See Harvey, "Dear Lyle," 337.

[92]Sherwood Anderson, letter to Lyle Saxon, [Jun. 1927], TU.

[93]Tynes, 4.

[94]Richard S. Kennedy, *The Window of Memory: The Literary Career of Thomas Wolfe* (Chapel Hill: U of North Carolina P, 1962), 181.

[95]"Society, Literati Hear Chorus Girl Defended," *Brooklyn Eagle*, 6 Dec. 1929, NSU.

[96]Joseph Blotner summarizes a story, told to him by Carl Carmer, about Faulkner's looking up Saxon in New Orleans, for example, in the summer of 1927. See Blotner, 1: 555.

[97]Minter, 134; Karl, 344; and Blotner, 1: 583.

[98]Grimwood, 56.

[99]Blotner, 1: 587.

[100]Lyle Saxon, letter to Olive Lyons, 18 Feb. 1927, TU.

[101]Blotner, 1: 587.

[102]Blotner, 1: 597-98.

[103]Ben Wasson, *Count No 'Count: Flashbacks to Faulkner* (Jackson: U P of Miss., 1983), 91.

[104]Blotner implies that Faulkner composed the story in August or September of 1929. See Blotner, 1: 631-32.

[105]See Frederick L. Gwynn and Joseph L. Blotner, eds., *Faulkner in the University* (New York: Random House, 1959), 58.

[106]Dreyer, 162.

[107]*Father Mississippi* is the only volume by Saxon in Faulkner's library. See Joseph L. Blotner, *William Faulkner's Library—a Catalogue* (Charlottesville: U of Virginia P, 1964). For the discussion of Faulkner's two works and *Father Mississippi*, see Grimwood, 53-62.

[108]The "capsule history" of Doom in "Red Leaves" is what Blotner suggests Faulkner drew from Saxon's work. See Blotner, 1: 663.

[109]Blotner, 2: 1426.

[110]Grimwood, 56.

[111]Others with whom I spoke mentioned this copy of Faulkner's story as well. Although I do not discount Downey's claim that Saxon's copy of "A Rose for Emily" was "one of Lyle's prized possessions," I doubt that he recalls correctly the matter of a privately printed copy. I have not seen a reference to such a copy of the famous story elsewhere.

[112]Lyle Saxon, "Lizzie Balize," *The Dial* 85 (1928), 303-12. See references to the arrangements in Marianne Moore, letter to Lyle Saxon, 12 June 1928, TU.

[113]Lyle Saxon, "Have a Good Time While You Can: An Impression of the Carnival in New Orleans, I," *The Century Magazine* 116 (1928): 680-90. This article was continued the next month: "Have a Good Time . . . II," *The Century Magazine* 117 (1928): 85-94.

[114]Lyle Saxon, "The Gay Dangerfields," *The Century Magazine* 118 (1929): 489-95.

[115]Lyle Saxon, "Mardi Gras," *NYHT* magazine, 2 Mar. 1930: 16-18.

[116]Saxon writes in the newspaper, for example: "Canal Street is unusually wide; there is a double roadway . . . ." In the *Theatre Arts Monthly*, he writes: "Canal Street is a wide thoroughfare with a double roadway . . ." (cf. 16 and 685 respectively).

[117]Lyle Saxon, "Easter on the Plantation," *NYHT* magazine, 20 Apr. 1930: 14-16. The manuscript of this article is dated 1923. "Easter on the Plantation," ms., 1923, TU.

[118]Lyle Saxon, "Lafitte, the Pirate," *The New Orleanian,* 4 Oct. 1930: 16-17+; and "A New Rush for Pirates' Gold," *NYHT* magazine, 19 Oct. 1930: 14-16.

[119]See, for example: Lyle Saxon, "Voodoo in Haiti," rev. of *The Magic Island,* by W. B. Seabrook, *The Bookman* 68 (1929): 714; "Hushed Orchestra," rev. of *River House*, by Stark Young, *The Saturday Review of Literature,* 7 Dec. 1929: 520; and "Romances of Old New Orleans," rev. of *Old New Orleans,* by Edward Larocque Tinker, *NYHTB,* 15 Feb. 1931: 6.

[120]Karl, 382.

^{121}In later years, too, Saxon praised Faulkner consistently and lavishly. In 1934 Saxon called Faulkner an extraordinary artist and "already . . . a legend" ("Frank Recollections," NSU). Harris Downey, for several years a member of the English Department at L.S.U., told me that Saxon was indirectly responsible for the inclusion of Faulkner in the American literature courses at the university. Downey, who first read Faulkner at his friend Saxon's urging, said he convinced his chairman at L.S.U. to include the Mississippian's novels for study.

^{122}See, for example: Lyle Saxon, "Grand Days on the River," rev. of *The Pageant of the Packets*, by Garnett Laidlaw Eskew, *NYHTB*, 27 Apr. 1930: 17; and "Bad Men of the Natchez Trace," rev. of *The Outlaw Years*, by Robert M. Coates, *NYHTB*, 3 Aug. 1930: 3.

^{123}Lyle Saxon, "A Family Breaks Up," rev. of *The Sound and the Fury*, by William Faulkner, *NYHTB*, 13 Oct. 1929: 3.

^{124}Blotner, 1: 632; and David Minter, introduction, *The Sound and the Fury*, by William Faulkner (New York: W. W. Norton, 1987), [ix].

^{125}Jay B. Hubbell, *Who Are the Major American Writers?* (Durham: Duke U P, 1972), 319.

^{126}Lyle Saxon, letter to Sherwood Anderson, 12 Sep. 1926, Harvey, "Dear Lyle," 331.

^{127}Karl, 346.

^{128}Carvel Collins, personal interview, 10 May 1989.

^{129}Dormon, 65.

^{130}Dreyer, 148.

^{131}Lyle Saxon, "Fame," 9.

Chapter 4

^{1}Lyle Saxon, letter to Kate Scott, 30 Jan. 1928, Harvey, "Portrait," 299-300.

^{2}See, for example, "*Life* Visits the Pirate Country of Louisiana," *Life,* 10 May 1943: 93; and "Lyle Saxon: Author of *Old Louisiana*," *The Wilson Library Bulletin* 4 (1929): 148.

^{3}Cleveland B. Chase, "Fighting the 'Father of Waters,' " *NYTBR*, 27 Nov. 1927: 9.

^{4}Lyle Saxon, letter to Sherwood Anderson, 5 June 1927, Harvey, "Dear Lyle," 334-35. While Saxon's fatigue and sunburn surely made him unhappy, he was pleased with the phrase he wrote to Anderson. In a letter to Olive Lyons, written probably within a week of the other letter, he says, "I'm burned to a blister and sore as a boil . . . ." See Lyle Saxon, letter to Olive Lyons, [June 1927], Harvey, "Portrait," 288-89.

^{5}Lyle Saxon, letter to Caroline Dormon, 29 Aug. 1927, Harvey, "Portrait," 291-93.

[6]See Lyle Saxon, letter to Olive Lyons, 10 Aug. 1927, TU; and letter to Olive Lyons, 31 Aug. 1927, TU.

[7]John McClure, "*Father Mississippi*," *The New Republic* 53 (1927): 148.

[8]"Radio Program To Use Excerpts From Saxon Book," *BRST*, 6 Dec. 1951, LSL. "The International Broadcasting division of the U. S. State department" was the group that planned the program. According to this article, the date for this broadcast had not been set.

[9]Chase, 9.

[10]McClure, "*Father Mississippi*," 148.

[11]Chase, 9.

[12]Lyle Saxon, Notes for *Father Mississippi*, ms., May 1927, TU. This notebook contains several disjointed phrases and quotations, such as "What the hell can I do with six beehives on a refugee boat?" or "The people won't leave," which become meaningful when examined in light of the finished text. In these two instances, Saxon describes in his book the efforts of one man to take his beehives aboard the rescue boat (362) and comments on the reluctance of many to be taken away from the flooded areas (361). In his notes on the manner in which livestock was herded aboard and kept on one large rescue boat, Saxon writes: "They are crowded on with no regard to their torture. They pile up one rises above another—They gore each other and low incessantly." In the "Episode" chapter of *Father Mississippi*, Saxon writes: "The animals are crowded with no regard to their torture—this through direct necessity. So tight-packed are they, that they rise one above the other. The horses whinny; the cows low" (365).

[13]Grimwood, 57. Grimwood suggests, for example, that Faulkner "appropriated" Saxon's scenes involving the Indian mounds, a comparison of the animal refugees and Noah's ark, and the use of newspaper headlines to heighten the drama. Grimwood's article has been identified as one of the best Faulkner source studies of 1985 with "specific, provable connections" to the earlier work. See Karl F. Zender, "Faulkner," *American Literary Scholarship: 1985*, ed. James L. Woodress (Durham: Duke U P, 1987), 155.

[14]For reviews of *Father Mississippi* cited in this paragraph, see McClure "*Father Mississippi*," 148; Arthur Kellogg, "Ol' Davil River," *The Survey* 59 (1927): 163; Mary Katharine Reely, ed., "A Selected List of Current Books," *Wisconsin Library Bulletin* 23 (1927): 287; "*Father Mississippi*," *The Mississippi Valley Historical Review* 15 (1927): 133; Charles J. Finger, "Validity and Vision," *NYHTB*, 11 Dec. 1927: 5; and "In Brief Review," *The Bookman* 66 (1927): xviii.

[15]For reviews cited in this paragraph, see May Lamberton Becker, ed., "The Reader's Guide," *The Saturday Review of Literature*, 17 Dec. 1927: 461; "*Father Mississippi*," *The Mississippi Valley Historical Review*, 133; and Chase, 9. Saxon's 1937 comment about the book is found in McGraw, 2.

[16]Sherwood Anderson, letter to Lyle Saxon, [late 1927], TU.

[17]Lyle Saxon, letter to Olive Lyons, 31 Aug. 1927, TU.

[18]Leisure, 509.

[19]See Lyle Saxon, letter to Olive Lyons, May 1928, TU; letter to Olive Lyons, [April 1928], TU; and letter to Olive Lyons, 8 May 1928, TU.

[20]Lyle Saxon, Edward Dreyer, and Robert Tallant, letter to Paul Brooks [an editor at Houghton Mifflin], 19 Feb. 1944, TU.

[21]Others in the series, all of which were illustrated by Suydam, included Charles Caldwell Dobie's *San Francisco: A Pageant* and Lucius Beebe's *Boston and the Boston Legend.*

[22]Tallant, *The Romantic New Orleanians,* 302.

[23]Daryl W. Davis, "Lyle Saxon: Twentieth-Century Champion of Louisiana's Heritage," thesis, Midwestern [Texas] U, 1960, 36.

[24]B. W., "*Fabulous New Orleans,*" *Outlook and Independent* 150 (1928): 1374.

[25]Edmund Wilson, letter to Hamilton Basso, 25 Jan. 1927, *Letters,* 132.

[26]Blake Touchstone, "Voodoo in New Orleans," *Louisiana History* 13 (1972): 381.

[27]Harvey feels that this obsession "arose from his fundamental temperament." See Harvey, "Portrait," 45, 235n, 337.

[28]The discussions of Marie Laveau and of voodoo, for example, are ten chapters apart. At the end of Chapter 17, moreover, Saxon nicely introduces the subject of the quadroon balls (172), but Chapter 18 is "The River," without a mention of the dances. Chapter 19 is "The Quadroon Balls." Much of this awkwardness, of course, indicates the Century editors' carelessness as well as Saxon's.

[29]For the reviews that comment on the lack of organization, see Worth Tuttle, "*Fabulous New Orleans,*" *The New Republic* 58 (1929): 103; and R. L. Duffus, "New Orleans Is Still a Story City," *NYTBR,* 25 Nov. 1928: 4.

[30]George Washington Cable, *Strange True Stories of Louisiana* (New York: Scribner's, 1889), 22. Edmund Wilson wrote John Peale Bishop that he should find a copy of *Strange True Stories of Louisiana* before he visited New Orleans. Wilson mentioned that the book was hard to find and that Saxon loaned him a copy. See Edmund Wilson, letter to John Peale Bishop, 4 Dec. 1934, *Letters,* 252.

[31]Sherwood Anderson, letter to Lyle Saxon, [late 1927], TU.

[32]For reviews cited in this paragraph, see Arthur Warner, "All Roads Lead to Paris," *The Nation* 128 (1929): 23; "Classified Books," *The Booklist* 25 (1929): 159; Josiah Titzell, "Mardi Gras," *NYHTB,* 23 Dec. 1928: 15; and Duffus, "New Orleans," 4.

[33]See Evans Wall, letter to Lyle Saxon, 8 Mar. 1929, TU; Bernard De Voto, letter to Lyle Saxon, 2 Nov. 1928, TU; and Carl Carmer, letter to Lyle Saxon, 25 Mar. 1929, TU.

[34]Dillon, 6, 21.

[35]Dale Warren, letter to Lyle Saxon, 17 May 1929, TU.

[36]See Lyle Saxon, letter to Olive Lyons, 15 Jun. 1929, TU; and Evans Wall, *The No-Nation Girl* (New York: The Century Co., 1929), n. pag. Wall, in his dedication, says that Lyle Saxon "knows the truth of the types and scenes presented in these pages."

[37]Tynes, 4.

[38]Lyle Saxon, letter to Noel Straus, 21 Dec. 1925, TU.

[39]Lyle Saxon, letter to Olive Lyons, 15 Jun. 1929, TU.

[40]See Lyle Saxon, letter to Lyman B. Sturgis [book editor at Century], 12 Mar. 1929, TU; letter to Lyman B. Sturgis, 8 May 1929, TU; and letter to Olive Lyons, 15 Jun. 1929, TU.

[41]R. L. Duffus, "That Lost Garden of Eden Which Was Old Louisiana," *NYTBR*, 17 Nov. 1929: 8.

[42]One of Elaine's poems, the narrator points out, caused a discussion that lasted several hours. The final line—"To get some water, to make some paste!"—is an explanation of why the little girl in the poem is running. The aunts are especially perplexed as to one point, the resolution of which takes a great deal of time. What must be determined first is whether the water was to be used to make the paste or if two separate activities were planned: getting water and making paste. Whatever the proper reading, this is surely the "most difficult line of the verse" (41). I am tempted to add that this is a sticky point indeed.

[43]Dormon, 26.

[44]Herschel Brickell, "The Good Old Days," *The Saturday Review of Literature,* 21 Dec. 1929: 583.

[45]Saxon points out that two of these chapters, dealing with Christmas and with New Year's Eve on plantations, are rewrites of earlier *Times-Picayune* works (ix). Although not acknowledged as adapted from the newspaper, the chapters on black superstitions are also adaptations of Saxon's "Cane River Superstitions," *NOTP,* 20 Sep. 1925: 3.

[46]Within five pages in *Old Louisiana*, Saxon writes the same sentence; "Fortunes were made in three or four years" appears on pages 132 and 137. The second such flaw is his discussion of Robert McAlpin (365-66) apparently without regard to his earlier exploration of this topic in some detail (253-66).

[47]Henry Steele Commager, "Levee Land," *NTHTB,* 24 Nov. 1929: 25.

[48]For reviews cited in this paragraph, see Stark Young, *"Old Louisiana," The New Republic* 61 (1929): 43; John McClure, *"Old Louisiana," NOTP,* 17 Nov. 1929, NSU; Burton Rascoe, "Among the New Books," *Arts and Decoration,* Jan. 1930: 92; and Howard Mumford Jones, "The Literary Lantern," *The Asheville Citizen,* 8 Dec. 1929, NSU.

[49]Duffus, "That Lost Garden," 8.

[50]Brickell, 583.

[51]J. Frank Dobie, letter to Mrs. C. J. [Cammie] Henry, 25 Mar. 1930, NSU.

[52]Lyle Saxon, letter to Cammie Henry, [summer 1930], NSU. Saxon herein refers to Henry's scrapbooks he has borrowed for his work on Lafitte.

[53]Lyle Saxon, letter to Caroline Dormon, 14 Sep. 1930, Harvey, "Portrait" 319-21.

[54]Lyle Saxon, *Lafitte the Pirate* (New York: The Century Co., 1930), ix. Subsequent references are to this edition and will appear parenthetically in the text.

[55]For example, in his notebook Saxon writes: "Atmosphere 'Grande Isle.' Gnarled oak trees, twisted by gulf winds, scalded by salt spray . . . ." In the book he elaborates: "Dwarfed oak-trees, curiously twisted by the wind and their outer leaves scalded by the salt spray, grew in dense groves, their gnarled trunks leaning all in one direction . . ." (40). For other comparisons, see Lyle Saxon, Notes for *Lafitte the Pirate*, ms., [1930], TU.

[56]Rose C. Feld, "Lafitte, Picturesque Brigand of Old New Orleans," *NYTBR*, 30 Nov. 1930: 7.

[57]Lyle Saxon, letter to Cammie Henry, [summer 1930], NSU.

[58]J. Fair Hardin, "Saxon's *Lafitte the Pirate*," *The Louisiana Historical Quarterly* 14 (1931): 442.

[59]For reviews cited in this paragraph, see Charles J. Finger, "Blacksmith Turned Pirate," *NYHTB*, 9 Nov. 1930: 3; Feld, 7; "Classified Books," *The Booklist* 27 (1931): 205; "*Lafitte the Pirate*," *The Bookman* 72 (1930): v; Stark Young, "Deep South Notes, V: Ars Longa," *The New Republic* 72 (1932): 71; and Hardin, 441.

[60]Julia Peterkin, letter to Lyle Saxon, 10 Jan. 1931, NSU.

[61]Grace King, letter to Lyle Saxon, 18 Nov. 1930, NSU.

[62]See Lyle Saxon, "A Child Looks at the River," *American Scrap Book: The Year's Golden Harvest of Thought and Achievement* (New York: W. H. Wise, 1928), 34-40; "Crevasse," *Contemporary Literature*, ed. Russell Blankenship, R. L. Lyman, and Howard C. Hill (New York: Scribner's, 1938), 468-81; "The Great Mississippi Flood," *Cypress Knees*, ed. Clarence R. Stone (St. Louis: Webster, 1942), 190-207; "Refugee," *A Treasury of Mississippi River Folklore*, ed. B. A. Botkin (New York: Crown, 1955), 285-88; "America in Europe," *Southern Treasury of Life and Literature*, ed. Stark Young (New York: Scribner's, 1937), 39-44; and "The Time of their Lives," *The World From Jackson Square*, ed. Etolia S. Basso (New York: Farrar, Straus and Co., 1948), 47-52.

[63]See Lyle Saxon, "The Gay Dangerfields," *Stories of the South: Old and New*, ed. Addison Hibbard (Chapel Hill: U of NC P, 1931), 361-72; and "The Gay Danger-fields," *A Southern Harvest*, ed. Robert Penn Warren (Boston: Houghton Mifflin, 1937), 332-41.

[64]The first edition of *Lafitte the Pirate*, five thousand copies, sold out quickly; Saxon's book was listed among the "Best Sellers" in *The New York Times*. See "Best Sellers of 1930," *NYTBR*, 21 Dec. 1930: 24. The serialized installments of his story in *The Times-Picayune* appeared daily from May 25 through June 29, 1931. Each daily article consisted, essentially, of a chapter of the Century volume.

[65]See "Newsboys Dress Like Buccaneers," *NOTP*, 25 May 1931: 2; "Announc-ing the 'Lafitte the Pirate' Essay Contest for All School Children," *NOTP*, 18 May

1931, NSU; and "Student Pastor Unearths Chest in Lafitte Hunt," *NOTP,* 31 May 1931, NSU. The treasure was eventually unearthed by a Baptist preacher near Pontchartrain Beach. The final clue told readers of this locale, and "thousands" looked frantically there for the treasure. A near-riot erupted when the huge crowd caught sight of the chest.

[66]Lyle Saxon, *Lafitte the Pirate,* trans. Andrhee Vaillant (Paris: Gallimard, 1935), 187.

[67]Lyle Saxon, "The General and the Pirates," *North, East, South, West: A Regional Anthology of American Writing,* ed. Charles Lee (New York: Howell Soskin, 1945), 312-14.

[68]See Lyle Saxon, letter to Mary Bird Perkins, 4 Nov. 1937, LSL; and "Editors, Writers Speak at L.S.U. Jubilee Program," *BRST,* 12 Apr. 1935, NSU.

[69]These figures appear in Roberta Gilkison, "Lyle Saxon Here on Brief Holiday Visit is Busy With Plans for His Next Book, Which Will Be a Novel," *BRST,* 30 Dec. 1930, LSL; and "Lyle Saxon, Famous Louisiana Author," 1.

[70]See Louis J. Nicolosi, "The Teaching of Louisiana History in the School Curriculum," *Louisiana History* 13 (1972): 39.

[71]Ray M. Thompson, 19.

[72]Dreyer, 164.

[73]See Lyle Saxon, "Hail Rex!" *A Southern Reader,* ed. Willard Thorp (New York: Knopf, 1955), 234-41; and "Ghosts in Gallatin Street," *A Treasury of Mississippi River Folklore,* ed. B. A. Botkin (New York: Crown, 1955), 257-61.

[74]Bennett Cerf, "Trade Winds," *The Saturday Review of Literature,* 10 Apr. 1948: 4.

[75]In 1988 *Fabulous New Orleans* and *Old Louisiana* were reissued as paperbacks by the Pelican Publishing Company of Gretna, Louisiana.

[76]Robert Cantwell, letter to the author, 22 Aug. 1974.

[77]Jay B. Hubbell, *"Old Louisiana," American Literature* 1 (1930) 465.

[78]Stuvyesant, 19.

[79]"Lyle Saxon, Famous Louisiana Author," 1.

[80]Lyle Saxon, letter to Olive Lyons, May 1928, TU.

[81]Arlin Turner, "Fiction of the Bayou Country," *The Saturday Review of Literature,* 30 Apr. 1938: 3.

Chapter 5

[1]See Lyle Saxon, letter to Cammie Henry, 4 Apr. 1923, NSU; and 1925 Diary, 10 Apr. entry, ms., NSU.

[2]See "South: New Orleans Literary Mentor Weeps for Mulattoes," *Newsweek,* 10 Jul. 1937: 20; Jo Thompson, 3; and Saxon's letter to Mary Bird Perkins, 4 Nov. 1937, LSL. In the Thompson interview Saxon claims that he had worked on the

novel for twelve years; in the letter he says he formulated the overall plan of the book in 1925.

[3]See Saxon's comments about the novel in "Lyle Saxon: Author of *Old Louisiana*," 148; Titzell, "Chronicler of the Fabulous," 495; [untitled clipping], *BRST,* 3 Jan. 1930, NSU; Mary Daggett Lake, "Meet Mr. Lyle Saxon of Louisiana and New York," *Texas Outlook* 14 (1930): 38; and Gilkison, LSL.

[4]Francois Mignon, "Cane River Memo: Letter to the Editor," *Natchitoches Enterprise,* 18 Feb. 1960: 4.

[5]Lyle Saxon, letter to Caroline Dormon, 14 Sep. 1930, Harvey, "Portrait," 319-21.

[6]See, for example, Lyle Saxon, letter to Olive Lyons, 6 May 1931, Harvey, "Portrait," 328-331; and Melrose Diary, 20 Nov. 1933 entry, ms., TU.

[7]Doris Ulmann, letter to Cammie Henry, 13 Mar. 1932, NSU.

[8]Tynes, 4.

[9]See Lyle Saxon, letter to Grace Arny, 8 Jun. 1933, LSU; letter to Elizabeth and Maude Chambers, 25 Jul. 1933, Harvey, "Portrait," 377-78; and letter to Grace Arny, 10 May 1934, LSU.

[10]McGraw, 2.

[11]Blotner, 1: 583.

[12]Carl Carmer told at least two publishers of Saxon's work on the novel. See Cleveland B. Chase, letter to Lyle Saxon, 11 Apr. 1929, TU; Ben Wasson, letter to Lyle Saxon, 4 Jun. 1929, TU; and William Rose Benét, letter to Lyle Saxon, 6 Feb. 1929, TU.

[13]See Ben Wasson, letter to Lyle Saxon, 4 Jun. 1929, TU; and Stuvyesant, 19.

[14]Hal Smith, letter to Lyle Saxon, 13 Feb. 1921, NSU.

[15]Gary B. and Elizabeth Mills, *Melrose* (Natchitoches: The Association of Natchitoches Women for the Preservation of Historic Natchitoches, 1973), 52.

[16]Harnett Kane, *Plantation Parade: The Grand Manner in Louisiana* (New York: Morrow, 1945), 276.

[17]Blotner makes no mention of Faulkner's travels to northern Louisiana, and Carvel Collins told me recently that he knows of "no proof" that Faulkner ever traveled to Melrose. Nevertheless, Collins added that it is entirely possible that Faulkner could have gone there. Joseph Henry told me he was "positive" the novelist visited Melrose.

[18]Mignon, *Plantation Memo,* 41.

[19]Lyle Saxon, letter to Olive Lyons, 24 Jul. 1933, Harvey, "Portrait," 374-76.

[20]Mignon describes some of the contents of Yucca House during Saxon's years there. He recalls a "unique" painting by Louisiana artist Jules Lion, "a punkah, a little bidet, a cotton stencil," and a personalized set of andirons bearing an "L" and an "S" (Mignon, *Plantation Memo,* 3, 17).

[21]See Mignon, "Cane River Memo: Birth of a Book," *Natchitoches Times,* 28 Feb. 1971: 2; and Mignon, *Plantation Memo,* 200.

[22]Saxon's Melrose Diary entries are sporadic; occasionally more than a month elapsed between the times he would keep this account.

[23]Lyle Saxon, Melrose Diary, 5 Dec. 1933 entry, ms., TU.

[24]Lyle Saxon, letter to Mary Bird Perkins, 4 Nov. 1937, LSL.

[25]Lyle Saxon, Melrose Diary, 1 Jan. 1934 entry, ms., TU.

[26]Lyle Saxon, letter to Mary Bird Perkins, 4 Nov. 1937, LSL.

[27]Regarding Saxon's difficulties cited in this paragraph, see Lyle Saxon, letter to Olive Lyons, 6 May 1931, Harvey, "Portrait," 362-64; letter to Caroline Dormon, 13 Oct. 1932, Harvey, "Portrait," 370-71; Melrose Diary, 25 Oct. 1933 and 31 Oct. 1933 entries, NSU; and Harvey, "Portrait," 496.

[28]Lyle Saxon, Melrose Diary, 6 Nov. 1933 entry, ms., TU.

[29]Lyle Saxon, letter to Cammie Henry, 11 Jan. 1934, NSU.

[30]Lyle Saxon, Melrose Diary, 20 Jan. 1934 entry, ms., TU.

[31]See Lyle Saxon, "Merry Moods of Carnival—Then and Now," *NOTP* magazine, 11 Feb. 1934: 3; "The Flaming Career of Adah Menken of New Orleans," *NOTP* magazine, 18 Feb., 25 Feb., and 4 Mar. 1934; "Shin-kicking Gets Countess Court Call," *NOTP* magazine, 11 Mar. 1934: 3; "Explosion on Steamboat *Louisiana* Shocked All New Orleans," *NOTP* magazine, 18 Mar. 1934: 3; "Sunrise and Easter Morning on a Louisiana Plantation," *NOTP* magazine, 1 Apr. 1934: 3; "How an Insult to 'Old Man River' was Expiated Under the Dueling Oaks," *NOTP* magazine, 8 Apr. 1934: 3; and "When Jackson, the General, and Lafitte, the Corsair, Hobnobbed in New Orleans," *NOTP* magazine, 15 Apr. 1934: 3.

[32]Lyle Saxon, letter to Grace Arny, 10 May 1934, LSL.

[33]Lyle Saxon, letter to Olive Lyons, 16 Mar. 1934, Harvey, "Portrait," 391-96.

[34]Saxon's bank balance in March 1934 was $5.59; in November he had over $750 (Chase National Bank of New York, letters and statements to Lyle Saxon, 9 Mar. 1934 and 30 Nov. 1934, NSU).

[35]Lyle Saxon, "Vanished Paradise," *Country Life*, Nov. 1934: 34-41+. Saxon's comment is in his letter to Grace Arny, 26 Sep. 1934, LSL.

[36]Lyle Saxon, "The Amazing Career of Myra Clark Gaines," *New Orleans Delphinian Oracle*, Nov. 1934: 6-7.

[37]Lyle Saxon, letter to Grace Arny, 26 Sep. 1934, LSU.

[38]See, for example, Lyle Saxon, letter to Caroline Dormon, 18 Mar. 1935, Harvey, "Portrait," 398-400; and letter to Olive Lyons, 21 Mar. 1935, Harvey "Portrait," 400-01.

[39]Lyle Saxon, letter to Grace Arny, 26 Sep. 1934, LSU.

[40]Lyle Saxon, letter to Mary Bird Perkins, 4 Nov. 1937, LSL.

[41]Lyle Saxon, letter to Grace Arny, 10 May 1934, LSU.

[42]See Jo Thompson, 3; and Lyle Saxon, letter to Mary Bird Perkins, 4 Nov. 1937, LSL.

[43]Tynes, 6.

[44]"Lyle Saxon, Famous Louisiana Author," 3.

[45]"Editors, Writers Speak at L.S.U.," NSU.

[46]Lyle Saxon, letter to Mary Bird Perkins, 4 Nov. 1937, LSL.

[47]Lyle Saxon, Melrose Diary, 1 Jan. 1934 entry, ms., TU.

[48]The word *mulatto* is used throughout this chapter in the sense that Saxon uses it in the novel: to denote any person of mixed Caucasian and African ancestry. The more limited meaning of *mulatto* (to denote only a person who is half-Caucasian, half-African) and the use of such terms as *griffe*, *quadroon*, or *octoroon*, seem not only outdated but needlessly complicated in regard to the novel.

[49]Saxon's name for the fictional plantation, "Yucca," should not be confused with the name of the actual cabin, "Yucca House," at Melrose. The entire plantation was actually once called Yucca. The Henrys renamed it Melrose after Sir Walter Scott's burial place, Melrose Abbey.

[50]Lyle Saxon, *Children of Strangers* (Boston: Houghton Mifflin, 1937), 33. Subsequent references are to this edition and will appear parenthetically in the text.

[51]Although certainly not as isolated or clannish as in Saxon's day, many of these people still live on or near the same spot. Some still intermarry and remain aloof from the town of Natchitoches. Recent telephone directories for Cane River, Louisiana, still include several names that appear in Saxon's book, such as Metoyer, Monette, Rocque, and Le Cour.

[52]Saxon chose the title for his novel from Leviticus 25: 45, which he quotes from the Authorized Version: "Moreover of the children of the strangers that do sojourn among you, of them shall ye buy, and of their families that are with you, which they begat in your land: and they shall be your possessions." The phrase "children of . . . strangers," aptly descriptive of the Louisiana mulattoes, refers in Leviticus to those offspring of foreigners in Israel whom the Israelites could purchase as slaves.

[53]Mills and Mills, 41.

[54]Mills and Mills, 41.

[55]Saxon refers to the visit to Madame Rocque in Melrose Diary, 6 Nov. 1933 entry, ms., TU. Joseph Henry and Francois Mignon told me about Tyler.

[56]In his notes Saxon writes: "Aunt Cammie is making preserves. Magnificent. She does this as she does everything else, with dash . . . . Aunt Cammie, her skirts caught up, goes from kettle to kettle, stirring with a great iron spoon" (Lyle Saxon, Notes for *Children of Strangers*, [1928 or 1929?], ms., TU). In the novel he writes: "Mr. Guy's wife was making preserves. She did this as she did everything else—with dash. . . . Miss Adelaide, her skirts caught up, went from kettle to kettle, stirring with a large iron spoon" (238-39).

[57]For example, Saxon writes that Josephine had at least six children and two mulatto husbands (Notes for *Children of Strangers*, [1928 or 1929?], ms., TU).

[58]The priest at the St. Augustine church from 1894 to 1908 was Father B. Regis. In the early 1970s, when Joseph Henry asked the priests to allow him to see documents

from this period, he was told "that all church records between 1894 and 1908 are missing—quite a coincidence" (Joseph Henry, letter to the author, 30 Oct. 1974; and letter to the author, 13 Nov. 1974).

[59]McGraw, 2

[60]Hamilton Basso quoted in Newton Arvin, ed. *The Grandissimes*, by George Washington Cable (New York: Hill and Wang, 1957), v-vi.

[61]Dillon, 33.

[62]See, for example, "A Visit to Avoyelles" and "A No-Account Creole" in Kate Chopin, *The Awakening and Other Stories*, ed. Lewis Leary (New York: Holt, Rinehart and Winston, 1970).

[63]Saxon mentioned cutting at least one major character out completely (see Leisure, 509), and the manuscript of the novel at L.S.U. indicates that others, such as Numa, were once more fully developed. The account of Numa's death, for example, was apparently at least three pages longer at one time (see Lyle Saxon, Draft of *Children of Strangers*, ms., LSU, 196-200).

[64]The reader occasionally encounters a somewhat unfortunate alliteration, for example, such as, "Famie's fingers fumbled for the lamp" (99). Also, the passage in which Saxon has Mr. Guy mention the title of the book in describing the Cane River mulattoes is particularly unnatural and awkward (177); and Saxon "nods" on occasion, such as when he again explains who Guy Randolph is several chapters after readers first encounter the planter (153). On the other hand, for Saxon's adroit handling of the four dialects, see 14-17, 117-18, 120-24, and 175-77.

[65]Roark Bradford, "Disintegration of 'Famie,' " *New Orleans Item*, 19 Jul. 1937, NSU.

[66]The novelist usually employs rhetorical questions in such instances. In the scene wherein Numa lies to Famie, for example, Saxon writes: "Why did he go on talking, lying, damning himself further?" (98). In describing Famie's wedding night, he writes: "Why was she afraid? Why did she dread this moment?" (138). Another example of Saxon's focusing on a single consciousness is the "Long Furrow" chapter, wherein several passages are found that are more typical of Henry Tyler than the sophisticated narrative voice elsewhere. Saxon, for example, writes: "Yes, sir, that's what sickness does to you. Sickness comes on horseback but it goes away on foot" (159).

[67]Lyle Saxon, letter to Mary Bird Perkins, 4 Nov. 1937, LSL.

[68]See E. P. O'Donnell, "An Arrangement in Decay," *The Washington Post*, 11 Jul. 1937, NSU; "Mixed Strains," *The Times Literary Supplement*, 4 Dec. 1937: 927; and Hamilton Basso, "Bayou People," *The New Republic* 92 (1937): 108.

[69]Saxon repeatedly points out her passion for the man's hair (see 65, 67, 71, 72, 73). The suggestion here seems to be not only of Famie's love of the sexual union they enjoy, but of an affinity too for this hair color not unusual among whites but very rare among her own people.

[70]Philip A. Tapley, "Negro Superstitions in *Children of Strangers*," *Louisiana Folklore Miscellany* 4 (1976-80): 65-66.

[71]See Edward Larocque Tinker, "A Dramatic Novel of Louisiana," *NYTBR*, 11 Jul. 1937: 1; and Harry Hansen, "The First Reader," New York *World Telegram*, 6 Jul. 1937, NSU.

[72]Davis, 34.

[73]O'Donnell, NSU.

[74]A passage dealing with Joel's likes and dislikes as a child, for example, is crossed out in the manuscript of the novel at LSU.

[75]George Stevens, "A Poignant Story of the 'Free Mulattoes,' " *The Saturday Review of Literature*, 10 Jul. 1937: 6.

[76] Roark Bradford, NSU.

[77]The bad luck omens Saxon incorporates among the superstitions mentioned in the novel almost invariably work. Previously the owl is heard before Joe is discovered and shot (73) and before a character contracts smallpox (199). In his study of Saxon's superstitions, Tapley writes: "If the owl's hooting does not portend death, then, at minimum it brings bad luck" (Tapley, 69).

[78]Lyle Saxon, letter to Arthur G. Draper, 13 Aug. 1937, NSU.

[79]See Carl Van Doren, " 'Children of Strangers' Shows Its Working With Unusual Skill," *Boston Herald*, 10 Jul. 1937, NSU; and George W. Healy, Jr., "Novel by Lyle Saxon Is Distinguished Work," *NOTP*, 11 Jul. 1937, LSL.

[80]See Ward Greene, "*Children of Strangers*," *NYHTB*, 18 Jul. 1937: 3; Tinker, 1; Hansen, NSU; Basso, 108; and Stevens, 6.

[81]See Kate O'Brien, "Fiction," *The Spectator* 159 (1937): 1016; "*Children of Strangers*," *Scotsman*, 23 Dec. 1937, NSU; "*Children of Strangers*," *The Birmingham Post*, 28 Dec. 1937, NSU; and "Mixed Strains," 927.

[82]Tess Crager and Muriel Saxon Lambert both stressed this point to me.

[83]Healy, "Novel," LSL.

[84]Lyle Saxon, letter to Noel Straus, 12 Aug. 1937, NSU.

[85]Gwen Bristow, letter to Lyle Saxon, 27 Jul. 1937, TU.

[86]See McGraw, 2; and Jo Thompson, 3.

[87]"Frank Recollections," NSU.

[88]John R. Egle, letter to the author, 21 Jun. 1974.

[89]See, for example, Shirley K. Sullivan, "Lyle Saxon's Novel of South From Thirties," *Savannah News*, 31 Mar. 1974; Iris McNeer, "Take a Trip Into the Old South But Watch Out for the Trapdoor," *Mebane* [North Carolina] *Enterprise-Journal*, 4 Apr. 1974; and Monty Simmons, "Novel of Old South Shallow," *Roanoke World-News*, 17 Apr. 1974.

[90]Anne Goodwyn Jones, "*Gone With the Wind* and Others: Popular Fiction, 1920-1950," *The History of Southern Literature*, ed. Louis D. Rubin, Jr., et al (Baton Rouge: LSU P, 1985), 368.

Chapter 6

[1]Jerre Mangione, *The Dream and the Deal: The Federal Writers' Project* (Boston: Little, Brown, 1972), ix.

[2]Mangione, 4.

[3]Mangione, ix.

[4]William F. McDonald points out that salaries ranged from $1,800 to $3,800, and Saxon very probably was nearer the higher end of this scale due to his reputation. See William F. McDonald, *Federal Relief Administration and the Arts: The Origins and Administrative History of the Arts Projects of the Works Progress Administration* (Columbus: Ohio State U P, 1969), 680.

[5]McDonald, 743.

[6]Lyle Saxon, letter to Cammie Henry, 18 Oct. 1935, NSU.

[7]Lyle Saxon, letter to Cammie Henry, 7 Jan. 1936, NSU.

[8]Caroline Durieux, personal interview, 28 Aug. 1974. Subsequent references to Durieux are to this interview unless otherwise noted.

[9]Saxon's published works from the period include *A Walk Through the Vieux Carré and a Short History of the St. Charles Hotel* (New Orleans: Dinkler Hotels, 1935); "Lyle Saxon Tells of the Haunted House of Old New Orleans (The Lalaurie Mansion)," *Southern Architectural Review,* Aug. 1936: 13-15+; "History of the New Orleans Underworld," rev. of *The French Quarter,* by Herbert Asbury, *NYHTB,* 4 Oct. 1936: 5; "A Novel Bitter, Brutal, Compassionate," rev. of *Death in the Deep South,* by Ward Greene, *NYHTB,* 25 Oct. 1936: 6; "Uneasy Blood in Their Veins," rev. of *Courthouse Square,* by Hamilton Basso, *NYHTB,* 1 Nov. 1936: 8; "Novelist of the Mississippi Delta," rev. of *St. George of Weldon,* by Robert Rylee, *NYHTB,* 4 Apr. 1937: 6; "Recipe for Aristocracy," rev. of *The Three-Headed Angel,* by Roark Bradford, *NYHTB,* 25 Apr. 1937: 4; *"The Share-Cropper,* by Charlie May Simon," *NYHTB,* 19 Sep. 1937: 18; and *"Son of Haman,* by Louis Cochran," *NYHTB,* 26 Sep. 1937: 12.

[10]See Lyle Saxon, "Editorial," *Little Theatres of the South Magazine,* Dec. 1935: 1. This editorial laments the decline of the theater in New Orleans and recommends the support of the new little theaters throughout the South; and "Hotel [St. Charles] Also Celebrating Its Centennial, Was Hailed as World's Greatest in 1837," *NOTP,* 25 Jan. 1937: 18.

[11]Frank Vreeland, *Foremost Films of 1938* (New York: Pitman, 1939), 63.

[12]Edwin Justus Mayer, Harold Lamb, and C. Gardner Sullivan, "The Buccaneer," ms., LSU.

[13]Charles P. Jones, "Tamiroff Steals Show as Lafitte Returns to Life," *NOTP,* 8 Jan. 1938: 10.

[14]Frank S. Nugent, *"The Buccaneer," The New York Times,* 17 Feb. 1938: 17.

[15]*The Buccaneer* was remade in 1958, with Yul Brenner as the pirate and Charles Boyer as You. Although Saxon's name again appeared in the credits, this film is clearly a reincarnation of De Mille's, not Saxon's, Lafitte.

[16]Saxon comments favorably on the film in Leisure, 509; Several of those whom I have interviewed, however, mentioned Saxon's making great fun of the film.

[17]Vreeland, 64.

[18]Lyle Saxon, ed., *New Orleans City Guide* (Boston: Houghton Mifflin, 1938), 371-78. Subsequent references are to this edition and will appear parenthetically in the text.

[19]Edna Ferber, letter to Lyle Saxon, 11 Nov. 1940, Harvey, "Portrait," 430.

[20]See Edward Larocque Tinker, "A Well-Planned Guide to New Orleans," *NYTBR*, 22 May 1938: 5; and Thad St. Martin, "Crescent City," *The Saturday Review of Literature*, 23 Apr. 1938: 19.

[21]Saxon's writing during this time includes a few lines of doggerel in Olive Leonhardt, *New Orleans Drawn and Quartered* (Richmond: Dale Press, 1938)—Saxon writes, "The pen of Olive Leonhardt/ Has a cruel, catlike touch;/ It drips with gall and venom,/ Lewdness, lechery and such./ The result is simply awful,—/ And I like it very much!"; *Gwen Bristow: Author of Two Remarkable Novels, Deep Summer, 1937, The Handsome Road, 1938, A Sketch of Her Life* (n.p., 1938)—Bristow had worked with Saxon in the 1920s on *The Times-Picayune* and at the time the pamphlet was written lived in Hollywood with her husband Bruce Manning; "Saxon Finds Priestley View of New Orleans Shallow," *NOTP*, 15 May 1938: 3—In this piece Saxon defends his city, regrets that the Englishman did not enjoy his recent stay, and expresses a hope that Priestley will return and, upon further reflection, write of Orleanians in the future with "a little more tolerance and humor"; and "Madison Street," *Click*, Sept. 1938: 13.

[22]Stark Young, *Feliciana* (New York: Scribner's, 1935). In a letter to Saxon, Young even says that without Saxon's help the book could not have been done (Stark Young, letter to Lyle Saxon, 29 Mar. 1935, TU).

[23]Charles Elder, personal interview, 13 Apr. 1974.

[24]See Andrew Turnbull, *Thomas Wolfe* (New York: Scribner's, 1967), 252-53; and Dreyer, 133.

[25]Katy Dos Passos, letter to Lyle Saxon, 8 Sep. 1938, TU.

[26]Richard Bradford, letter to the author, 12 Nov. 1974.

[27]Dreyer, 170.

[28]Dreyer, 152.

[29]Richard Bradford, letter to the author, 12 Nov. 1974.

[30]See Sherwood Anderson, letter to Lyle Saxon, [1939], TU; and Hamilton Basso, letter to Lyle Saxon, 21 Mar. 1939, NSU.

[31]Lyle Saxon, letter to Cammie Henry, 23 Mar. 1939, NSU.

[32]Lyle Saxon, 1939 Diary, 28 Mar. entry, ms., TU.

[33]Dillon, 22.

[34]Richard Bradford, letter to the author, 12 Nov. 1974.

[35]See "Cane River," *Louisiana in the Short Story*, ed. Lizzie Carter McVoy (Baton Rouge: LSU P, 1940); "Traditional and Romantic Jefferson," *Jefferson Parish Yearly Review*, 1939: 93-103+; and "Their Faces Tell the Story," *Jefferson Parish Yearly Review*, 1940: 32-56.

[36]Hugh Saxon, letter to Lyle Saxon, 14 Aug. 1939, Harvey, "Portrait," 442.

[37]Alfred Kazin, *On Native Grounds*, 2nd ed. (Garden City: Anchor Books, 1956), 392.

[38]Lyle Saxon, ed., *Louisiana: A Guide to the State* (New York: Hastings House, 1941), 3. Subsequent references are to this edition and will appear parenthetically in the text.

[39]For reviews of *Louisiana* cited in this paragraph, see Pierre Crabitès, "*Louisiana*," *The Catholic World* 153 (1941): 630; Gilbert Govan, "Is It True What They Say About Dixie," *NYHTB*, 31 Aug. 1941: 5; and Frances Bryson, "Saxon's Book Best of State Guide Series, Says Carmer," *New Orleans Item*, 6 Mar. 1941, LSU.

[40]"Guide Credit Given to WPA by Saxon," *New Orleans Item*, 7 Mar. 1941, LSU.

[41]James B. La Fourche, "Lyle Saxon, Friend of Negro Passes," *The Louisiana Weekly*, 20 Apr. 1946, NSU.

[42]Leisure, 510.

[43]La Fourche, NSU.

[44]See Marcus B. Christian, ed., *From the Deep South* (New Orleans: n.p., 1937).

[45]Langston Hughes, letter to Lyle Saxon, 17 Nov. 1933, NSU.

[46]Octave Lilly, personal interview, 25 Aug. 1974. Subsequent references to Lilly are to this interview unless otherwise noted.

[47]Richard Bradford, letter to the author, 12 Nov. 1974.

[48]See "A Tourist Looks at Jefferson," *Jefferson Parish Yearly Review* 1941: 122-44; and "The Spaniard's Beard," *Jefferson Parish Yearly Review* 1942: 34-48.

[49]Dillon, 23.

[50]Mangione, 368.

[51]See Dillon, 23; and *FJG*, 93-95. In a brief reminiscence about the Washington assignment in *The Friends of Joe Gilmore*, Saxon also admits that he did not do his job well and that it "practicaly destroyed my mind . . . and put out my eyes."

[52]Mangione, 368-69.

[53]Mangione, 369.

[54]Lyle Saxon, letter to Cammie Henry, 8 Jun. 1943, NSU.

[55]Mignon, "Cane River Memo: Letter to the Editor," 4.

[56]McDonald, 698.

[57]Paul Streger [agent for Leland Hayward, Inc.], letter to Lyle Saxon, 22 Jul. 1937, NSU.

[58]Francois Mignon, "Cane River Memo: Lyle Saxon, Twenty-Five Years Later," *Natchitoches Times,* 10 May 1970: 2.

[59]Lyle Saxon, letter to T. S. Stribling, 13 Aug. 1937, NSU.

[60]Malcolm Cowley, letter to Lyle Saxon, 8 Nov. 1937, NSU.

[61]The request for a contribution to the Thurber-Benchley-Broun volume (*For Men: and Men Only*) is in Fred J. Feldkamp, letter to Lyle Saxon, 9 Dec. 1937, NSU; the *Saturday Review* offer is in George Stevens, letter to Lyle Saxon, 24 Feb. 1938, NSU.

[62]Fred J. Feldkamp, letter to Lyle Saxon, 12 Jan. 1938, NSU.

[63]Letters and telegrams from Stevens, now at Northwestern State University, continued throughout January and February of 1938 soliciting this article from Saxon. Eventually Stevens seems to have given up on the author. Arlin Turner's "Fiction of the Bayou Country" appeared on April 30, 1938.

[64]The *Southern Literary Messenger* offers are in F. Meredith Dietz, letter to Lyle Saxon, 22 Nov. 1938, NSU; Saxon had "The Centaur" illustrated about 1939 and was told by a publisher, probably Hastings House, that if he could complete a companion piece, a similar story, and have it illustrated as well, both would be published in "a small expensive book." Saxon planned the second story, but evidently never found the time to write it. The plans surrounding the venture are summarized in a letter Saxon wrote to a woman who was interested in illustrating some of his stories. See Lyle Saxon, letter to Mrs. Ralph Ellis, 23 Mar. 1939, NSU.

[65]Bernard Geis, letter to Lyle Saxon, 27 Sep. 1940, LSL.

[66]Ken McCormick, letter to Lyle Saxon, 3 Mar. 1942, NSU.

[67]Saxon told a reporter that the second book was already outlined in his mind. See Jo Thompson, 3.

[68]Lyle Saxon, letter to Mary Bird Perkins, 4 Nov. 1937, LSL.

[69]Leisure, 509.

[70]Lyle Saxon, letter to Noel Straus, 8 Aug. 1937, NSU.

[71]See Lyle Saxon, letter to Cammie Henry, 8 June 1943, NSU; and Ralph D. Paine, Jr., letter to Lyle Saxon, 4 June 1943, TU.

[72]Lyle Saxon, letter to David Ruml, 11 June 1943, TU.

[73]Lyle Saxon, letter to Mrs. Sam Jones, 4 June 1943, TU.

[74]See Lyle Saxon, "Bucks, Six-a-Week to Song Composer," *Inn Dixie,* Oct. 1943: 13+; and "Fame," *South,* Mar. 1945: 7+.

[75]Dillon, 23.

[76]See Hope Ridings Miller, "Hope Ridings Miller," *The Washington Post,* 8 Jun. 1943, TU.

[77]This is also the assumption of R. W. Clayton, who did a 1974 doctoral dissertation on the W.P.A. in Louisiana. Clayton told me that he felt Saxon's part in *Gumbo Ya-Ya* was more that of an overseer than an author (R. W. Clayton, personal interview, 20 May 1974).

[78]Lyle Saxon, letter to Marge Hunter, 7 Oct. 1940, Harvey, "Portrait," 455-56.

[79]Lyle Saxon, Edward Dreyer, and Robert Tallant, letter to Paul Brooks, 19 Feb. 1944, TU.

[80]For reveiws of *Gumbo Ya-Ya* cited in this paragraph, see Arna Bontemps, "Louisiana Folk Tales: Lively and Exotic, Strange and Wonderful," *The Chicago Sun Book Week,* 9 Dec. 1945: 14; David L. Cohn, "Everybody Talks at Once," *The Saturday Review of Literature,* 22 Dec. 1945: 11; and Eudora Welty, "Creole Get-Together," *NYTBR,* 20 Jan. 1946: 5.

[81]Lyle Saxon, letter to Noel Straus, 12 Aug. 1937, NSU.

[82]Dreyer, 173.

[83]Lucius Beebe, "This New York," *NYHT,* 13 May 1944, NSU.

[84]John Steinbeck, letter to Lyle Saxon, 5 Jan. 1942, TU.

[85]Gwyn Steinbeck, letter to Lyle Saxon, 8 Mar. 1944, TU.

[86]John Steinbeck, letter to Nunnally Johnson, [Apr. 1943], *Steinbeck: A Life in Letters,* ed. Elaine Steinbeck and Robert Wallsten (New York: Viking, 1975), 251.

[87]George Sessions Perry, "The Cities of America: New Orleans," *The Saturday Evening Post,* 1 Jun. 1946: 75.

[88]Robert Tallant, "Salute to Saxon," *South,* June 1946: 28.

[89]Tallant, "My Fabulous Friend," 9.

[90]Walter Frese, letter to the author, 19 Aug. 1974. Frese provided me with pertinent information regarding Saxon's dealings with Hastings House publishers.

[91]Richard Bradford, letter to the author, 12 Nov. 1974.

[92]For reviews of *The Friends of Joe Gilmore* cited in this paragraph, see "*The Friends of Joe Gilmore,*" *The New Yorker,* 22 Jan. 1949: 82; Hodding Carter, "Background for Laughter," *NYHTB,* 20 Feb. 1949: 6; and Ernest Gueymard, "Lyle Saxon Book Issued Posthumously," *BRST,* 16 Dec. 1948: 16.

[93] Sales moved very slowly; about five thousand copies sold over a long period of years (Walter Frese, letter to the author, 19 Aug. 1974).

[94]Dillon, 31.

[95]Dillon, 31.

[96]Tallant, "My Fabulous Friend Lyle Saxon," 9.

[97]See Maude Chambers, letter to Mrs. Frank Johnson, 21 Oct. 1944, LSL; and Lyle Saxon, letter to Maude Chambers, 7 Apr. 1945, LSL.

[98]Lyle Saxon, letter to Cammie Henry, 16 Oct. 1945, NSU.

[100]See Lyle Saxon, "Foreword," *Voodoo in New Orleans,* by Robert Tallant (New York: MacMillan, 1946), v; and " 'You Must Mask For Mardi Gras,' Says Saxon," *NOTP,* 6 Feb. 1946, NSU. This *Times-Picayune* article is evidently the last thing Saxon wrote that was published in his lifetime. It is a very short, one-column piece on what the tourist should see and do at carnival time in New Orleans.

[101]Robert Tallant, letter to Cammie Henry, 14 Apr. 1946, NSU.

[102]Robert Tallant, letter to Cammie Henry, 14 Apr. 1946, NSU.

[103]For the obituaries cited in this paragraph, see "Lyle Saxon," *BRST,* 11 Apr. 1946: 4; "Noted Historian Lyle Saxon Dies," *NOTP,* 10 Apr. 1946: 1; "Lyle Saxon," *NOTP,* 11 Apr. 1946: 10; "Milestones," *Time,* 22 Apr. 1946: 92; "Transition," *Newsweek,* 22 Apr. 1946: 60; "Obituary Notes," *The Publishers' Weekly* 149 (1946): 2459; and "Notes and Quotes," *The Wilson Library Bulletin* 20 (1946): 696.

[104]Perry, 75.

[105]Tallant "Salute to Saxon," 28.

[106] Saxon quoted in Tallant "My Fabulous Friend Lyle Saxon," 9.

[107]Saxon quoted in "South: New Orleans' Literary Mentor," 20.

Chapter 7

[1]Lewis Simpson, letter to the author, 9 Apr. 1974.

[2]Adaline Samuel, personal interview, 24 Aug. 1974.

[3]Walter L. Mosley, letter to the author, 29 Apr. 1974.

[4]Ed Tunstall, letter to the author, 10 Oct. 1974.

[5]See Baldridge, 14.

[6]Pat Baldridge, personal interview, 28 Aug. 1974.

[7]Joan Samuel, personal interview, 28 Aug. 1974.

[8]The illustrated "Centaur" was to have been issued in a limited edition after Saxon's death; but, after several years, the project was canceled by Hastings House, who returned the story and drawings (Walter Frese, letter to the author, 19 Aug. 1974).

[9]Harris Downey, personal interview, 25 Aug. 1974.

[10]Francois Mignon recalled how aptly Saxon's friends thought this phrase described him. It was quoted in Saxon's *Times-Picayune* obituary and was the title of another article (Begbie's *Shreveport Times* article is "A Writer Without an Enemy").

[11]Robert Tallant, letter to Cammie Henry, 14 Apr. 1946, NSU.

[12]"Lyle Saxon, Noted Louisiana Author, Dies in Orleans," *BRMA,* 10 Apr. 1946, LSL.

[13]Tallant, "Introduction," xiv.

[14]"Lyle Saxon, Famous Louisiana Author," 3.

[15]Saxon quoted in Tynes, 4.

[16]See Jo Thompson, 3.

[17]Stuvyesant, 19.

[18]Lyle Saxon, letter to Noel Straus, 21 Dec. 1925, TU.

BIBLIOGRAPHY

NOTE: Part I of this bibliography is a chronological listing of Saxon's works. I have attempted a complete list with the exception of his routine news assignments and less significant articles and reviews. Part II is a listing of the works I consulted for this study. Included here are all items dealing with Saxon that I have been able to locate over the years. The various clippings and the considerable amount of unpublished Saxon material cited in this study (letters, diaries, and manuscripts) that are identified with the designations LSL, LSU, NSU, and TU can be found at the following libraries:

LSL   Saxon Collection
       Louisiana State Library
       Baton Rouge

LSU   Saxon Archives
       Louisiana State University Library
       Baton Rouge

NSU   Melrose and Saxon Collections
       Eugene P. Watson Memorial Library
       Northwestern State University of Louisiana
       Natchitoches

TU   Saxon Collection
       Howard-Tilton Memorial Library
       Tulane University
       New Orleans

I. Published Works by Lyle Saxon

"Fire Leaves Home of Lyric Opera Heap of Ruins." *NOTP*, 5 Dec. 1919: 1+.

"At the Gates of Empire." *NOTP*, 24 Apr.-14 Aug. 1921.

"The General Remembers, Recollections of Gen. John McGrath of Baton Rouge." *NOTP*, 21, 28 Aug., 4, 11 Sept. 1921.

[Series on Spanish Architecture in New Orleans—various titles]. *NOTP*, 9-19 Apr. 1922.

"Unusual Ways of Making a Living." *NOTP*, 26 Jul.-17 Aug. 1922.

"Easter Sunday at Aunt Cammie's." *NOTP* magazine, 22 Apr. 1923: 1.

"An Interlude" and "The Forgotten Cigarette." *NOTP* magazine, 20 May 1923: 4, 7.

"Fingers in the Dark." *NOTP*, 27 May 1923, NSU.

"The One Thing." *NOTP* magazine, 27 May 1923: 1+.

"After All These Years." *NOTP* magazine, 24 Jun. 1923: 1+.

"Two Writers Do Time for Story 'Behind Bars' " [coauthored with Wilbur Wright]. *NOTP*, 15 Jul. 1923: 1+.

"Epitaph: A Play in One Act." *NOTP* magazine, 16 Sept. 1923: 2+.

"The Perfume of Her Presence." *NOTP* magazine, 30 Sept. 1923: 1.

"A Breath from the Vieux Carré." *House and Garden*, Nov. 1923: 72+.

"The Mistletoe Trail: Christmas on a Louisiana Plantation." *NOTP* magazine, 23 Dec. 1923: 1+.

Introduction. *Picturesque New Orleans*. By William Spratling. New Orleans: TU P, 1923.

"Gallatin Street." *NOTP* magazine, 6 Jan. 1924: 1+.

"Jewels of a Century." *NOTP* magazine, 17 Feb. 1924: 5.

"Blackmail." *NOTP* magazine, 30 Mar. 1924: 1+.

"The Toil of Worship." *NOTP* magazine, 27 Apr. 1924: 1+.

"The Man Who Hated Women." *NOTP* magazine, 25 May 1924: 1+.

"The Return." *NOTP* magazine, 13 Jul. 1924: 1+.

"Cane River Superstitions." *NOTP*, 20 Sept. 1925: 3.

"Cane River." *The Dial* 80 (1926): 207-221.

"Brilliant Throng Meets Movie Folk at Opening of Loew's State Theater." *NOTP*, 4 Apr. 1926, TU.

"Baroness Pontalba Goes Home." *NOTP* magazine, 10 Oct. 1926: 7.

"Voodoo." *The New Republic* 50 (1927): 135-39.

"Cane River." *O. Henry Memorial Award Prize Stories of 1926*. Ed. Blanche Colton Williams, et. al. Garden City: Doubleday Page, 1927. 213-38.

"Fame." *New Orleans Life*, May 1927: 9-11.

"Down on the Levee: A True Story of the Mississippi Tragedy." *The Century Magazine* 114 (1927): 292-98.

"Acadians in the Flood: Waiting for Safety and Sunrise and Dry Land." *The Century Magazine* 114 (1927): 462-68.

"And the Waters Receded: But What about Bigger and Better Floods Next Year." *The Century Magazine* 114 (1927): 583-89.

"The Centaur Plays Croquet." *The American Caravan*. Ed. Van Wyck Brooks, Alfred Kreymborg, Lewis Mumford, and Paul Rosenfeld. New York: Literary Guild, 1927. 344-69.

Father Mississippi. New York: The Century Co., 1927.

"The Long Furrow." *The Century Magazine* 114 (1927): 688-96.

"Cane River." *The Best Short Stories of 1927 and the Yearbook of the American Short Story*. Ed. Edward J. O'Brien. New York: Dodd, Mead, 1927. 240-54.

"Make This a Book Christmas." *The Publishers' Weekly* 112 (1927): 2021-24.

"Lizzie Balize." *The Dial* 85 (1928): 303-12.

"Have a Good Time While You Can: An Impression of the Carnival in New Orleans, I." *The Century Magazine* 116 (1928): 680-90.

"Have a Good Time While You Can: An Impression of the Carnival in New Orleans, II." *The Century Magazine* 117 (1928): 85-94.

Fabulous New Orleans. New York: The Century Co., 1928.

"A Child Looks at the River." *American Scrap Book: The Year's Golden Harvest of Thought and Achievement*. New York: W. H. Wise, 1928. 34-40.

"Voodoo in Haiti." Rev. of *The Magic Island*, by William Seabrook. *The Bookman* 68 (1929): 712-14.

"The Gay Dangerfields." *The Century Magazine* 118 (1929): 489-95.

"A Family Breaks Up." Rev. of *The Sound and the Fury*, by William Faulkner. *NYHTB*, 13 Oct. 1929: 3.

Old Louisiana. New York: The Century Co., 1929.

"Hushed Orchestra." Rev. of *River House*, by Stark Young. *The Saturday Review of Literature*, 7 Dec. 1929: 520.

"Mardi Gras." *NYHT* magazine, 2 Mar. 1930: 16-18.

"Easter on the Plantation." *NYHT* magazine, 20 Apr. 1930: 14-16.

"Grand Days on the River." Rev. of *The Pageant of the Packets*, by Garnett Laidlaw Eskew. *NYHTB*, 27 Apr. 1930: 17.

"The South Parades: Mardi Gras." *Theatre Arts Monthly* 14 (1930): 683-88.

"Bad Men of the Natchez Trace." Rev. of *The Outlaw Years*, by Robert M. Coates. *NYHTB*, 3 Aug. 1930: 3.

Lafitte the Pirate. New York: The Century Co., 1930.

"Lafitte the Pirate." *The New Orleanian*, 4 Oct. 1930: 16-17+.

"A New Rush for Pirates' Gold." *NYHT* magazine, 19 Oct. 1930: 14-16.

"Romances of Old New Orleans." Rev. of *Old New Orleans*, by Frances and Edward Larocque Tinker. *NYHTB*, 15 Feb. 1931: 1+.

"Lafitte the Pirate." *NOTP*, 25 May-29 Jun. 1931.

"The Gay Dangerfields." *Stories of the South: Old and New*. Ed. Addison Hibbard. Chapel Hill: U of NC. P, 1931. 361-72.

[Remarks on the Death of Grace King] "Death of Grace King." Ed. Henry P. Dart. *Louisiana Historical Quarterly* 15 (1932): 330-38.

"Merry Moods of Carnival—Then and Now." *NOTP* magazine, 11 Feb. 1934: 3.

"The Flaming Career of Adah Menken of New Orleans." *NOTP* magazine, 18, 25 Feb., 4 Mar. 1934.

"Shin-kicking Gets Countess Court Call." *NOTP* magazine, 11 Mar. 1934: 3.

"Explosion on Steamboat *Louisiana* Shocked all New Orleans." *NOTP* magazine, 18 Mar. 1934: 3.

"Sunrise and Easter Morning on a Louisiana Plantation." *NOTP* magazine, 1 Apr. 1934: 3.

"How an Insult to 'Old Man River' was Expiated Under the Dueling Oaks." *NOTP* magazine, 8 Apr. 1934: 3.

"When Jackson, the General, and Lafitte, the Corsair, Hobnobbed in New Orleans." *NOTP* magazine, 15 Apr. 1934: 3.

"Vanished Paradise." *Country Life,* Nov. 1934: 34-41+.

"The Amazing Career of Myra Clark Gaines." *New Orleans Delphinian Oracle,* Nov. 1934: 6-7.

"Editorial." *Little Theatres of the South Magazine,* Dec. 1935: 1.

A Walk Through the Vieux Carré and a Short History of the St. Charles. New Orleans: Dinkler Hotels, 1935.

"Lyle Saxon Tells of the Haunted House of Old New Orleans (The Lalaurie Mansion)." *Southern Architectural Review,* Aug. 1936: 13-15+.

"History of the New Orleans Underworld." Rev. of *The French Quarter,* by Herbert Asbury. *NYHTB,* 4 Oct. 1936: 5.

"A Novel Bitter, Brutal, Compassionate." Rev. of *Death in the Deep South,* by Ward Greene. *NYHTB,* 25 Oct. 1936: 6.

"Uneasy Blood in Their Veins." Rev. of *Courthouse Square,* by Hamilton Basso. *NYHTB,* 1 Nov. 1936: 8.

"Hotel [St. Charles] Also Celebrating Its Centennial, Was Hailed as World's Greatest in 1837." *NOTP,* 25 Jan. 1937: 18.

"Novelist of the Mississippi Delta." Rev. of *St. George of Weldon,* by Robert Rylee. *NYHTB,* 4 Apr. 1937: 6.

"Recipe for Aristocracy." Rev. of *The Three-Headed Angel,* by Roark Bradford. *NYHTB,* 25 Apr. 1937: 4.

Children of Strangers. Boston: Houghton Mifflin, 1937.

Children of Strangers. London: John Lane, 1937.

"*The Share-Cropper,* by Charlie May Simon." *NYHTB,* 19 Sept. 1937: 18.

"*Son of Haman,* by Louis Cochran." *NYHTB,* 26 Sept. 1937: 12.

"America in Europe." *Southern Treasury of Life and Literature.* Ed. Stark Young. New York: Scribner's, 1937. 39-44.

"The Gay Dangerfields." *A Southern Harvest.* Ed. Robert Penn Warren. Boston: Houghton Mifflin, 1937. 332-41.

New Orleans City Guide. Ed. Lyle Saxon. Boston: Houghton Mifflin, 1938.

Foreword. *New Orleans Drawn and Quartered.* By Olive Leonhardt. Richmond: Dale P, 1938.

Gwen Bristow: Author of Two Remarkable Novels, Deep Summer, *1937,* The Handsome Road, *1938, A Sketch of Her Life.* N.p.: n.p., 1938.

"Saxon Finds Priestley View of New Orleans Shallow." *NOTP,* 15 May 1938: 3.

"The Federal Writers' Project in Louisiana." *Louisiana Library Association Bulletin,* Sept. 1938: 2-3.

"Madison Street." *Click,* Sept. 1938: 13.

"Crevasse." *Contemporary Literature.* Ed. Russell Blankenship, Rollo L. Lyman, and Howard C. Hill. New York: Scribner's, 1938. 468-81.

"Traditional and Romantic Jefferson." *Jefferson Parish Yearly Review* 1939: 93-103+.

"Cane River." *Louisiana in the Short Story.* Ed. Lizzie Carter McVoy. Baton Rouge: LSU P, 1940. 129-46.

"Their Faces Tell the Story." *Jefferson Parish Yearly Review* 1940: 32-56.

Louisiana: A Guide to the State. Ed. Lyle Saxon. New York: Hastings House, 1941.

"A Tourist Looks at Jefferson." *Jefferson Parish Yearly Review* 1941: 122-44.

"The Spaniard's Beard." *Jefferson Parish Yearly Review* 1942: 34-48.

"The Great Mississippi Flood." *Cypress Knees.* Ed. Clarence R. Stone. St. Louis: Webster, 1942. 190-207.

"Bucks, Six-a-Week to Song Composer." *Inn Dixie,* Oct. 1943: 13+.

"Fame." *South* Mar. 1945: 7+.

"The General and the Pirates." *North, East, South, West: A Regional Anthology of American Writing.* Ed. Charles Lee. New York: Howell Soskin, 1945.

Gumbo Ya-Ya. Ed. Lyle Saxon, Edward Dreyer, and Robert Tallant. Boston: Houghton Mifflin, 1945.

Foreword. *Voodoo in New Orleans.* By Robert Tallant. New York: MacMillan, 1946.

" 'You Must Mask for Mardi Gras,' Says Saxon." *NOTP,* 6 Feb. 1946, NSU.

The Friends of Joe Gilmore. New York: Hastings House, 1948.

"The Time of their Lives." *The World From Jackson Square.* Ed. Etolia S. Basso. New York: Farrar, Straus, 1948. 47-52.

"The Centaur Plays Croquet." *The World From Jackson Square.* Ed. Etolia S. Basso. New York: Farrar, Straus, 1948. 277-300.

"Culpepper's Pride." *A Treasury of Southern Folklore.* Ed. B. A. Botkin. New York: Crown, 1949. 61-63.

"The Devil's Mansion." *A Treasury of Southern Folklore.* Ed. B. A. Botkin. New York: Crown, 1949. 547-48.

My Love: From Lyle Saxon's 1924 Scrapbook and By the Fire: From Lyle Saxon's 1925-26 Scrapbook. Baton Rouge: n.p., 1950.

"Hail Rex!" *A Southern Reader.* Ed. Willard Thorp. New York: Knopf, 1955. 234-41.

"The Creoles of New Orleans." [By Lyle Saxon, Edward Dreyer, and Robert Tallant]. *A Southern Reader.* New York: Knopf, 1955. 90-98.

"Ghosts in Gallatin Street." *A Treasury of Mississippi River Folklore.* Ed. B. A. Botkin. New York: Crown, 1955. 257-61.

"Refugee." *A Treasury of Mississippi River Folklore*. Ed. B. A. Botkin. New York: Crown, 1955. 285-88.

"Pirogue Races." *A Treasury of Mississippi River Folklore*. Ed. B. A. Botkin. New York: Crown, 1955. 440-41.

" 'Stuck Good.' " *A Treasury of Mississippi River Folklore*. Ed. B. A. Botkin. New York: Crown, 1955. 482-83.

II. Works Cited and Other Works Related to Lyle Saxon

Aldrich, Ella V. "Lyle Saxon." *Louisiana Library Association Bulletin* 9 (1946): 108.

"Among the Publishers." *The Publishers' Weekly* 132 (1937): 1421.

Anderson, Viola. "Louisiana in Print." *Louisiana Library Association Bulletin*, June 1942: 7-11.

"Announcing the 'Lafitte the Pirate' Essay Contest for All School Children." *NOTP*, 18 May. 1931, NSU.

Arvin, Newton, ed. *The Grandissimes*. By George Washington Cable. New York: Hill and Wang, 1957.

Asbury, Herbert. *The French Quarter*. New York: Knopf, 1936.

Baldridge, Pat. "Memorial Service Will Honor Writer Lyle Saxon on Sunday." *BRST*, 25 Jan. 1974: 14.

Barnes, Pat M. "Saxon Relates Stories About Noted Writers." *The Houston Post*, 15 Mar. 1935, NSU.

Basso, Hamilton. "Bayou People." Rev. of *CS*. *The New Republic* 92 (1937): 108.

Becker, May Lamberton, ed. "The Reader's Guide." Rev. of *FM*. *The Saturday Review of Literature*, 17 Dec. 1927: 461.

Beebe, Lucius. "Mardi Gras Missed Lyle Saxon But It Was Still 'Gayest Ever.' " *NYHT*, 23 Feb. 1947: 1+.

———. "This New York." *NYHT*, 13 May. 1944, NSU.

Begbie, Viva. "A Writer Without an Enemy." *Shreveport Times*, 23 Mar. 1969: 14-15.

"Best Sellers of 1930." *NYTBR*, 21 Dec. 1930: 24.

Blotner, Joseph. *Faulkner: A Biography*. 2 vols. New York: Random House, 1974.

———. *William Faulkner's Library—a Catalogue*. Charlottesville: U of Virginia P, 1964.

"Body of Saxon Due Here Today." *BRST*, 10 Apr. 1946: 1+.

Bontemps, Arna. "Louisiana Folk Tales: Lively and Exotic, Strange and Wonderful." Rev. of *GYY*. *The Chicago Sun Book Week*, 9 Dec. 1945: 14.

Bowen, Frances Jean. "*The New Orleans Double Dealer*, 1921-May 1926: A Critical History." Diss. Vanderbilt U, 1954.

Bradford, Mary Rose. "The Story of Annie Christmas." *A Treasury of Mississippi River Folklore*. Ed. B. A. Botkin. New York: Crown, 1955. 35-36.

Bradford, Roark. "Disintegration of 'Famie.' " Rev. of *CS*. *New Orleans Item*, 19 July 1937, NSU.

Brickell, Herschel. "The Good Old Days." Rev. of *OL*. *The Saturday Review of Literature*, 21 Dec. 1929: 583.

Brogan, D. W. "Uncle Sam's Guides." Rev. of *NOCG*. *The Spectator* 161 (1938): 226-27.

Bryson, Frances. "Saxon's Book Best of State Guide Series, Says Carmer." *New Orleans Item*, 6 Mar. 1941, LSU.

"*Buccaneer, The*." *Filmfacts* 1 (1959): 279-81.

Burke, Marianne Turpin. "The Black Knight: The Negro as the Hero in the Twentieth Century American Novel." Thesis. U of Tennessee, 1944.

Burton, Robert. *The Anatomy of Melancholy*. Ed. and trans. Floyd Dell and Paul Jordan-Smith. New York: Tudor, 1927.

Bush, Robert. *Grace King: A Southern Dynasty*. Baton Rouge: LSU P, 1983.

Butcher, Philip. *George W. Cable*. New York: Twayne, 1962.

B. W. "*Fabulous New Orleans*." Rev. of *FNO*. *Outlook and Independent* 150 (1928): 1374.

Cable, George W. "The Freedman's Case in Equity." *Southern Writing: 1585-1920*. Ed. Richard Beale Davis, C. Hugh Holman, and Louis D. Rubin. New York: Odyssey, 1970. 673-91.

———. *Strange True Stories of Louisiana*. New York: Scribner's, 1889.

"Candidates for the Best Seller List." *The Publishers' Weekly* 132 (1937): 333.

Carmer, Carl. *The Hurricane's Children*. 1937. New York: David McKay, 1965.

Carter, Hodding. "Background for Laughter." Rev. of *FJG*. *NYHTB*, 20 Feb. 1949: 6.

Cerf, Bennett. "Trade Winds." *The Saturday Review of Literature*, 10 Apr. 1948: 4.

Chase, Cleveland B. "Fighting the 'Father of Waters.' " Rev. of *FM*. *NYTBR*, 27 Nov. 1927: 9.

"*Children of Strangers*." *The Birmingham Post*, 28 Dec. 1937, NSU.

"*Children of Strangers*." *Scotsman*, 23 Dec. 1937, NSU.

Chopin, Kate. *The Awakening and Other Stories*. Ed. Lewis Leary. New York: Holt, Rinehart and Winston, 1970.

Christian, Marcus B., ed. *From the Deep South*. New Orleans: n.p., 1937.

Claitor, Otto and Mrs. Claitor. "We Progress from Sidelines to Books." *The Publishers' Weekly* 132 (1937): 1412-14.

"Classified Books." Rev. of *FM*. *The Booklist* 24 (1928): 203.

"Classified Books." Rev. of *FNO*. *The Booklist* 25 (1929): 159.

"Classified Books." Rev. of *OL*. *The Booklist* 26 (1930): 200.

"Classified Books." Rev. of *LP*. *The Booklist* 27 (1931): 205.

"Classified Books." Rev. of *GYY*. *The Booklist* 42 (1946): 196.

"Classified Books." Rev. of *FJG*. *The Booklist* 45 (1949): 177.

Cohn, David L. "Everybody Talks at Once." Rev. of *GYY*. *The Saturday Review of Literature*, 22 Dec. 1945: 11.

Collins, Carvel, ed. *William Faulkner: New Orleans Sketches*. New York: Random House, 1958.

Commager, Henry Steele. "Levee Land." Rev. of *OL*. *NYHTB*, 24 Nov. 1929: 25.

Crabitès, Pierre. "*Louisiana*." Rev. of *LG*. *The Catholic World* 153 (1941): 630-31.

Culver, Essae M. "Lyle Saxon Memorial in the Louisiana State Library." *Louisiana Library Association Bulletin* 10 (1947): 36-37.

Dabney, Thomas E. *One Hundred Great Years: The Story of the* Times-Picayune *From Its Founding to 1940*. Baton Rouge: LSU P, 1944.

Dabney, Virginius. *Liberalism in the South*. Chapel Hill: U of NC P, 1932.

Davis, Daryl W. "Lyle Saxon: Twentieth-Century Champion of Louisiana's Heritage." Thesis. Midwestern [Texas] U, 1960.

Dillon, Catherine B. "Flickers through the Cypress Boughs: An Intimate Sketch of Lyle Saxon." *Inn Dixie,* Sep. 1946: 5-6+.

Dimmitt, Richard B. *A Title Guide to the Talkies*. New York: The Scarecrow Press, 1965.

Dormon, Caroline. "Southern Personalities—Lyle Saxon." *Holland's Magazine*, Jan. 1931: 26+.

Dreyer, Edward. "Some Friends of Lyle Saxon." *The Friends of Joe Gilmore*. By Lyle Saxon. New York: Hastings House, 1948.

Duffus, R. L. "New Orleans Is Still a Story City." Rev. of *FNO*. *NYTBR*, 25 Nov. 1928: 4.

———. "That Lost Garden of Eden Which Was Old Louisiana." Rev. of *OL*. *NYTBR*, 17 Nov. 1929: 8.

"Editors, Writers Speak at L.S.U. Jubilee Program." *BRST*, 12 Apr. 1935, NSU.

Enser, A. G. C. *Filmed Books and Plays: A List of Books and Plays From Which Films Have Been Made, 1928-1967*. London: Andre Deutsch, 1968.

"*Father Mississippi*." *The Mississippi Valley Historical Review* 15 (1928): 133.

Faulkner, William. "A Rose for Emily." *Collected Stories of William Faulkner*. New York: Random House, 1950.

———. *The Sound and the Fury*. Ed. David Minter. New York: W. W. Norton, 1987.

Feld, Rose C. "Lafitte, Picturesque Brigand of Old New Orleans." Rev. of *LP*. *NYTBR*, 30 Nov. 1930: 7+.

"Fiction." Rev. of *CS*. *The Booklist* 34 (1937): 11.

Finger, Charles J. "Blacksmith Turned Pirate." Rev. of *LP*. *NYHTB*, 9 Nov. 1930: 3.

———. "Validity and Vision." Rev. of *FM*. *NYHTB*, 11 Dec. 1927: 5.

"Frank Recollections of His Pals Told by Saxon." *Shreveport Times*, 8 Mar. 1934, NSU.

"*Friends of Joe Gilmore, The*." *The New Yorker*, 22 Jan. 1949: 82+.

Frost, Meigs O. "Annie Christmas." *NOTP* magazine, 23 May 1948: 16.

Gilkison, Roberta. "Lyle Saxon Here on Brief Holiday Visit is Busy With Plans for His Next Book, Which Will Be a Novel." *BRST,* 30 Dec. 1930, LSL.

"Good Loser." [c. Oct 1917]. LSL.

Govan, Gilbert. "Is It True What They Say About Dixie." Rev. of *LG. NYHTB,* 31 Aug. 1941: 5.

Greene, Ward. *"Children of Strangers." NYHTB,* 18 July 1937: 3.

Grimwood, Michael. "Lyle Saxon's *Father Mississippi* as a Source for Faulkner's 'Old Man' and 'Mississippi.' " *Notes on Mississippi Writers* 17 (1985): 55-62.

Gruening, Martha. "Between Castes." Rev. of *CS. The Nation* 145 (1937): 205.

Gueymard, Ernest. "Lyle Saxon Book Issued Posthumously." Rev. of *FJG. BRST,* 16 Dec. 1948: 16.

"Guide Credit Given to WPA by Saxon." *New Orleans Item,* 7 Mar. 1941, LSU.

Gwynn, Frederick L. and Joseph L. Blotner, eds. *Faulkner in the University.* New York: Random House, 1959.

Hamer, Alvin C. "Transcript of WXYZ Radio Broadcast." 8 Jul. 1937, NSU.

Hansen, Harry. "The First Reader." Rev. of *CS.* [New York] *World Telegram,* 6 Jul. 1937, NSU.

——, ed. *Louisiana: A Guide to the State.* 2nd. ed. New York: Hastings House, 1971.

Hardin, J. Fair. "Saxon's *Lafitte the Pirate." The Louisiana Historical Quarterly* 14 (1931): 441-42.

Harvey, Cathy. "Dear Lyle/ Sherwood Anderson." *Southern Studies* 18 (1979): 321-38.

——. "Lyle Saxon: A Portrait in Letters, 1917-1945." Diss. TU, 1980.

Healy, George W., Jr. "No Beck and Call for Bill." *William Faulkner of Oxford.* Ed. James W. Webb and Wigfall Green. Baton Rouge: LSU P, 1965. 57-60.

——. "Novel by Saxon Is Distinguished Work." Rev. of *CS. NOTP,* 11 Jul. 1937, LSL.

Hebert, F. Edward. "De Mille Comes to Plan Lafitte Film." *New Orleans States,* 18 Feb. 1937: 1+.

Hellman, Lillian. *Pentimento: A Book of Portraits.* Boston: Little, Brown, 1973.

Howard, Brian. "New Novels." Rev. of *CS. The New Statesman and Nation* 14 (1937): 1020.

Howe, Irving. *Sherwood Anderson.* Stanford: Stanford U P, 1951.

Hubbell, Jay B. *"Old Louisiana." American Literature* 1 (1930): 464-65.

——. *Who Are the Major American Writers?* Durham: Duke U P, 1972.

"In Brief Review." Rev. of *FM. The Bookman* 66 (1928): xviii.

"In the Bookmarket." *The Publishers' Weekly* 116 (1929): 263.

Jacobs, Howard. "Attacks on Cajun Humor Draw Variety of Responses." *NOTP,* 7 Jul. 1974: 4.

Jones, Anne Goodwyn. "*Gone With the Wind* and Others: Popular Fiction, 1920-1950."
    The History of Southern Literature. Ed. Louis D. Rubin. Baton Rouge: LSU P,
    1985.
Jones, Charles P. "Tamiroff Steals Show as Lafitte Returns to Life." *NOTP,* 8 Jan.
    1938: 1+.
Jones, Frances E. "Background of the Louisiana Short Story." Thesis. LSU, 1936.
Jones, Howard Mumford and Walter B. Rideout, eds. *Letters of Sherwood Anderson.*
    Boston: Little, Brown, 1953.
Jones, Howard Mumford. "The Literary Lantern." Rev. of *OL. The Asheville Citizen,*
    8 Dec. 1929, NSU.
Kane, Harnett T. "Indestructible, Careless New Orleans." *NYHTB,* 16 Dec. 1945: 5.
————. *Plantation Parade: The Grand Manner in Louisiana.* New York: Morrow,
    1945.
Karl, Frederick R. *William Faulkner: American Writer.* New York: Weidenfeld and
    Nicolson, 1989.
Kazin, Alfred. *On Native Ground.* 2nd. ed. Garden City: Anchor, 1956.
Kellogg, Arthur. "Ol' Davil River." Rev. of *FM. The Survey* 59 (1927): 163-64.
Kennedy, Richard S. *The Window of Memory: The Literary Career of Thomas Wolfe.*
    Chapel Hill: U of NC P, 1962.
Klevar, Harvey. "Image and Imagination: Flannery O'Connor's Front Page Fiction."
    Journal of Modern Literature 4 (1974): 121-32.
Krauss, Joe W. "Lyle Saxon's Footnotes to History: A Bibliography." *Louisiana
    Library Association Bulletin* 13 (1950): 15-18, 54-56.
Kunitz, Stanley J. and Howard Haycraft, eds. *Twentieth Century Authors.* New York:
    H. W. Wilson, 1942.
"*Lafitte the Pirate.*" *The Bookman* 72 (1930): v.
La Fourche, James B. "Lyle Saxon, Friend of Negro Passes." *The Louisiana Weekly,*
    20 Apr. 1946, NSU.
Lake, Mary Daggett. "Meet Mr. Lyle Saxon of Louisiana and New York." *Texas
    Outlook* 14 (1930): 38.
Lawrence, Alberta, ed. *Who's Who Among North American Authors, VI: 1933-35.* Los
    Angeles: Golden Syndicate, 1935.
Lea, Fanny Heaslip. "Yellow Roses." *Harper's Bazaar,* Apr. 1930: 88-89+.
Leisure, Harold L. "Presenting Lyle Saxon." *Southern Literary Messenger* 2 (1940):
    509-10.
"Letters to the Editor." *The Saturday Review of Literature,* 18 May 1946: 19.
Lewis, R. W. B. "Walt Whitman." *Major Writers of America.* Ed. Perry Miller, et. al.
    New York: Harcourt Brace, 1966. 567-83.
"*Life* Visits the Pirate Country of Louisiana." *Life,* 10 May 1943: 93.
"Lit'ry Lights Who Will Help Illumine the New Orleanian." *The New Orleanian,* 6 Sept.
    1930: 31.

"Lyddell A. Saxon." [*NOTP?*] [1901], LSL.

"Lyle Saxon." *BRST*, 11 Apr. 1946: 4.

"Lyle Saxon." *NOTP*, 11 Apr. 1946: 10.

"Lyle Saxon: Author of *Old Louisiana.*" *The Wilson Bulletin* 4 (1929): 148.

"Lyle Saxon Dead at 54." *NOSI*, 10 Apr. 1946, LSL.

"Lyle Saxon Dies at Home After Stroke." *Dallas Morning News* [Apr. 1939], NSU.

"Lyle Saxon, Famous Louisiana Author, Gives Opinions on Southern Literature." *Fair Park* [High School, Shreveport] *Pow Wow*, 21 Mar. 1934: 1+.

"Lyle Saxon Gift to Louisiana Library." *The Publishers' Weekly* 150 (1946): 60.

"Lyle Saxon Memorial." *Louisiana Library Association Bulletin* 10 (1946): 9.

"Lyle Saxon's New Book Dedicated to Miss Mercedes Garig, First Woman Ever on L.S.U. Faculty." *BRST*, 5 Nov. 1930, LSL.

"Lyle Saxon, Noted Louisiana Author, Dies in Orleans." *BRMA*, 10 Apr. 1946, LSL.

"Lyle Saxon Play 'Epitaph' Given at Petit Theatre." [*NOTP?*], TU.

"Lyle Saxon Rites to Be Held Today." *BRST*, 11 Apr. 1946, LSL.

McClure, John. "*Father Mississippi.*" *The New Republic* 53 (1927): 148.

———. "*Old Louisiana.*" *NOTP*, 17 Nov. 1929, NSU.

McDonald, William F. *Federal Relief Administration and the Arts: The Origins and Administrative History of the Arts Project of the Works Progress Administration.* Columbus: Ohio State U P, 1969.

McGraw, A. P. "Saxon, First Fiction Work Through, Has Guidebooks to Edit; Plans for Future Include Only 'More Writing.' " *BRMA*, 5 Aug. 1937: 2.

McNeer, Iris. "Fiction: Take a Trip into the Old South But Watch Out for the Trapdoor." Rev. of *CS. Mebane* [North Carolina] *Enterprise-Journal*, 4 Apr. 1974.

Mangione, Jerre. *The Dream and the Deal: The Federal Writers' Project, 1935-1943.* Boston: Little, Brown, 1972.

Mayer, Edwin Justus, Harold Lamb, and C. Gardner Sullivan. "The Buccaneer." Screenplay. LSU.

Mignon, Francois. "Beloved Cane River Character, Zeline Roque, Is Dead at Age of 95 Following Severe Stroke." *Natchitoches Enterprise*, 12 Oct. 1950: 1.

———. "Cane River Memo: Birth of a Book." *Natchitoches Times*, 28 Feb. 1971: 2.

———. "Cane River Memo: Letter to the Editor." *Natchitoches Enterprise*, 18 Feb. 1960: 4.

———. "Cane River Memo: Lyle Saxon, Twenty-Five Years Later." *Natchitoches Times*, 10 May 1970: 2.

———. *Plantation Memo.* Baton Rouge: Claitor's, 1972.

———. "Plantation Memo, 1968: *Children of Strangers.*" *Opelousas Daily World*, 21 Apr. 1968, LSL.

———. "Plantation Memo, 1969: High Society." *Opelousas Daily World*, 15 Jan. 1969, LSL.

"Milestones." *Time*, 22 Apr. 1946: 92.

Miller, Hope Ridings. "Hope Ridings Miller." *The Washington Post,* 8 Jun. 1943, TU.

Mills, Gary B. and Elizabeth S. Mills. *Melrose.* Natchitoches: The Association of Natchitoches Women for the Preservation of Historic Natchitoches, 1973.

Minter, David. *William Faulkner: His Life and Work.* Baltimore: Johns Hopkins U P, 1980.

"Mixed Strains." Rev. of *CS. The Times Literary Supplement,* 4 Dec. 1937: 927.

Modlin, Charles E., ed. *Sherwood Anderson: Selected Letters.* Knoxville: U of Tennessee P, 1984.

Moore, Opal. "The Development of the Negro Character in Louisiana Fiction." Thesis. LSU, 1942.

Mullins, Marion D. "The Glory That Was Old Louisiana Recaptured." Rev. of *OL. Texas Outlook* 14 (1930): 37.

"Newsboys Dress Like Buccaneers." *NOTP,* 25 May 1931: 2.

Nicolosi, Louis J. "The Teaching of Louisiana History in the School Curriculum." *Louisiana History* 13 (1972): 35-45.

"Noted Historian Lyle Saxon Dies." *NOTP,* 10 Apr. 1946: 1+.

"Notes and Quotes." *The Wilson Library Bulletin* 20 (1946): 696.

Nott, G. William. "The Charm of Old New Orleans." *The Mentor,* Mar. 1925: 27-46.

Nugent, Frank S. *"The Buccaneer." The New York Times,* 17 Feb. 1938: 17.

"Obituary Notes." *The Publishers' Weekly* 149 (1946): 2459.

O'Brien, Edward J., ed. *The Best Short Stories of 1927.* New York: Dodd, Mead, 1928.

O'Brien, Kate. "Fiction." Rev. of *CS. The Spectator* 159 (1937): 1016.

O'Donnell, E. P. " 'An Arrangement in Decay.' " Rev. of *CS. The Washington Post,* 11 Jul. 1937, NSU.

Pattee, F. L. "The Age of O. Henry." *Side-Lights on American Literature.* New York: The Century Co., 1922. 3-55.

Pearce, T. M. *Oliver La Farge.* New York: Twayne, 1972.

Perry, George Sessions. "The Cities of America: New Orleans." *The Saturday Evening Post,* 1 Jun. 1946: 24-25+.

Peterkin, Julia. "One Southern View-Point." *North American Review* 244 (1937-38): 389-98.

"Radio Program to Use Excerpts From Saxon Book." *BRST,* 6 Dec. 1951, LSL.

Rascoe, Burton. "Among the New Books." *Arts and Decoration,* Jan. 1930: 47+.

Reely, Mary Katherine, ed. "A Selected List of Annotated Books." *Wisconsin Library Bulletin* 24 (1928): 344.

———. "A Selected List of Current Books." *Wisconsin Library Bulletin* 23 (1927): 287.

———. "A Selected List of Current Books." *Wisconsin Library Bulletin* 25 (1929): 411.

Reilly, John M. "Jean Toomer: An Annotated Checklist of Criticism." *Resources for American Literary Study* 4 (1974): 27-56.

St. Martin, Thad. "Crescent City." Rev. of *NOCG*. *The Saturday Review of Literature*, 23 Apr. 1938: 19.

Saxon, Elizabeth Lyle. "The Rights of Women." *New Orleans Times*, 1879, TU.

———. *A Southern Woman's War Time Reminiscences*. Memphis: Pilcher Publishing Co., 1905.

"Saxon Known Everywhere—Best Here." *BRST*, 24 Mar. 1938: 7.

Schorer, Mark. *Sinclair Lewis: An American Life*. New York: McGraw-Hill, 1961.

Seldes, Gilbert. "An Enquiry into the Present State of Letters." *The Dial* 83 (1927): 434-38.

"Series and Editions." Rev. of *NOCG*. *The Booklist* 34 (1938): 364.

"Series and Editions." Rev. of *LG*. *The Booklist* 37 (1941): 389.

Simmons, Monty. "Novel of Old South shallow." *Roanoke World-News*,17 Apr. 1974.

"Society, Literati Hear Chorus Girl Defended." *Brooklyn Eagle*, 6 Dec. 1929, NSU.

"South: New Orleans' Literary Mentor Weeps for Mulattoes." Rev. of *CS*. *Newsweek*, 10 Jul. 1937: 20.

Sparks, Robert Branson. "The Melrose Library: An Annotated Bibliography of the Books." Thesis. Northwestern State U, 1973.

Spigelgass, Leonard, ed. *Who Wrote the Movie and What Else Did He Write: An Index of Screen Writers and Their Film Works, 1936-1969*. Los Angeles: The Writers' Guild, 1970.

Spratling, William. *File on Spratling: An Autobiography*. Boston: Little, Brown, 1967.

——— and William Faulkner. *Sherwood Anderson and Other Famous Creoles: A Gallery of Contemporary New Orleans*. 1926. Austin: U of Texas P, 1966.

"Steinbeck and Los Angeles Singer Married in Vieux Carre Courtyard." *NOTP*, 11 Mar. 1943, TU.

Steinbeck, Elaine and Robert Wallsten, eds. *Steinbeck: A Life in Letters*. New York: Viking, 1975.

Stevens, George. "A Poignant Story of the 'Free Mulattoes.' " Rev. of *CS*. *The Saturday Review of Literature*, 10 Jul. 1937: 6.

Stuart, Henry Longan. "The First 'American Caravan' Comes to the Bazaars." *NYTBR*, 18 Sep. 1927: 6+.

"Student Pastor Unearths Chest in Lafitte Hunt." *NOTP*, 31 May 1931, NSU.

Stuvyesant, Pieter. "Parnassus Under the Levee." *The New Orleanian*, 25 Oct. 1930: 18-19.

Sullivan, Shirley K. "Lyle Saxon's Novel of Sourh From Thirties." *Savannah News*, 31 Mar. 1974.

Tallant, Robert. Introduction. *Fabulous New Orleans*. By Lyle Saxon. 1928. New Orleans: Crager, 1950.

———. "My Fabulous Friend Lyle Saxon." *NOTP* magazine, 21 Nov. 1948: 8-9.

———. *The Romantic New Orleanians*. New York: E. P. Dutton, 1950.

———. "Salute to Saxon." *South,* Jun. 1946: 28.

———. *Voodoo in New Orleans.* New York: MacMillan, 1946.

Tapley, Philip A. "Negro Superstitions in *Children of Strangers.*" *Louisiana Folklore Miscellany* 4 (1976-80): 61-72.

Thomas, James W. "Lyle Saxon's Struggle with *Children of Strangers.*" *Southern Studies* 16 (1977): 27-40.

Thompson, Jo. "Lyle Saxon, Seasoned Reporter, Likes Reporting Far More than Writing Books—But Writes Books." *BRST,* 5 Aug. 1937: 3.

Thompson, Ray M. "The Three Decades of Lyle Saxon." *Down South,* May-June 1960: 5+.

"Three Collections of the 'Best Short Stories' of 1927." *NYTBR,* 11 Dec. 1927: 2+.

Tinker, Edward Larocque. "A Dramatic Novel of Louisiana." Rev. of *CS. NYTBR,* 11 Jul. 1937: 1.

———. "A Well-Planned Guide to New Orleans." Rev. of *NOCG. NYTBR,* 22 May 1938: 5.

Titzell, Josiah. "Chronicler of the Fabulous." *St. Nicholas* 56 (1929): 467+.

———. "Mardi Gras." Rev. of *FNO. NYHTB,* 23 Dec. 1928: 15.

Toomer, Jean. *Cane.* 1923. Ed. Darwin T. Turner. New York: W. W. Norton, 1988.

Touchstone, Blake. "Voodoo in New Orleans." *Louisiana History* 13 (1972): 371-86.

"Transition." *Newsweek,* 22 Apr. 1946: 60.

Turnbull, Andrew. *Thomas Wolfe.* New York: Scribner's, 1967.

Turner, Arlin. "Fiction of the Bayou Country." *The Saturday Review of Literature,* 30 Apr. 1938: 3-4+.

Tuttle, Worth. *"Fabulous New Orleans." The New Republic* 58 (1929): 103.

Tynes, Wendell. "A Talk with Lyle Saxon." *The Haversack,* 22 Jan. 1933: 4+.

Vaillant, Andrhee, trans. *Lafitte the Pirate.* By Lyle Saxon. Paris: Gallimard, 1935.

Van Doren, Carl. " 'Children of Strangers' Shows Its Working with Unusual Skill." *Boston Herald,* 10 Jul. 1937, NSU.

Veach, Damon A. "Two Literary Greats Recalled." *BRMA,* 9 June 1968, LSL.

Vreeland, Frank. *Foremost Films of 1938.* New York: Pitman, 1939.

Wall, Evans. *The No-Nation Girl.* New York: The Century Co., 1927.

Warner, Arthur. "All Roads Lead to Paris." Rev. of *FNO. The Nation* 128 (1929): 23.

Warren, Robert Penn, ed. *A Southern Harvest.* Boston: Houghton Mifflin, 1937.

Wasson, Ben. *Count No 'Count: Flashbacks to Faulkner.* Jackson: U P of Miss., 1983.

Welty, Eudora. "Creole Get-Together." Rev. of *GYY. NYTBR,* 20 Jan. 1946: 5+.

Williams, Blanche Colton, et al., eds. *O. Henry Memorial Award Prize Stories of 1926.* Garden City: Doubleday, Page, 1927.

Wilson, Edmund. *Letters on Literature and Politics.* Ed. Elena Wilson. New York: Farrar, Straus and Giroux, 1977.

———. *The Twenties.* Ed. Leon Edel. New York: Farrar, Straus and Giroux, 1975.

Woods, Sister Frances Jerome, C.D.P. *Marginality and Identity: A Colored Creole Family Through Ten Generations.* Baton Rouge: LSU P, 1972.

Young, Stark. "Deep South Notes, V: Ars Longa." *The New Republic* 72 (1932): 71-72.

———. *Feliciana.* New York: Scribner's, 1935.

———. "*Old Louisiana.*" *The New Republic* 61 (1929): 43.

Zender, Karl F. "Faulkner." *American Literary Scholarship: 1985.* Ed. James L. Woodress. Durham: Duke U P, 1987. 147-68.

INDEX